The Art of Teaching with Humor

This book is part of the Peter Lang Education list.
Every volume is peer reviewed and meets
the highest quality standards for content and production.

PETER LANG
New York • Bern • Berlin
Brussels • Vienna • Oxford • Warsaw

Teri Evans-Palmer

The Art of Teaching with Humor

Crafting Laughter

PETER LANG
New York • Bern • Berlin
Brussels • Vienna • Oxford • Warsaw

Library of Congress Cataloging-in-Publication Data
Names: Evans-Palmer, Teri, author.
Title: The art of teaching with humor: crafting laughter / Teri Evans-Palmer.
Description: New York: Peter Lang, 2021.
Includes bibliographical references.
Identifiers: LCCN 2021013508 (print) | LCCN 2021013509 (ebook)
ISBN 978-1-4331-8657-8 (hardback) | ISBN 978-1-4331-8656-1 (paperback)
ISBN 978-1-4331-5494-2 (ebook pdf) | ISBN 978-1-4331-5495-9 (epub)
Subjects: LCSH: Teaching—Humor. | Teaching—Psychological aspects. | Wit
and humor in education. | Classroom environment.
Classification: LCC LB1027 .E824 2021 (print) | LCC LB1027 (ebook) |
DDC 371.102—dc23
LC record available at https://lccn.loc.gov/2021013508
LC ebook record available at https://lccn.loc.gov/2021013509
DOI 10.3726/b18500

Bibliographic information published by **Die Deutsche Nationalbibliothek**.
Die Deutsche Nationalbibliothek lists this publication in the "Deutsche
Nationalbibliografie"; detailed bibliographic data are available
on the Internet at http://dnb.d-nb.de/.

© 2021 Peter Lang Publishing, Inc., New York
80 Broad Street, 5th floor, New York, NY 10004
www.peterlang.com

All rights reserved.
Reprint or reproduction, even partially, in all forms such as microfilm,
xerography, microfiche, microcard, and offset strictly prohibited.

For Larry, whose abiding support and laughter keep me sane, and for my joyful friends in the teaching profession, whose light and laughter resound across time in the hearts and minds of their students.

Table of Contents

List of Figures	xi
List of Tables	xiii
Preface	xv

Introduction	1
Why Did I Write This Book? My Testimony, My Study	1
Teaching Is Challenging, Humor Is Strengthening	3
Who Should Read This Book?	8
Chapter One: Humor's Place in Art Education	11
Humor and Laughter Are Essential to Teaching and Learning Art	11
Humor Makes Teaching Fun	12
Humor Triggers Innovative Thinking	13
Humor Distances Us From Stressors	15
Humor Builds Student Rapport	17
What Exactly Is Humor, a Sense of Humor and Laughter?	18
Teacher Sense of Humor	23
Effective Forms of Teacher Humor	26
Effective Humor for the Right Student	27
How to Have a Sense of Humor Even if You Don't Think You Are Funny	29
Achievable Teacher Behavior Sequence	29

When Good Humor Goes Bad: Appropriate and Inappropriate Teacher Humor ... 32
Chapter Two: What Good Humor Can Do for Art Teachers ... 41
   Why Good Humor Will Save Your Career ... 41
   Humor to Manage Classroom Procedures ... 42
      Five to Thrive Classroom-Based Behavior Strategies ... 42
      Rules to Inaugurate Behavior Expectations ... 43
      Consequences to Equitably Deter Misbehavior ... 44
      Routines to Guide Student Activities ... 46
      Devices to Redirect Misbehavior ... 48
      Incongruous Teacher Responses to Stop Student Distractions ... 49
      Thwart Annoying Behavior with Inanimate Objects ... 50
      More Annoying Behavior ... 51
      Engagement Strategies to Foster Student Attention and Active Learning ... 55
   Humor to Relieve Stress and Anxiety ... 59
      Raising Resilience: When Bad Things Happen to Good Teachers ... 60
      Humor Helps with External, Adverse Impingements ... 63
      Threats and Attacks on Teachers ... 64
      Humor Minimizes Our Perception of Threats and Attacks ... 65
      Humor Maximizes Internal Emotional Health ... 66
      Humor to Build Confidence in Your Teaching (Self-Efficacy) ... 68
Chapter Three: Humor Connects Teachers with Students ... 75
   Our Intuition ... 76
   Our Emotional Intelligence ... 77
      Self-Awareness and Self-Monitoring ... 78
      Developing Emotional Intelligence Capabilities ... 79
   Our Physicality ... 83
   Types of Teacher Humor ... 83
   Humor-Enhancing Dialogue ... 85
   Student Response to Your Humor ... 87
      Humor's Positive Effect on Student Emotions ... 87
      Engagement and Interest ... 88
      Learning ... 89
      Memory and Recall ... 90
   Humor Reaches Out to Students with Diverse Identities and Challenges ... 91

Culture	92
Gender	93
Autism	93
Perfectionism	94
Anger	96
Humor Engages Students with Art	98
The Big Picture about Teaching with Humor	100
Chapter Four: Humor Invites Play, Divergent Thinking and Creativity	107
Play	108
It All Adds Up: Interconnectedness of Play, Humor and Creativity	111
Go Bananas! An Example of Play, Humor and Creativity	111
Useless New Inventions: A Playful Activity for Emerging Artists	112
Playful Inventing and Divergent Thinking	113
Brain Thunder	114
Linking Thinking	116
A Method for Teaching Successful Inventing	117
Teaching Divergent Thinkers	117
PTDS: A Factor Hindering Successful Inventing	118
Analog Abstract Drawings: Nonthreatening First	
Drawing Challenge	119
The Dead Fly Story	119
Thumbnail Sketches of Four Themes	120
Final Drawing of One Selected Sketch	121
Class Critique of Final Drawings	122
Teacher Feedback	124
What Humor, Play, Inventiveness, and Divergent Thinking	
Means for Teachers	125
Tale of Two Teachers	125
Artists Play to Create	126
The Call for Creativity from the Future	128
Conclusion: Our Best Bet for Teaching Tomorrow: Encouragement and	
Empathy for Educators	133
To Art Teachers	133
To Teacher Educators	135
To Educational Policy Makers	137
Bibliography	139

Figures

Figure 0.1. Affective Dispositions Relative to Humor and Self-Efficacy   4
Figure 0.2. Emergent Themes of Construct Intersection   4
Figure 2.1. Rules of Thumb, Fingers and Hand   44
Figure 2.2. Classroom Conduct Gauge   53
Figure 2.3. The Eye Can Enabler   54
Figure 2.4. The Magic Wand Motivator   57
Figure 2.5. The Big Word Club   60
Figure 3.1. Laocoön and His Sons Sculpture Comes to Life   94
Figure 4.1. Useless New Inventions Everyday Objects   114
Figure 4.2. Divergent vs. Convergent Thinking   115
Figure 4.3. Preliminary Thumbnail Sketches for the Analog Abstract Drawing   123
Figure 4.4. The Final Analog Abstract Drawing   123

Tables

Table 1.1. Definitions of Humor Terms 25
Table 2.1. Definition of Self-Efficacy Terms 68
Table 2.2. A Few Humor Strategies 70
Table 4.1. Operational Definitions of Creativity-Related Terms 127

Preface

What I remember most about the days spent with my students in the art classroom are the times when something funny made things happen. A sense of humor has both saved me and served me as a teaching resource, a way to live connected to others, and as a source of strength and triumph. This book is a guide to teachers everywhere (with specifics for visual art teachers). My hope is it will be a safety net, a lifesaver, an instructional resource or simply a soft place to land when the burden of teaching knocks you over with the weight of it.

Introduction

Why Did I Write This Book? My Testimony, My Study

You might be asking yourself, "Why a book on humor for art teachers?" My response to you is directly related to my tortuous struggle teaching art in public schools that led to a serious dependency on humor. There were plenty of days when I felt like running into the woods screaming. My best days, however, were tinkling moments enrobed in rollicking laughter, days I would happily relive again and again. This book is for teachers who may share my need to laugh in the classroom in order to thrive and survive teaching as a career.

Just before I entered academia in higher education, I taught art for 7 years in a high school infamous for gang entanglements, truancy, student disengagement, and apathetic administrators. I had to do something to shield myself from spiralling disillusionment. (I was certainly not willing to join the herd of teachers running out the back door to seek employment elsewhere). So, I began to play with quirky teaching approaches to gain my equilibrium and motivate reluctant students at the same time. I tried warming up "cold" pencils, brought out the "I Can" (a soda can covered with magazine photos of eyes), came down with a British accent, leapt onto desks, sported a magic wand, and pulled a number of metaphors out of the air to clarify concepts. In doing so, I felt a strange sense of control, felt lighter, happier, more connected to my students.

Looking back, I have known that humor has had a resounding effect on my life as a teacher, kicking in as a default mechanism to override pressures outside of my control in the workplace. As a veteran K-12 art teacher in rural, urban and overseas military schools, I grasped at humor regularly as a lifesaver when I was drowning in a sea of stress. Stressors common to all art teachers flood into classrooms from a considerable number of sources: classrooms teeming with students operating with a broad spectrum of skills, reduced class time, minimized respect for the teaching profession, and the shrinking art curriculum attributed to accountability testing. I will be the first to tell teachers that teaching with humor as a Pollyanna, sunny-sky, everything's-okay practice is not what I propose in this book. Failure happens. Some classes are just hard to teach. Some teaching days are super sad. At a low point in my life, I left a very trying teaching position midpoint in the school year. No amount of good humor could accomplish what a good hard look at my teaching situation did. (Read about it Chapter Two).

My appeal to teachers in this book is to allow humor to shift their perspective. Much of what I learned about humor came to me at the height of art educator anxiety, while serving 7 years in the aforementioned high school, (you know, the one infamous for gang fights). After I had accumulated a toolbox full of humor devices to live by, a soft-eyed freshman looked up from his work and said solemnly, "You know, Mrs. Evans-Palmer, you really ought to get a Ph.D." His counsel remained lodged in my heart for the next 2 years. After a dodgy few months in a middle school art room dubbed the "snake pit" by the principal, I cheerfully accepted an adjunct position at a nearby university and enrolled in a doctoral program.

Earning a doctoral degree is like enjoying dessert after dutifully eating your vegetables. It is a privilege, a path to pondering all things yet to be pondered. There, I reflected on a list of issues that mattered the most to me as a teacher. At the top of the list was humor's power to bail me out of tough situations with students. I remembered how humor helped restore me to "whole health" teaching when teaching is robust, clicking into place in a way that makes students eager to learn. I recalled how weightless laughter made me feel as I trudged through tiresome tasks that felt like pushing rocks uphill. I remembered colleagues who modeled humor so well that their students would rush to class. They enjoyed a wonderful connection with their students, who I might add, were high-achievers. These teachers shared personality traits that perpetuated their success no matter how difficult their jobs. My observations, coupled with my experiences linking humor to emotional health, propelled me to investigate the relationship of humor to good teaching. I wanted to know, "What behaviors of teachers with high humor orientation encouraged positive perceptions of their teaching performance?" I also wanted to know, "Which of these traits were interrelated?"

My journey to find answers launched a study focusing on the possible relationship between social humor and instructional self-efficacy. Instructional, or teaching self-efficacy is an academic term for what a teacher believes about their capability to perform teaching tasks well. I collected survey data from 354 elementary and secondary art teachers in public schools across the state of Texas and found there to be a moderately positive relationship ($r = .29, p < .001$) between teachers' social use of humor and instructional efficacy (Evans-Palmer, 2009). More clearly, the statistics tell me that teachers using social humor as an effective social lubricant in their practice found it to be a coping function and an instructional resource. It helped them stay resilient when stress reared its ugly head (Evans-Palmer, 2010; Thorson & Powell, 1993). I call the capability to move forward after anxious assaults in the daily battle of teaching as "stepping over the dead horse" after it has been shot from underneath you. A bit harsh, I agree, but this book is for teachers who are perhaps seeking solutions for their own professional fatigue. They know what I am talking about.

After analyzing data, I compared my results with the findings of other studies focused on either teacher humor or teacher self-efficacy and discovered common behavior traits interrelating humor with teaching effectiveness! The five traits emerging from the interrelationship, fall into themes we consider to be "people skills" and are classified as teaching behaviors identified as either cognitive, emotional or social. These are: social connectedness, emotional intelligence, resilience to adversity, self-monitoring, and divergent thinking. I might add that we see these traits in the behaviors of comedians guiding them to success with engaged and happy audiences. (See Figure 0.1 for traits common to teacher self-efficacy and sense of humor.) Once I identified the themes, I could then assign humor approaches guiding teachers to effective teaching. (See Figure 0.2 for the traits for traits as they are contextualized in social, cognitive and emotional behaviors.)

You are reading the guidebook evolving from my research. Contextualized by published research, it offers relevant, effective, doable teaching strategies that promise to engage and motivate your students.

Teaching Is Challenging, Humor Is Strengthening

What we teachers need most to teach well is not an instructional technique, but internal capacities that come from the core of our identity (Palmer, 2007). These parts of ourselves —beliefs, and personality dispositions that we bring with us into the classroom every day are components in our being that are not taught in teacher education programs. Technique is like a vehicle a teacher climbs into to

4 | THE ART OF TEACHING WITH HUMOR: CRAFTING LAUGHTER

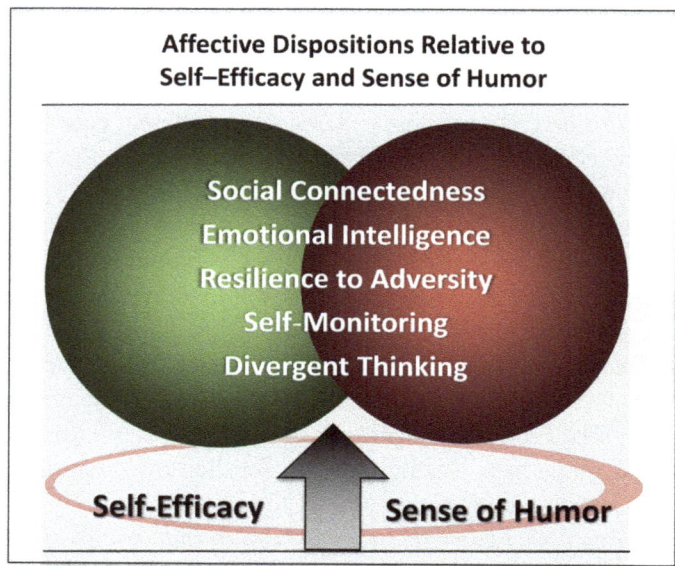

Figure 0.1. Affective Dispositions Relative to Humor and Self-Efficacy

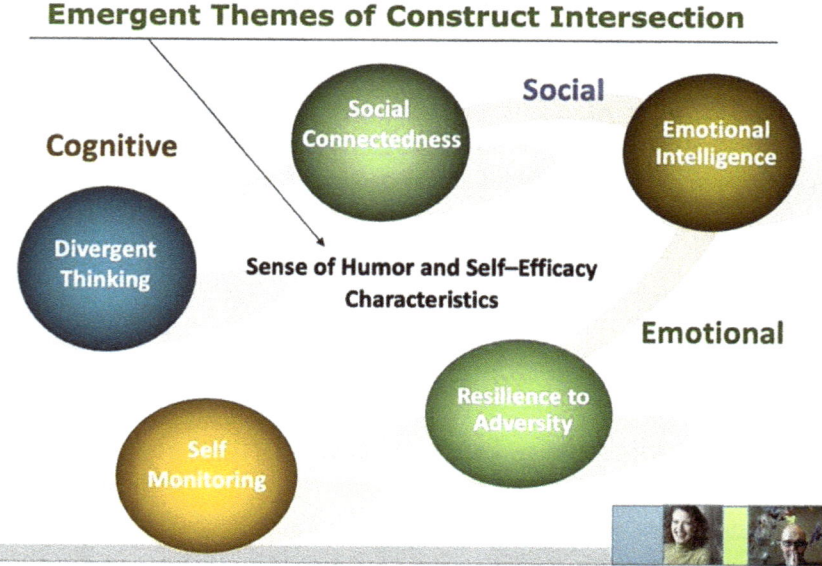

Figure 0.2. Emergent Themes of Construct Intersection

steer students to a learning destination. It is the teacher driver, and most certainly the heart of the teacher driver (resolve, resilience, optimism, tenacity) that guides a teacher's ability to carry students forward on bumpy roads, in all kinds of weather. However, when a frantic teacher overwhelmed by anxiety bails out of the moving vehicle, the result is either a collision or a break down in heavy traffic. No heart, no driver, no reaching the destination. Sources such as The Wall Street Journal tell of teachers exiting the profession in record numbers due to "small raises, budget frustration and opportunities elsewhere" (Hackman & Morath, 2018). Added to references. When asked which aspects of teaching contributed the most to leaving the profession, the majority of teachers replied, "lack of administrative support, teacher workload, and student discipline." Adding to data tied to these tiresome issues are comments centered around student discipline (yes, mentioned again), excessive paperwork, and pressures related to state testing (Thibodeaux, 2014).

I am amazed that our society does not comprehend the emotional labor teachers must exert just to manage daily life in the classroom. Resilience is paramount for teachers in crises and is critical to career longevity (Bobek, 2002). A high school art teacher shared with me a shortlist of assailing events occurring in her classroom on a particular day for which she thought she was prepared. She had assembled the materials, cued up a presentation, and rehearsed an introduction to a ceramics lesson. Within 3 minutes after the door flew open, she greeted a mob of students pushing in, separated two students locked in a passionate embrace, caught a flying pen, encouraged a whiner, hushed a cursing senior and answered a visiting administrator's question. Unfazed, she chuckled, "Laughter makes me strong." When teachers are laughing, they are embodied with a suit of armor, shielding the vulnerable parts of their being from flaming missiles of discouragement.

Finding humor in small skirmishes keeps us buoyant, but what happens when behavior brawls supervene relentlessly day after day? Our self-efficacy perceptions give way to helplessness, that's what. Either we are equipped with dispositions enabling us to persevere in the classroom in spite of dynamic challenges we face, or we buckle under pressure over time. Some theorists say what we believe we can accomplish as teachers (self-efficacy) is far more potent than the reality of our performance (Bandura, 1997; Pajares, 2002). Humor can equip us for good teaching just as breathing equips us for life. My intent for this book is to offer content that is relevant and valuable to art teachers' experience in education. It also delivers to teachers a toolkit of helpful humor strategies that unites teachers with their students, their students to art, preserves their emotional well-being and raises their teaching confidence in the process.

We all love to laugh. Often, we do not know what makes us laugh but we do know that laughter makes us feel good. Laughing is a pleasurable social process we develop from childhood (Morreall, 2009). The intensity of laughter noticeably increases the visible expression of emotion from smiles to grins to giggles and finally, to convulsive guffaws (Ruch, 1998). Genuine laughter vents the soul and the nostrils of the heart (Berk, 2003). It is for us as necessary to health and happiness as sunshine is for flowers to grow. The smallest gestures can provoke us to laughter if we've a mindset to enjoy ourselves.

While traveling through a particularly tiresome trial in my life, I created a Pandora station capturing over a dozen stand-up comedians for driving entertainment. I made an 8-hour trip to Dallas and back listening to their monologues and found I was impervious to driving aggravation. I hooted when people tailed me or cut me off. I chortled while I waited in long construction lines on the interstate. It was amazing that laughter could place me in such a euphoric state of anesthetizing laughter that nothing whatsoever bothered me. Most of the time when I drive, I find myself next to aggressively enraged drivers. Now, drivers were looking at me and smiling. They were smiling because I was laughing. The best part is that I arrived at my destination feeling unfettered, light, and uplifted.

Wouldn't it be wonderful if we could tap into a similar euphoria laughing with our students? What would make us laugh in an art classroom? I certainly do not propose we saturate instruction with witty Jimmy Fallon monologues (although wouldn't *that* be fun?) What I am advocating for is simply allowing ourselves to capitalize on the comical situations incubating right in front of us every day as we teach. Truly, if you look around, you will see what I am talking about. The most engaging humor outcomes occur naturally from the interaction of our own teaching personality with students. My sanguine self makes me prone to perform. I also put on various accents while delivering pedantic dialogue. The point I hope to make is that we teach from who we are; what we find funny in our classrooms is so very related to our own lives. "Teaching, like any truly human activity, emerges from one's inwardness, for better or worse" (Palmer, 2007, p. 2). Teaching can be like holding up a mirror to our soul; we reflect ourselves and in that same mirror, we see our students.

I have collected a hearty inventory of situations occurring in my classroom across time that I find deliciously silly. Allow me to share three humor snapshots, which you might find amusing. There was the Kinder student who exclaimed, "I am finnershed with my drawring!" There was the first-grader who ate a few bites of Playdough because he wanted to find out if a substance that looked and smelled good also tasted good. There was also the Art 1 student who composed a rap to help her memorize the art elements: "My boyfriend fed me a LINE, I got all bent out of SHAPE, I shot into outer SPACE," etc. These glimpses capture spontaneous classroom humor that I cherish. Since then, I have adopted the word, "finnershed" into my daily talk. I ask students who eat art materials if they "would like to see the dessert menu?" I also share the art element rap often when teaching art vocabulary. In a sense, humor that happens while I teach becomes part of who I am as a teacher. It helps me to know myself. Good teaching "is a secret hidden in plain sight" (Palmer, 2007, p. 3). Not everyone's mirror will be the same.

My soft-spoken, more reserved colleagues, who are uncomfortable with high-drama delivery find they achieve an appreciation for humor when they do something totally unexpected. For example, I knew of a rather proper high school English teacher whose straps on her undergarment slip (remember those?) gave way while she was writing on the board with her back to the class. After the slip settled into a fluffy white cloud around her ankles, she turned around, picked it up and deposited it in her desk drawer. Then, she announced with cool composure, "That is the only item of clothing I will be removing for you this semester." Her response was so unpredictably amusing that students watched her like prison guards for weeks that followed.

Whatever leads us our instructional journey to joy, we must pursue it. We also must talk about what not to do. We teachers have a tendency to run our classrooms with a "sage on the stage" approach: we talk, students listen. Certainly, small doses of direct teaching are useful when demonstrations of technical procedures or direct instruction are required. Unfortunately, the cyber-savvy student will not attend to a long-winded exposé for more than 20 minutes max. Instead, I suggest we prepare our classrooms for a harvest of healthy humor, such as sprinkling teacher talk with wordplay, frisky puns, silly gestures, personal stories, clever wit, acerbic irony, gentle teasing and spontaneous drama (Keith-Spiegel, 1972; Martin, 2007). Be relieved that research does not validate joke-telling as a major player in modern-day humor so no need to memorize jokes (Derks, 1996; Morreall, 1997; Wrench & McCroskey, 2001).

This book offers teachers a safety net for leaping into the unknown, four chapters that illuminate the dimension of humor to assist teachers in the classroom. Within each chapter are plenty of funny stories from classroom situations that help to contextualize applicable meaning to the message content for retrievable recall. Chapter One—Humor's Place in Art Education, defines, describes teacher humor, and even suggests how to have a sense of humor even if you do not think you are funny. Chapter Two—What Good Humor Can Do for Art Teachers, offers humorous procedures and processes you may adopt to run your art room. These methodologies should support your emotional, mental, physiological and professional well-being. Chapter Three—Social Connectedness with Students and Subject, rationalizes humor's value as a connector of teachers to the learners in their classroom through the capacities of emotional intelligence and self-monitoring that engage, encourage, motivate and disarm widely diverse students. Finally, in Chapter Four—Humor That Invites Divergent Thinking and Creativity, joins humor to play, divergent thinking and creativity of artists, art students and art teachers.

Who Should Read This Book?

My hope is that this book will serve a consortium of art education stakeholders as a sourcebook for research and praxis. Many art teachers I have encountered want to raise their level of levity so they may enjoy teaching (in spite of the stress) to make what they are teaching mean something to students. I would be honored if art teachers searching to fan the dying flame of fun and meaning would use it as a guide for directing activities in their classrooms. Among these are teachers who are new, teachers who are tired, and perhaps teachers who are anticipating "re-tirement."

This book would also serve teacher educators concerned with preparing new art teachers emotionally for the tenuous "edu-scape" of K-12 education—beyond the didactic delivery of knowledge and skills. Higher education's research interest in humor is high. More and more, scholars in the fields of communication, health, design, theater, music are conducting studies on humor. A few recent examples include NYU's Department of Art and Art Professions, offering a program to 9–12 grade students entitled, "It's No Laughing Matter" (NYU Steinhardt, 2019). The 9-week course takes students through a study of humor as a complex subject for artworks. Also, RMCAD featured a comedic performance on what makes artists great comedians: "Decoding Humor in Art and Design" (RMCAD, 2019). The list goes on.

Finally, this book could influence educational leaders to design professional development that impacts teacher effectiveness and retention. Eager to raise student achievement scores, they must know how incredibly powerful humor can be for both teachers and students. Public-school administrators must consider how laughter acts as a social salve on the machinery of classroom management. Many school districts require teachers to attend continuing education seminars each year. For these sessions, this book could be a viable resource for training as it offers tangible tools that promise to undergird teacher resilience and instructional efficacy with social humor skills.

Bibliography

Bandura, A. (1997). *Self-efficacy: The exercise of control*. New York, NY: W. H. Freeman.

Berk, R. (2003). *Professors are from Mars; Students are from Snickers*. Sterling, VA: Stylus Publishing.

Bobek, B. (2002). Teachers' resiliency: A key to career longevity. *Clearing House, 70*(4), 176–178.

Derks, P. (1996). Twenty years of research on humor: A view from the edge. Introduction in A. Chapman & H. Foot (Eds.), *Humor and laughter: Theory, research, and applications* (p. cm). New Brunswick, NJ: Transaction Publishers.

Evans-Palmer, T. (2009). *The relationship between sense of humor and self-efficacy: An exploration of the beliefs of art teachers* (Doctoral dissertation). University of the Incarnate Word, San Antonio, TX. Available from ProQuest Digital Dissertation. (TX 6-697-683).

Evans-Palmer, T. (2010). The potency of humor and instructional self-efficacy on art teacher stress. *Studies in Art Education, 52*(1), 69–83.

Hackman, M. & Morath, E. (2018, December 28). Teachers quit jobs at highest rate on record. *The Wall Street Journal*. https://www.wsj.com/articles/teachers-quit-jobs-at-highest-rate-on-record-11545993052

Keith-Spiegel, P. (1972). Early conceptions of humor: Varieties and issues. In J. H. Goldstein & P. E. McGhee (Eds.), *The psychology of humor: Theoretical perspectives and empirical issues* (pp. 3–39). New York, NY: Academic Press.

Martin, R. (2007). *The psychology of humor; An integrative approach*. Burlington, MA: Elsevier Academic Press.

Morreall, J. (2009). *Comic relief: A comprehensive philosophy of humor*. Chichester, UK: Wiley-Blackwell.

NYU Steinhardt. (2019, July 30). *No laughing matter*. Retrieved from https://steinhardt.nyu.edu/art/education/high_school/curriculum2010/no_laughing_matter

Palmer, P. (2007). *The courage to teach: Exploring the inner landscape of a teacher's life*. San Francisco, CA: Jossey-Bass.

Pajares, F. (2002, June 18). *Overview of social cognitive theory and self-efficacy*. Retrieved from June 18, 2008. http://www.emory.edu/EDUCATION/mfp/eff.html

RMCAD. (July 30, 2019). Decoding humor in art and design. Retrieved from https://www.rmcad.edu/vasd-lecture/dr-peter-mcgraw-chelsey-delaney-decoding-humor-art-design/

Ruch, W. (1998). *Humor research 3: The sense of humor—Explorations of a personality characteristic*. New York, NY: Mouton de Gruyter.

Thibodeaux, J. (2014). Three versions of constructionism and their reliance on social conditions in social problems research. *Sociology, 48*(4), 829–837.

Thorson, J., & Powell, F. (1993). Development and validation of a multidimensional sense of humor scale. *Journal of Clinical Psychology, 49*(1), 13–23.

Wrench, J., & McCroskey, J. (2001). A temperamental understanding of humor communication and exhilaratability. *Communication Quarterly, 49*(2), 142–159.

CHAPTER ONE

Humor's Place in Art Education

Humor and Laughter Are Essential to Teaching and Learning Art

Humor is critical to teaching. Just ask any art teacher on a Friday afternoon after a long, intense week. You can bet they are headed somewhere to laugh with friends. Why? Because laughter motivates us, revives us, relieves us, encourages us and inspires us to teach art with fresh new insights in the weeks to come. Artful humor, that is speech and behavior that evokes creative ideas and free laughter, is more appropriate for an art classroom than any other educational venue. Art teachers who laugh at themselves and laugh with (never at) students are well on the way to eliminating much of the tension that inherently resides in highly interactive art classrooms in our schools. With humor, teachers create a space that positively nurtures learning, a place where joy supports human endeavors (Banas, Dunbar, Rodgriquez, & Liu, 2011; Perrez, Huber, & Geissler, 2001), and helps students become the unique human beings they were born to be.

Teachers are now competing with "a range of portable electronic devices that are often switched on and fully operational" (Tait, Lampert, Bahr, & Bennett, 2015). We must work harder to gain the attention of a student audience hypersensitive to keeping one eye on a screen. Gone are the pedagogic expectations for full-on attention. Whoosh! Instead, educators, have adapted their autocratic approach from an absolute master possessor of knowledge to a more hybrid mix of performance. We have become "edutainers" and humor is a perfect means for "edutainment" (2015). If we are going to use humor, we must first explore what humor looks like in a classroom and what the benefits are for it being there.

Learning, like all human experience, is an emotional affair that involves discovery and delight if we are lucky. When learning is enjoyable, it is touched by entertainment, synthesis, and personalized new ideas. It is not the robotic acquisition of concepts that holds little meaning for us when learning is *not* enjoyable. The former processes are more likely activated in a classroom where both teachers and students feel safe and function without fear of failure. I argue for humor-evoked instruction, teaching behaviors that powerfully and effortlessly generate a sense of fun, stirring up emotions such as joy and laughter—emotions that make us feel present (and safe). Delicious, delightful and deeply embedded concepts served with a side of humor like a good entrée, more effectively connect students to concepts, motivates them to attend, achieve, and recall more easily than rigid, robotically delivered content. (Opplinger & Zillman, 2003; Teslow, 1995; Wanzer & Frymier, 1999).

Ask anyone and they will tell you that their favorite teacher was one who made them laugh, who bent the rules to make class fun and told self-deprecating, personal stories while teaching. Those anecdotal insights our teachers shared with us were so filled with learning we cannot help but remember what made us laugh (Glasser, 1986, 1997). If we are wise, we will do everything in our power to get their attention, entertain them and inspire them. In doing so, we will feel like the plane has left the classroom runway after tiresome taxying for long stretches on the tarmac.

Humor Makes Teaching Fun

There are manifold reasons why humor works well for art teachers in an art classroom, but the first reason for engaging students with humor is that it makes teaching gratifyingly fun! Our need for fun is one of five primary needs driving our behavior, along with survival, belonging, power, and freedom (Glasser, 1986). I do not have to convince anyone that having fun is essential to living:

> We are all driven by four psychological needs embedded in our genes: the need to belong, the need for power, the need for freedom, and the need for fun. We can no more ignore these needs than we can ignore the food and shelter we must have for survival. Satisfying one or more of these needs feels very good. In fact, the biological purpose of pleasure is to tell us a need is being satisfied. (Glasser, 1997, p. 17)

Fun resides where we play and where we play, we laugh. Laughter is something we do with other people—it is a socially exhilarating, liberating group activity. Shared laughter reinforces many aspects of learning, while, at the same time removing academic and social barriers that thwart learning (Shade, 1996). We can expect humor to bring emotional pleasure to teaching but I have found that pleasure comes even if students do not "get it." When I was an elementary art teacher years ago, I introduced a rather wrangly group of fourth-grade students to the judicious use of glue with a silly saying, "A little bit of glue will do.... whoo!" Upon hearing this, a self-assured fourth-grader coolly reminded me that I had already taught them the glue ditty. I responded with, "Well then, you must be having déjà glue." The obtuse comment sailed over students' heads and did not liberate their resistance to cooperate, but it did adjust *my* attitude. Chuckling to myself, I noticed students eyeing me curiously as if to say, "What are you going to do next?" I thrive on throwing students off balance by shifting the staged, rigid pedagogical paradigm from sober to spirited. Humor helps me do this.

On the flip side of fun are conditions essential to good art teaching. These being freedom to investigate and learn, fairness, honesty, esteem, orderliness and respect. These conditions are critical because their absence makes satisfying the five basic needs impossible. Imagine, e.g., trying to satisfy your belongingness and love needs or your esteem needs in an atmosphere characterized by dishonesty, unfair punishment, and restrictions on freedom of speech.

Humor Triggers Innovative Thinking

Second, laughter and play entertained in a community space such as an art classroom empower members to depart or diverge from the expected. After all, aren't the unexpected results of innovative thinking a principal goal for art education curriculum? In the same way that we make humorous connections between two unrelated concepts (like joke punchlines), divergent thinking helps us to join incongruous ideas together to create something unconventional. "The way artists think, learn, and engage in the world involves deep questioning, comfort with ambiguity, and a sophisticated understanding of play as process" (Foley, 2014, p. 144).

Playing in school can be scary for teachers because we love to be in control. Playful humor that hurls us and our students into a vortex of creative chaos can be a wild and wooly ride. We hang on tight and close our eyes but are delighted to discover our "what ifs?" have crystallized into "wows!" Vibrancy comes from this kind of chaos, whereas too much order marches in predictable habits. In turn, too much habit gives birth to unexceptional thinking. Boring. Humor to the rescue! Laughter with play highjacks our inhibitions, pushing us forward across the lines of convention. (More on play in Chapter Four). Teaching from a point of playfulness constructs a natural safety net that allows for human misstep and failure. Students offered the freedom to explore, play, and take risks, will come to accept that they will make mistakes. The "uh-oh!" moment is sister to the "ah-ha!" event. Both earmark a creative learning process summit, a summit where shame from making mistakes cannot reside.

Any artist will tell you that to be liberated from the fear of failure is a major catalyst for creative advancement, even for very young artists (see Chapter Four for a deep dive into creativity). I substituted several days for a friend who taught art at a K-8 Montessori school. The schedule for her art classroom offered chunks of time dedicated to "open studio" in which kids can elect to explore whatever has captured their interest. During one period, an adorable Kinder student whom I will call Megan appeared in the art room giggling. She proclaimed, "I feel like doodling!" We smiled at each other and I replied, "You do? Well, the doodling tools are over there and here is some paper." The young artist worked effusively for about 15 minutes, then jumped up and ran to me with her drawing. Proudly holding the paper inches from my face, Megan announced, "Hey! I was doodling and look what showed up!" This joyful, spontaneously combustible child artist had captured the most amazing shapes and lines I had ever seen. She was on to something and that something escaped while playing freely with materials. She was given the freedom to play and was able to share her joyful journey with someone like me, a teacher observer on the paper playground.

As art educators and advancers of creativity, we embrace the processes of idea cultivation with imagination, synthesizing and critically evaluating those ideas with the hope of doing something valuable with the creative outcomes (Foley, 2014). How can we expect superlative outcomes for creative ideas (innovation) that hold the potential to impact the world if we are not comfortable with not knowing what the results will be? Children are. I affirm that playful humor's part in these processes it that it removes the fear of not knowing. Children are okay with not knowing. They are willing to "just have a go" as Sir Kenneth Robinson, an authority on creativity in American schools, would say (Robinson, 2006).

Sir Ken would also say that we are educating our children out of the creativity they are born with, at a time when we should be preparing them for a workforce which will rely on the creativity humor can produce. A national study conducted across 100 of the largest corporations found 84% of their personnel directors believed people with a sense of humor were more creative, more flexible, and more willing to try new ideas (Scriven & Hefferin, 1998). As Megan exemplified, humor supported by joy are indisputably necessary behaviors for teachers who wish to be effective with their students. Humor fertilizes young minds in our art classrooms to generate unconventional ideas, the process associated with divergent thinking.

We discover a great many more optional paths around "dead end" ways of thinking when we are operating with lateral, not linear, thinking (more about this in Chapter Four). Fearless idea-proliferation, exploration and investigation processes are the performance of studio art making.

Truly, teaching is a performance akin to stand-up comedy. Good comedians are always good teachers (Glasser, 1997). I would argue that good teachers are also comedians (Evans-Palmer, 2010). The goal for both the teacher and the comedian is to attain an interactive relationship with their audience through the use of performative strategies that achieve a desired response (McCarron & Savin-Baden, 2008). It is no surprise that students who were asked to identify characteristics that describe excellent teachers they remember offer a sense of humor as one of the first descriptors (Pollack & Freda, 1997). I can think of many effective teachers who have much in common with good comedians. Enter, Pat Harris, a seventh-grade English teacher voted Teacher of the Year for her humorous and effective teaching practices that could be adopted by art teachers for their sheer accessibility. Her principal affirmed, "Mrs. Harris has a knack for making learning fun" (Pannell, 2009, p. 53). Pat confesses to joking with her seventh-grade students, using different voices and accents because she believes that using humor encourages higher-level thinking.

Committing to making school fun, Pat professes "I feel like I do stand-up comedy—seven shows a day, five days a week" (Pat Harris, personal communication, August 17, 2009). Her playful attitude and willingness to use appropriate humor directly relates to her instructional efficacy; 87% of Mrs. Harris' students achieved proficient to advanced scores in the state benchmark test (Pannell, 2009, p. 54). Although her students scored well, Pat discloses they will tell you her class is easy (Pat Harris, personal communication, August 17, 2009). Strategies Pat practices are saturated with silliness. For example, she holds up a pair of baby jeans claiming they are "happy pants" for students who complain, are depressed or simply surly. She also suspends wires from the ceiling with clothespins attached at the end. When students are finished or have a question about their work, they clip it to the clothespin to signal they are "up in the air" and would like feedback. Pat sits in the ideological bleachers with creativity research rock stars like Torrance (1970), who discovered humor and playfulness are characteristics of creative people, and humor researchers like, Murdock and Ganim (1992), who proclaimed humor as a subset of creativity.

Humor Distances Us From Stressors

The third reason humor belongs in the art classroom is the contribution it makes to teachers' emotional well-being by moderating stressors. Let's face it, teaching while traveling through personal adversity can take you to the edge of good reason. Years ago, I was teaching art in an elementary school and feeling acutely tense a week before my wedding. While guiding needy Kindergarteners through a drawing activity, I asked students to kindly refrain from calling out my name with the promise that I would be moving around the room to assist them in every way. An awkward silence blanketed the classroom until one bright youngster chirped out, "911, 911!" How clever, I thought. (I wanted to ask the young comedian to determine if the issue was indeed a 911/emergency or a 411/information). Nevertheless, the incident unshackled tension in my body as laughter bubbled into my being. There is nothing like laughing during the hectic teaching day to uncap relief as an operational safety valve while under duress. It is amazing how a playful appreciation for what is funny evokes positive emotions for everyone in the classroom. It is utterly magical.

Consider laughter as a way to run away without leaving the classroom. The more frequently we use humor as teachers, the more likely we are to see sources of stress as less threatening, swatting problems away like flies (Martin, 2007). Emotionally positive humor is a coping mechanism for stress in any workplace because it powerfully relaxes those in the environment, reduces tension, buffers disappointments (Lippitt, 1982) and eases tense social interactions (Martin, Puhlik-Doris, Larsen, Gray, & Weir, 2003; Mesmer-Magnus & Glew, 2012).

Now let's talk about burnout, a condition that creeps up on us if we are not mitigating the stress that swarms around us. As a caring professional, you know you are approaching burnout when you feel a slow-leaking loss of empathy, a rise in cynicism and are inclined to cite your students as the source of your problems (Intrator & Kunzman, 2007). You find yourself distanced from your job, reaching for any coping mechanism that offers relief. Relief theory humorists recommend laughter as a means for venting nervous energy to bring about liberation (Morreall, 1983). They assert that when we are frustrated, angry or fearful we make movements to prepare to run away, move closer to our enemy, or attack! We stand staring them down rooted in a challenging position with clenched fists and jaws. The movements we make while laughing, although not the movements of fleeing or fighting, relieve the excessive strain in our muscles with relaxed breathing (Morreall, 2009). Education reformer, John Dewey reasoned "the laugh is thus a phenomenon of the same general kind as the sigh of relief" (1894, p. 558).

Seriously, if we do not find what renews us as educators, we are at risk of burnout, the "prolonged response to chronic and interpersonal stressors on the job" (Maslach, 2003, p. 189), stemming from the inability to cope with breaking down (Jennings & Greenberg, 2009). Burgeoning job tasks, standardized tests influencing curriculum have now been overshadowed by real fears and concerns about physical safety and bodily injuries, i.e., contusions (59.2%), sprains (19.6%), abrasions (6%), fractures (5%), and anxiety or stress (3%; Williams, Billingsley, & Banks, 2018). Alongside fears of physical safety is the overwhelming call on teacher emotional labor. As job stress is on the rise and mental health is declining: 58% of teachers testified that their mental health was eroding, while only 34% made the same confession in 2015 (2018). Teacher renewal matters not only for teacher retention but also for nurturing teachers as a way to stir up spontaneous innovation (keeps learning "messy" open-ended vs. "perfect" finite with predictable outcomes, and places you, the teacher, back in control).

Not surprisingly, the teacher attrition rate is escalating well beyond the 15% attrition rate of almost a decade ago; the frequency of younger teachers (1–5 years of experience, 30 years of age or younger) leaving the profession is five times greater than more experienced teachers 31 years and older (Borman & Dowling, 2008). Does the unsettling rise in attrition rates among young teachers point to their inadequate emotional preparation for the trials that accompany the business of teaching art? As a veteran teacher remaining in the profession for the long haul, I have observed a contingency of seasoned teachers capable of escaping emotional meltdown and burnout from job stress. These teachers are able to distance themselves from the effects of intense job heat with the robust resilience that humor provides (Darwich, 2018).

Sixteenth-century relief theory essayists persuaded those entangled with life to break free of constraints by laughing at constraining forces. Further, Freud asserted humor to be a "rare and precious gift" that has the power to liberate us from anxiety (1928, p. 220), essentially acting like a parent telling our childlike hearts that life is not as dangerous as it seems (Martin, 2007). We do not need a theorist's rationale to know that laughter helps us escape whatever anxiety or fear is overpowering us.

Humor Builds Student Rapport

The fourth reason for humor in the art classroom is what humor can do to build student rapport. As the leader of learning, highly effective teachers "cooperate, inspire, and earn student trust" through social interactions (Yatvin, 2008, p. 71). In the same way, humorous teachers possess a capacity for immediacy or quickly connecting with students (Martin, 2007; Torok, McMorris, & Lin, 2004). Glasser's choice theory (1997) encourages teachers to positively charge the classroom's social environment by laughing with their students, priming them for learning (Evans-Palmer, 2009).

I, among others, have found humor to be extremely useful in constructing human connectedness, as opposed to social disengagement. Rather like a social glue. In classroom communities, humor humanizes, defuses, encourages bonding, reduces anxiety, and promotes higher-order cognitive skills that keep students end with one another to share critical thinking (Bryant & Zillman, 1989; Coleman, 1992; Torok et al., 2004; Ziv, 1983). If we hope to operate in a pleasant classroom environment with happily engaged students, we must rely on either affiliative or self-disparaging humor, steering clear of aggressive humor that creates an environment where students feel anything but connected.

What Exactly Is Humor, a Sense of Humor and Laughter?

Humor. Humor, the word related to all things laughable, is a universally pleasurable behavior phenomenon experienced by every person in every culture since time began. The subject of humor is very popular. A 2019 Google search for "humor" netted a total of 991,000,000 results, "a sense of humor" fetched 485,000,000 results and a search for "laughter" scored 169,000,000 hits. The word humor is derived from the Latin word, *humoreum*, meaning fluid, referring to four bodily fluids or *humors* that are balanced when one was in good health (Martin, 2007). The phrases, *of good humor*, or *a good sense of humor* denote an individual's state of physiological balance. *Humorous* came to denote a personality trait that was out of the norm, odd, or eccentric; associated with being peculiar. Humor psychologist, Rod Martin concurs pleasurable humor allures us in every area of our life because it fuses a kind of mental play with social, emotional, cognitive and expressive components. "Humor is a positive emotion called mirth, which is typically elicited in social contexts by a cognitive appraisal process involving the perception of playful, nonserious incongruity, and which is expressed by the facial and vocal behavior of laughter" (Martin, 2007, p. 29). The overarching definition of humor indicates that it is always present in situations that trigger laughter.

"In humor, we experience a sudden change of mental state—a cognitive shift, that would be disturbing under normal circumstances, that is if we took it seriously" (Morreall, 2009, p. xii). The sudden, cognitive shift is present in all types of humor, in fact, that is what makes us laugh. It is what comedians call "timing" because we do not expect the suddenness of the shift (Ziv, 1984). We laugh as we swiftly swing from one state of being to another, like moving from serious to playful (Morreall, 1983). The shifting permits us to exit reality, to soar over our problems on the wings of pleasure.

To provide a school-embedded scenario of this phenomenon, I share this story. While on hall duty during classes at the high school where I taught, I encountered a student with seriously sagging pants. Although it was the style at the time, we teachers were nevertheless admonished to instruct students to "pull up their pants" as stipulated by the student dress code. When I asked this particular student to comply, he instead pulled *down* his pants. (That is the first and only time I have been "mooned" in a school setting.) Instead, of a reprimand, I offered an assessment, "I will give it a 4!" He stopped, without turning around, pulled up his pants—all the way—and walked on without missing a beat. Mission accomplished by the old sudden shift maneuver. I can tell you that by handling this particular misbehavior with humor enticed me to seek situations to make the shift happen, again and again. (Do we love to be comedians, or what?)

Our society has grappled with understanding humor for some time now, hence, the presence of humor theories, four of which situate why something is perceived as funny enough to make us laugh. These are incongruity theory, arousal relief theory, disparagement or superiority theory, and an amalgamation of the other theories into a new theory (Wolff, Smith, & Murray, 1934). First, incongruity theory, the most widely accepted explanation promoted by philosophers Aristotle and Kant, supposed that laughter was "an intellectual reaction to an unexpected, illogical, or inappropriate" event (Morreall, 1983, p. 15). We find something humorous if it is jolts us out of the ordinary pattern of life. A sudden shift from what expected occurs. Second, arousal relief theorists put forth the idea that laughter was evoked when a person was forbidden to act in a certain way, creating frustrated desire and pent-up nervous energy (Morreall, 1983). Laughter arouses in us a pleasant emotional state that vents our nervous energy setting us free from constraints and bringing relief (Berylne, 1969; Morreall, 1983). Adding to this thought was education reformer, Dewey (1894) who postulated that instantaneous relaxation of strain occurred when individuals were laughing; Freud (1928) interpreted the mechanics of laughter as a discharge of surplus psychic energy (as cited in Morreall).

Third, the disparagement or superiority theory, beginning with Plato, proposed that we feel superior when we laugh at others' weaknesses. Spawned from this notion are writings that cited laughter as controlled, aggressive, and observable human behavior compared to dogs showing their teeth while challenging an enemy (Morreall, 1983). In succinct social terms: "Laughing equals winning" and for every humorous situation, there is a winner, a loser, and the suddenness in which something is won or lost (Gruner, 1997, p. 8). The fourth theory, a new theory, combining important features of the previous three, offered distinct situations that triggered laughter: (1) a change from a serious pattern of thinking to a nonserious state brought about by incongruity; (2) a sudden psychological shift in perspective followed by laughter; (3) anxiety replaced by a relaxing, pleasurable feeling of mirth (Morreall, 1983).

Epistemologically speaking, all that is written suggests extrapolating humor theories only allows us to peer into the yawning chasm of what we do not know about humor and laughter. Research continues and even the humor connoisseurs are updating the information as we speak. For example, Morreall maintains that laughter can be elicited without the presence of humor. He came to this conclusion after watching children. He first observed that 4-month-old infants laughing in response to sensory stimuli not because they experienced a cognitive or psychological shift. Later, he became convinced that laughter was not associated with humor until children had matured enough to associate concepts with acquired language patterns. As teachers, we have observed this ourselves and can attest how much more literal small children are than adolescents when they laugh at literal statements such as "I am so hungry I could eat a horse" or "It is raining cats and dogs." Youth only roll their eyes.

Sense of humor. We know what humor looks and feels like, but what does it mean to possess a sense of humor? A "good sense of humor is an important social skill that we admire in others," as they are easy-to-be-with individuals who do not take themselves too seriously (Martin, 2007, p. 131). Those who possess a sense of humor are equipped with an ability to see life, especially problems, with a playfully childlike perspective (Davis, 1999). We generally prefer to be with humorous people because they are charming, engaging, communicative and skilled at making mundane tasks fun. However, humor researchers exploring personality dimensions found less than desirable characteristics associated with high-humor people—such as boastfulness, restlessness, impulsiveness, and immaturity—than their more conscientious, low-humor counterparts (McCrae & John, 1992). Roses have thorns, too.

Art teachers and artists are admired for their ability to operate effortlessly in their endeavors with creativity. Common traits shared among creative people are both positive and negative, with a sense of humor as one of the most positive traits (Cayirdag & Acar, 2010). A sense of humor in creative people enables them to see life, especially problems, with a playfully childlike perspective (Davis, 1999; Koestler, 1964; O'Quin & Derks, 1997).

Playing with problems in the classroom activates the delivery of instructional content from different angles. At one point in my middle school teaching career, I was teaching a painting unit to seventh graders who were behaving badly with brushes. So, I initiated the institution of Painting Licenses that gave students the right to paint. To earn a license, students were required to pass two parts of a painting assessment: a written color theory test and a "driving" painting performance assessment. I evaluated their performance on five tasks: (1) mixing paint on a palette, (2) mixing tints and shades, (3) painting defined edges with the side of a brush, (4) painting a gradual tonal scale with blended colors and, (5) washing and storing the brush appropriately. I printed their pictures on a driving license-like card, laminated them and ceremoniously distributed them to exemplary students. No license, no painting. I was also free to revoke their license, even writing up a painting citation if their painting efforts threatened a crash. They had to complete a Defensive Painting mini-course to win their license back. I enjoyed it and the students willingly played along. Little did they know that the licenses resolved the misbehavior problem.

Although this example may not be wildly creative, it nevertheless demonstrates how unconventional approaches to instructional issues can join instruction with humor. It also captures another positive trait common to both humor and creativity: resolution—the impulse to be creative, to have an idea, to act, or produce something unique that is appropriate, relevant, and best-fit response to a problem (O'Quin & Derks, 2017). The balance we achieve when we depart from one idea and jump to another as we accomplish resolution in teaching requires both relevance and incongruity. Note: slapstick humor may be surprisingly incongruous but it isn't intelligently relevant.

We can understand the concept sense of humor concept more clearly by breaking it down into three separate behaviors in which we are engaged. We can appreciate humor, we can produce humor or we can possess humor as a personality trait (O'Quin and Derks, 1997). Anyone who generates humor is one who appreciates humor, however, not everyone who appreciates humor is capable of producing humor. To explain further, an orientation toward humor could either be a genetically inherited personality trait or a communication skill that can be learned. Genetic sense of humor proponents argue that we are all born with a biological humor fingerprint that can develop as we grow (Berlyne, 1971). Others argue that an orientation toward humor can be nurtured in us if we are cheerfully inclined to find humor in most situations (Booth-Butterfield & Booth-Butterfield, 1991; Merolla, 2006), and are adept at communicating effectively with humor (Wrench & McCroskey, 2001). Then there is the idea that people perceived as humorous are extroverted, sociable, assertive, dominant, carefree, and venturesome, and more inclined to sport a happy outlook than a sullen mood (Ruch & Köhler, 1999; Wrench & McCroskey, 2001).

A reliable self-report survey I employed to determine teachers' sense of humor in my search for a relationship with humor and self-efficacy is The Multidimensional Sense of Humor Scale (MSHS) (Thorson & Powell, 1993). The survey assessed a teacher's overall sense of humor with 24 items representing four dimensions of humor: (a) the creation or production of humor, (b) humor used as a coping mechanism, (c) humor used socially, and (d) humor appreciation. The MSHS score indicates the level of perceived sense of humor assessed on a five-point scale with response anchors from 1 (*strongly disagree*) to 5 (*strongly agree*).

Laughter. Laughter is strange. It is familiar, yet when we think about it, the sounds we make while laughing are like no other communication. When we laugh, all body parts participate, and we are out of control in a way unmatched by any other state (save insanity):

> Our eyebrows and cheeks go up, as the muscles around our eyes tighten. The corners of our mouths curl upward, baring our upper teeth. Our diaphragms move up and down in spasms, expelling air from our lungs and making staccato vocal sounds. If the laughter is intense, it takes over our whole bodies. Our eyes tear. We may wet our pants. (Morreall, 2009, p. 2)

Only humans laugh and when we do, we do not do it alone. In fact, hearing other people laugh (especially children giggling) ignites our own laughter. Laughter that makes us laugh is like a "behavioral chain reaction that sweeps through a group, creating a crescendo of jocularity" (Provine, 2000, p. 129). Truly, laughter is contagious. A bizarre account of an outbreak of contagious laughter was reported in 1962 at a Tanzanian girls' boarding school:

> What began as an isolated fit of laughter (and sometimes crying) in a group of 12- to 18-year-old schoolgirls rapidly rose to epidemic proportions. Contagious laughter propagated from one individual to the next, eventually infecting adjacent communities. The epidemic was so severe that it required the closing of schools, lasting for six months. (Provine, 1992, p. 38)

Laughter makes us healthy. The benefits of laughter appear in the literature of many cultures, including the Bible. "A merry heart doeth good like a medicine" (Proverbs 17:22). Immanuel Kant testified that laughter massaged the organs, while physician, James Walsh, observed laughing after surgery reduced pain and accelerated healing (Morreall, 1997). Norman Cousins (1991), a writer experiencing chronic spinal pain, abandoned traditional medical treatment to watch hours of funny videos and movies. His joyful experiment discovered a significant pain-to-laughter ratio: 10 minutes of spasmatic belly laughing produced 2 hours of painless sleep. The physiological benefit of laughter for teachers and students aids learning by easing anxiety through improved respiration and circulation, lowering pulse and blood pressure, oxygenating the blood, releasing "feel good" endorphins into the bloodstream and even elevating activity in the immune system (Berk, 1998; Garner, 2006).

Yes, laughter makes us and others laughing with us feel good. If there was such a thing as a "laughter-stat" that could gauge the extent to which laughter made us connect with those around us, we could better determine what humor to cultivate. While working in a difficult teaching assignment in a school where administrative support was tragically negligible, I initiated the institution of Friday afternoon "Laughter Hour." I invited my colleagues to join me off campus to share the stories from the week that made us feel depleted, helpless, discouraged or assaulted. I will admit that sometimes adult beverages were shared along with the stories, but the goal of Laughter Hour was to flip flop the bad times into something laughable. The telling of the story usually began with a whining woe-is-me pitch but almost always ended with disclosure of some laughable aspect coming to light. The transformation of turning mourning into mirth gave us all a sense of distance from the problems we faced in the classroom.

I promote laughter with students to accomplish all tasks but have learned that not everyone is convinced laughing in the workplace is beneficial. There is a small contingency of teachers who believe laughter holds little value for productive work, in fact, they insist laughter and goal-oriented behavior are incompatible (Apter & Smith, 1977). At the university where I teach instructors' offices are next to each other along the hall leading to the classrooms. Students stopping in my office for counsel inevitably engage in laughter with me. (I do admit to helping that along). We are not insipidly, raucously engaged but our hushed conversation does often erupt into occasional chortles. The instructor whose office was next to mine at one point would become inflamed with anger at the sound of our laughter. Sometimes they were known to appear in my doorway scowling and saying to the student, "Selena, don't you have somewhere else you should be?" I did some research into why this person harbored such aversion to laughter and found that, while laughter to most listeners induces positive effect there may be a conscious or unconscious interplay of the emotional (affective) state of the listener that permits them to like or dislike the sound of laughter (Kipper & Todt, 2001).

In other words, the mood of the listener determines whether the sound of laughter is pleasant or unpleasant. I will take one for the team on this issue and try to keep laughter in my office low key but everything in me wants to shout, "Laughing is legal and it is free. It offers no penalties, no calories, or any other health concern!" (For clarity of humor terms, definitions associated with humor in this book are included in Table 1.1.)

Teacher Sense of Humor

On good days, students in art classrooms of humorous teachers eagerly join their teacher in the task at hand. Effective, relevant, humor-oriented teachers win over students with their rapport-building teaching strategies that feature unexpected, naturally engaging humor-embedded nuggets. They are adept at pulling people into their sphere by sharing personal anecdotes, playing with words, vividly illustrating concepts punctuated with dramatic demonstrations. Similar to comedians, teachers are especially sensitive to the audience/student response and can adjust their delivery accordingly. These stand-out, socially connected teachers make students care about what they are teaching.

The role of teacher humor and its effect on education within the past two decades has produced some interesting findings. For the benefit of hurried art teachers reading this chapter to tap into the "relevant good stuff" researchers have discovered about humor, I have extracted the most salient studies from educational, philosophical, physiological, sociological and psychological perspectives and added them contextually in the chapters to follow. Regrettably, there are but a few published investigations connecting laughter, humor, and sense of humor to benefits specifically for art educators. Since my observations and collected data as an art teacher and research offer some substantive validity, I will share these in context as well.

Studies that most relevant to the goal of this book were conducted decades ago in university environments, a far cry from what could be useful for primary and secondary teachers (Neuliep, 1991). Who knows why humor has been passed over for serious academic examination? Perhaps it is because academia associates it with pleasure and fun (Martin, 2007). Go figure. I have, however, have done some digging to uncover research that applies humor to teaching.

Humor that shows up in a teacher is portrayed as spontaneity, goodwill, joy in relating to others, a willingness to explore alternatives before making serious overtures, as well as an ability to see through pretensions and deceptions (Kane, Suls, & Tedeschi, 1977). Humor-oriented teachers appreciate and generate humor, believing they are more effective and *are* more effective than those who are not humor-oriented (Gorham & Christophel, 1990; Korobkin, 1988; Martin, 2007; Sveback, 1974; Torok, McMorris, & Lin, 2004; Wrench & McCroskey, 2001; Ziv, 1984, 1988). Humor is linked to positive teacher evaluations, greater student enjoyment of the subject, and greater student retention (Martin, 2007). Students learn most effectively from teachers who deliver humor in a manner compatible with their personality, especially when high humor-oriented students were paired with high humor-oriented instructors (Wanzer & Frymier, 1999).

Humor is potently effective as an instructional tool that advances learning for students at all levels (Berk, 2002, 2003; Bryant & Zillman, 1979; Civikly, 1986; Polio

& Humphreys, 1996), and most effective when there is an authentic connection to the concept (Downs, Javidi, & Nussbaum, 1988). But wait, humor researchers have revealed a few more reasons for humor's presence in our classrooms: laughter relieves classroom stress (Shibinski & Martin, 2010), enhances relationships with students (Nesi, 2012), makes subjects more enjoyable (Torok et al., 2004), as well as more memorable (Garner, 2006).

One study conducted in a college course correlated learning to teachers' sense of humor by randomly assigning students to one of two instructors (Ziv, 1988). The humorous instructor effectively amplified key concepts of the lecture with humor devices three or four times per lecture, while the not so humorous instructor did not. The humorous instructor employed mnemonic humor decises, such as jokes, cartoons, illustrations, or anecdotes not only engaged students but also increased retention (Martin, 2007). The final grades of students assigned to the instructor who used humor were nearly 10% higher than the grades of students assigned to the instructor who had not. Please note that healthy outcomes such as this are indeed influenced by how funny students find their instructor humor to be.

Table 1.1. *Definitions of Humor Terms*[1]

Term	Definition
Humor	A verbal or nonverbal activity eliciting a positive cognitive or affective response from listeners
Humorous	A genuine sense of fun and comedy, impersonal or gently personal; a humorous view of life
Humor appreciation	A positive attitude toward humor and humorous people
Humor production	Ability to create humor to amuse others
Humor used as a coping mechanism	Ability to use humor to cope with stress or adversity
Humor used socially	Ability to attract and maintain relationships with others using humor to obtain the mental and physical health benefits of social support
Sense of humor	Frequency in which individuals produce or display humor in a variety of life situations
Incongruity of humor	Humor involving making a connection with two disparate ideas, concepts, or situations in a surprising or unexpected manner

[1] Definitions attributed to Martin (2014).

Effective Forms of Teacher Humor

The majority of teachers use some form of humor in their classrooms from time to time but experienced teachers, and male at the use humor most frequently (Bryant, Cominsky, & Zillmann, 1979; Javidi & Long, 1989). Teacher humor, it would seem, is a composite of multiple behavioral messages coming from a teacher. To complicate the understanding of teacher humor even more, there are at least three factors that influence humor as it appears from teacher to teacher.

First, humor is very much an extension of a teacher's personality, their identity—cultural, racial, ethnic, socioeconomic, their beliefs, the dynamics of the family in which they were raised, their geographic grounding, even their present life circumstances. (Teachers may all be of the same species but they are *not* the same animal.) Second, teachers capable of engaging students quickly activate their attention with "immediacy" behaviors that enhance physical and psychological closeness and include use of humor and praise, vocal expressiveness, smiling, mobility, and eye contact (Gorham & Christophel, 1990). High-immediacy teachers may be more effective at making an impact with humor than those with low-immediacy. Finally, the third form of humor teachers use extends along an intellectual spectrum from slapstick silly at the lowest end, to global wit at the high end. Relevant, concept-rich humor that highlights ideas during instruction is by far the best form to foster superior student learning (Bryant et al., 1979).

To add to this, we believe that teacher humor is also multidimensional, belonging to one of two types that achieve varying effects in the classroom: (1) social, emotional and motivational effects, or (2) cognitive effects (Bieg & Dresel, 2018). Both types are easily influenced by students' perceptions of the teacher or their teaching (Ho, 2016; Kennedy, Ahn, & Choi, 2008; Kunter et al., 2013). The social, emotional and motivational effects appeal to students' sense of belonging to a group, of feeling good about being present and motivated to learn. The cognitive effects of humor drive divergent thinking and are a desirable source of intelligent humor that we call wit. Witty instruction leans on semantic transformations (puns and wordplay), that often triggers "aha" moment surprises (Guilford, 1961).

Researchers warn teachers to use humor in moderation, lest they lose stature and are perceived as nonserious jokers (Zillmann, 1977). Surely there is a threshold for humor anecdotes (funny stories) students may hear from the same instructor over time. Moreover, teachers who lean too much on funny stories—even if they are related to the topic—lose student attention and motivation to learn if it is not balanced with a focused, serious complement. Some students perceive humor unrelated to course content as "wasting time and contrary to learning and achievement goals" (Bieg et al., 2017, p. 30).

The range of humor-oriented forms of instruction is as diverse as the teachers who are using humor and all have been shown to engage and elevate retention (Martin, 2007). Pedagogical humor related to the subject enhances students' ability to process, to synthesize and understand. Self-efficacious teachers use germane humor messages embedded in instruction to incite students to attend to the resolution of incongruity relating to the concept (Evans-Palmer, 2010; Wanzer, Frymier, & Irwin, 2010). Humor devices include but are not limited to mnemonic aids, jokes, cartoons, illustrations, or anecdotal stories, word puns, metaphors, speaking with an accent, and even belting out songs mid lesson. Most teachers use humor purely for the pedagogical purpose of making content memorable (Martin, 2007), while others use humor to manage student behavior (Berk, 2002; Korobkin, 1988; Manning, 1982; Pigford, 2001). However humor is used, five conditions must be in action if something a teacher says or does is to be perceived as funny (Coleman, 1992). These are:

1. Humor must be understood within the social context in which it is delivered or there is a connection to the material in which it is presented.
2. Humor is cognitively challenging to receptive students.
3. Humor is an unexpectedly new concept or is unrelated to two diverse concepts.
4. Humor must be delivered at an appropriate point in time.
5. Humor must be impersonal, not encroaching on students' sensitivities. In other words, warm and fuzzy humor messages we send can mask aggressively hostile, openly sexual behavior (Gruner, 1997).

Effective Humor for the Right Student

Forms of teacher humor effect student audiences differently. For young pre-K and elementary audiences, fast-paced humor intermingled with content messages successfully holds children's attention longer than slower-paced or non-humorous messages (Zillman & Bryant, 1983). Small children operating at low intellectual levels enjoy obvious, slapstick humor, while witty wordplay appeals to the youth of higher intellectual levels. College students prefer witty over silly lectures as wittiness (the ability to employ integrated, relevant humor) has been judged to be pleasurably motivating. Humor in higher education may be present in a variety of strategies from a humorous context in a syllabus, clever online announcements, descriptively funny assignments, or self-disclosing anecdotes embedded in lectures and humorous exam responses (Berk, 2002; Downs, Javidi, & Nussbaum, 1988).

The way students receive and decode teacher humor are worthy of consideration as well. When well-liked students are the target of teacher humor, it is perceived to be negative, and therefore not funny. Conversely, when less liked students are the target, it is perceived to be positive and funny (Frymier, Wanzer, & Wojtaszczyk, 2008). In this way the presence of humor can directly affect the appraisals that underlie the humorous message. Attentive humor coming from a teacher can motivate students to learn if they are capable of processing the instructional humor messages sent (Gorham & Christophel, 1990; Neuliep, 1991; Wanzer et al., 2010).

Clearly, the capability to formulate messages to convey information is important, but *how* a teacher sends that message to make students feel pleasurably comfortable is just as important (Frymier & Houser, 2000). Three individual dispositional differences describe how individual students deal with being the focus of others' laughter. These are: (1) gelotophobia, fear of being laughed at, (from the Greek word, *gelos*, laughter and *phobia*, fear); (2) gelotophilia, joy in being laughed at is the opposite of *phobia* (*philia*, affection) and, katagelasticism, joy in laughing at others from *katagelao*, laughing at (Brauer et al., 2019; Ruch & Proyer, 2008).

Gelotophobes bear an almost paranoid sensitivity toward being laughed at, with a few fearing any kind of laughter-related behavior, even smiling (Brauer et al., 2020). They cope with their shame by negatively controlling or withdrawing from the laughter event (Platt, Ruch, Hofmann, & Proyer, 2012). Watch out for student gelotophobes who sink into their seats when you are slinging jokes in their direction. They would much rather laugh with or at someone else than bear the shame of targeted amusement.

Gelotophiliacs, extraverts of the emotionally stable kind truly revel in being laughed at, seeing laughter as an indication of their value to others (Ruch & Proyer, 2008). They actively seek situations that place them on an imaginary stage where their performance inspires pleasurable laughter from others. They do this by candidly sharing incidents or embarrassing feelings that make them targets, just as comedians volunteer self-deprecating humor to evoke audience laughter at their expense. Note to self: Class clowns are gelotophiliacs.

Katagelasticists (now that's a mouthful) enjoy laughing at others, actively seeking attributes in others that elicits laughter and ridicule directed at the target; thereby, accepting that they might feel hurt. They do not feel bad about laughing at others, but rather think that those who do not like being laughed at should just fight back (Ruch & Proyer, 2008). They see laughter and being laughed at as part of life and pursue an "eye-for-an-eye"-principle when it comes to ridicule. The joy in laughing at others is particularly pronounced in younger males.

Another group of students teacher should consider as receptors of humor in the art classroom are international or ESL students recently assimilating into

American culture. These students may find the humor we take for granted difficult to understand. They may feel alienated and isolated when they are not laughing along with everyone else (Walker, 2006). Humor tied to universal subjects that come up in everyday conversations should stand out more clearly to students with diverse frames of reference. Subjects aligned with basic human conditions, parental/boyfriend/girlfriend issues, movies, songs, and exams are mainstream enough to be understood by students of all ethnicities and languages.

> In this sense, humor activates intercultural understanding and can assist in the understanding and deconstructing of social and cultural expectations. It can function as a social lubricant, as well as be an antidote to inter-ethnic tensions. Humor promotes mental flexibility, which can help people to first understand, then adopt, new aspects of culture and communication, which can then be further developed through education. (Oshima, 2018, p. 205)

How to Have a Sense of Humor Even if You Don't Think You Are Funny

Okay, you may be saying to yourself, "How can I use humor comfortably as a teacher if I am not a funny person?" "If I start telling jokes to students, I will lose control and we will not get any work done!" I get it but you are misguided if you think humor-evoked laughter elicits wildly uncontrollable unproductive activity. Quite the contrary. Humor in any social situation is as authentically human as talking with your friends (Wanzer & Frymier, 1999). You are probably wrong about your perception of yourself anyway. Just ask your family and friends. Because you see, everyone appreciates humor. If this were not so, then why are comedians so popular? Why is a sense of humor so high on the list of most desirable qualities in a mate? Why is the pleasure of laughter something we want to do again and again?

I suggest here that you begin easing into humor as a viable part of your teaching practice by first becoming comfortable with being funny. Comfort with humor is the key. A sequence of teacher behaviors you can adopt can gradually move your students' responses from low receptivity (soft chortles) to rip-roaring attentiveness and explosive guffaws (Weaver & Cotrell, 1987). The following list sequences teacher behavior with contextual explanations achievable for any teacher:

Achievable Teacher Behavior Sequence

1. Smile. Do it a lot. Smile no matter what your morning was like before you left home. Seriously, why does teaching have to be so serious? Why not teeter in space with a light-hearted attitude? How long can you attend to a serious speaker? Smiling does not mean you are not seriously dedicated to teaching all of the cognitive academics of visual arts. Puleeze, do not try to emulate your college art professor. You know the type, sensible shoes, scholarly voice, stern face, neutrally dressed. Mysterious but boring as watching wet paint dry. You thought he/she was so knowledgeable because they looked tucked-in serious and rarely smiled. (Picture this person up to their elbows in sloppy, wet clay).

Smiling is to human warmth like soft butter is to warm toast. It is a bit like spreading a fuzzy blanket over shivering students. I remember smiling at a little boy (probably 5 years old) in a grocery store. He was dancing to a song in his head, while his distracted mother standing next to him was preoccupied with looking through frozen meat in a waist-high freezer. I thought he was funny so I smiled. Do you know what he said to me, a smiling stranger? He said, "Thank you for being so happy!" That made me smile even more. As I walked away I realized that the subtle human gesture of smiling is always appreciated, especially by children. "Smiling is an instant communicator and motivator, and that is what teaching and learning is all about" (Walker, 2006, p. 121).

2. Be yourself. Just "do" you because "doing" you is the best person you can be. Good teaching comes from real people. We teach from who we are. As new teachers enter the profession they are not aware of the part of their identity that is their "teacher selves." This dimension of self comes into focus while they begin to teach and interact with students. Gradually they develop a teacher identity and presence that contributes to the feeling of authentically "owning" the classroom with integrity:

> By identity and integrity I do not mean only our best qualities, the edited version we wear in public. Identity and integrity have as much to do with our shadows and limits, our wounds and fears, as with our strengths and potentials. (Palmer, 2007, p. 13)

Do not expect to really know your students if you are not willing to be real with them. They will not trust you if your fear of their judgment holds the authentic you, prisoner. I dislike riding horses because I am uncomfortable with commandeering a large animal that has the power to harm me. Horses sense this and ride hard to buck me off. Kids are like horses; they sense when the person in charge is uncomfortable with being themselves. Horses gallop and buck, kids act out.

Talk *with* your students, naturally. Try not to talk *at* them. The things kids say are funny so listen to them. The more relaxed you are with them, the more frank and candid they will be with you. Go ahead and laugh at what they say. They will appreciate that you think *they* are funny. Humor energizes conversations.

Try to use loose, informal conversation as you follow the lesson trajectory. Keep a ping-pong dialogue going related to the subject. If you think of any, respond to student side comments with relaxed comebacks of your own. Do not hesitate to improvise your funny thoughts into subject-related add-ins. "Spontaneous" humor is often planned. You may think that the stand-up comedian you so admire is able to spontaneously call out clever comebacks to unanticipated audience heckles. They probably are reusing the first response they thought of fifty shows ago to a similar retort. You will remember your funny comebacks the more classes (or shows) you teach.

3. Cultivate a playful attitude. Laughter happens in relaxed environments where laughter and fun are easily triggered from somewhere unexpected. I have found that operating from a place of surprise permits you, the teacher, to be playful. If students never know what you will do next, they will pay attention to what you are doing now. The classroom then becomes primed for play from play that happened in the past. If you cultivate a playful approach (joyful banter, etc.) to teaching from time to time, the payoff is magnificent. Conversely, if you are stiff and formal while trying to joke with your students, they will be uncomfortable and your attempt to engage will fall flat.

If play is difficult for you because you have been too long an adult, I advise you to remember playing games in your childhood. Remember how carefree and lighthearted you felt? To pull students into my "playground" I have often asked a room full of education students during our first class together if they would like to play hide and seek with me. I explain that I will be "It," will count to 50, and they can hide anywhere on the ground floor of the building. I will then come find them. When I ask who will join me in the game, only 5 or 6 volunteer. I then say, "If you will not play with me, do not expect to have fun in this course. Playing is required for effectively teaching children." I have not to date truly played the Hide and Seek game with my students as described here, but the point is made.

4. Dare to be vulnerable. Tell personal (and appropriately professional) stories about your life. Self-disclosure is a powerful tool of engagement. Students are more actively and personally engaged when teachers talk about themselves (Downs et al., 1988). Further, teachers who share humorous personal experiences maximize student perception of teacher clarity (Wambach & Brothen, 1997). Teaching is an act of transparency. As we connect ourselves and our subject with our students, "we make ourselves and our subject vulnerable to indifference, judgment, ridicule" and rejection. (Palmer, 2007, p. 18)

5. *Warm-up students with humor on the first day.* Meet your students at the door on the first day. As cheesy as it may sound, introduce yourself to each student, smiling and shaking their hand as they enter. (I still do this at the university level.) A direct gaze and an enthusiastically strong hand squeeze not only communicates "I care about you enough to meet you face to face" but also haptically sends the message, "I may look small but I am a strong person in charge of the learning in this classroom. Do not even think of messing with me!" After introductions, initiate group cohesion with an art-related ice-breaker activity, a funny story, or a cartoon embedded in your "Expectations" presentation that you planned for the first class day. Another first-day favorite is to gather a number of household items you will call "New Use Inventions" into a canvas bag. Paired students reach into the bag and grab an item, then decide: (1) a new use for this everyday object (can be irrelevant to its current use), (2) a clever name, (3) a targeted market of persons who might buy it, and (4) how they will present the item to the class in a mock commercial. It is hilarious. Some examples that have come from this activity include a cardboard toilet paper roll touted as a pet "Hamster Hotel," a mesh zippered laundry bag as a "Flexi-Spaghetti Strainer" and an automatic lamp timer as a "Authentic Activity Activator."

When Good Humor Goes Bad: Appropriate and Inappropriate Teacher Humor

As teachers, we are aware our teaching affects the social and emotional experiences of our students. Humor not only dynamically drives instruction to a place of positive influence on student learning but also secures a positive relationship with our students (Wanzer et al., 2010). Happy and amused students are more motivated to learn and retain information than anxious and threatened students (Opplinger, 2003). Even when facing the unflinching hostility of an antagonistic student, humor can effectively neutralize, convert and control hostility, while still allowing it to be expressed (Coser, 1960). See Chapter Three for highly descriptive stories detailing classroom episodes.

A colleague of mine was teaching in a challenging high school where the profanity flying through the air is so thick, it almost drips down the walls. A student entering her art room asked (explicit content ahead) "What kind of f—ing sh-t are we going to do today?" She responded without missing a beat, "Well, what kind of f—ing sh-t would you *like* to do?" It stopped the student in his tracks because he did not expect to hear a teacher repeat his profanity. For an instant, she threw him off balance with off-color humor. I am not going to preach here but I will say that teachers are expected to operate with a higher standard of language probity than students.

I advocate for appropriately non-offensive humor over humor that is inappropriately offensive but how do we know where to draw the line? One censoring parameter that might guide your selection of humor content by movie ratings. For example, "G" for elementary audiences, "PG" for middle school and "PG-13" for high school. You will also know whether the humor you use is appropriate for your art classroom if it is something you would say to students with an administrator in the room. Do not be enticed to sling street-talk humor just because students and faculty talk that way outside of class and talking that way makes you "liked." Let me make this clear. By leaning on inappropriate slang, including trashy dialogue from movies or songs, you are essentially demonstrating your lack of creativity. It is not necessary. It is not professional and, believe me, it will go home with your students. You and your students can do better. You are also setting a bar for humor in your classroom that belongs in a bar. Conversely, reaching for wit, rising to high levels of strategically rendered humor, playing with words, even making up words, these are the kinds of humor that model the keenness students in research applaud.

To determine if humor is good or bad, we examine the message, the way it is delivered and how it makes recipients feel. Good humor sends positive messages that make receivers feel good, bad humor sends negative messages that make students feel horrible; humor types lead to quite different outcomes (Bieg & Dresel, 2018; Frymier et.al., 2008; Martin et al., 2003; Wanzer et al., 2006). Appropriate teacher humor not only dynamically drives instruction to a place of positive influence on student learning but also secures a positive relationship with our students (Wanzer et al., 2010). Happy and amused students are more motivated to learn and retain information than anxious and threatened students (Opplinger, 2003). Relevant, content-specific humor eased into serious content relaxes the atmosphere, enlightens new perspectives, which lead to cognitive insights and provide mental breaks for students (Korobkin, 1988); Ziv, 1988).

Arguably, different types of teacher humor impact how we relate to students in unique ways (Martin et al., 2003). When we use positive, appropriate, non-tendentious social humor to communicate with students in our classes, we draw them to us, generate harmony and psychological well-being. Good humor is always inclusive. Laughing together creates a shared bond of harmonious unity. Good humor even stimulates a protective function against the negative effects of anxiety that hinders free creativity (Cann, Cann & Jordan, 2001). Emotionally positive, non-tendentious, or unbiased teacher humor that does not favor a particular point of view, such as funny stories, funny comments, clever jokes, professional humor, puns, cartoons, and riddles are more effective in teaching than negative, tendentious, biased instructor humor perceived as sarcastic, aggressive, hostile, pejorative toward sex, gender or ethnicity (Torok, McMorris & Lin, 2004).

On the other hand, a significant amount of social humor has an aggressive component (superiority theory). When we communicate with negatively charged, negative, inappropriate, tendentious, aggressive and self-defeating humor, we push students away by denigrating, even harming them. Negative aggressive humor is inappropriate on so many levels: its use violates social and classroom expectations, provokes anger or sadness, stimulates anxiety, opens the door to depression, hostility and psychological unease (Bieg & Dresel, 2018; Martin et al., 2003; Wanzer et al., 2006). Aggressive teacher humor produces negative effects on all dimensions of instruction "because this type of humor is used by teachers to enhance the self at the expense of others (namely students) and is achieved at the cost of their social relationships with students" (Bieg & Dresel, 2018, p. 810).

Bad humor modeled by teachers (the divisive weapons of sarcasm, irony, insults that belittle and humiliate) are divisive weapons that train students to propagate bad student humor, consequently, dividing and disbanding unity within the classroom community (Frymier et al., 2008). Bad humor damages and corrodes a teacher's effectiveness, contributing to students' negative perceptions of their teacher (2008). Now that's a boatload of damage! To add to this rebuke is the evidence supporting that negative, aggressive humor suppresses creativity—an effect art teachers would certainly regard as detrimental (Apter, 1991).

How do you turn bad student behavior into good humor? A high school art teacher in one of my professional development sessions told of a tense situation in her classroom when a female student unabashedly called her a "bitch." The teacher motioned to the perpetrator to come to her, then looked her sternly in the eye and announced, "That is Mrs. Bitch to you, please." There was an intense frontal showdown, then suddenly, both burst out laughing. Surprising, yes? Recommended for professionals, no. Nonetheless, their shared laughter defused the ticking bomb and the teacher reported there has not been a hostile incident with that student since. I would guess the offending student has chosen not to break the pleasurable connection she felt while laughing with her teacher.

Bibliography

Apter, M. (1991). A structural-phenomenology of play. In J. H. Kerr & M. J. Apter (Eds.), *Adult play: A reversal theory approach* (pp. 13–29). Amsterdam, the Netherlands: Swets & Zeitlinger.

Apter, M. (Ed.). (2001). *Motivational styles in everyday life: A guide to reversal theory*. Washington, DC: American Psychological Association.

Apter, M., & Smith, K. (1977). Humour and the theory of psychological reversals. In A. Chapman & H. Foote (Eds.), *It's a funny thing, humour* (pp. 95–100). Oxford, UK: Pergamon Press.

Banas, J., Dunbar, N., Rodriquez, D., & Liu, S. (2011). A review of humor in educational settings. *Communication Education, 60*, 115–144.

Berk, R., & Nanda, J. P. (1998). Effects of jocular instructional methods on attitudes, anxiety, and achievement in statistics course. *Humor: International Journal of Humor Research, 11*(4), 383–410.

Berk, R. (2002). *Humor as an instructional defibrillator*. Sterling, VA: Stylus Publishing.

Berk, R. (2003). *Professors are from Mars, students are from Snickers*. Sterling, VA: Stylus Publishing.

Berlyne, D. (Ed.). (1971). *Humor and its kin*. New York, NY: Academic Press.

Bieg, S., & Dresel, M. (2018). Relevance of perceived teacher humor types for instruction and student learning. *Social Psychology of Education, 21*(4), 805–825. Retrieved from https://doi-org.libproxy.txstate.edu/10.1007/s11218-018-9428-z

Bieg, S., Grassinger, R., & Dresel, M. (2017). Humor as a magic bullet? Associations of different teacher humor types with student emotions. *Learning and Individual Differences, 56*(2017), 24–33.

Booth-Butterfield, M., & Booth-Butterfield, S. (1991). Individual differences in communication of humorous messages. *Southern Communication Journal, 56*, 43–50.

Borman, G., & Dowling, N. (2008). Teacher attrition and retention: A meta-analytic and narrative review of the research. *Review of Educational Research, 78*(3), 367–409.

Brauer, K., Proyer, R. T., & Ruch, W. (2019). Extending the study of gelotophobia, gelotophilia, and katagelasticism in romantic life toward romantic attachment. *Journal of Individual Differences*.

Bryant, J., Comisky, P., & Zillmann, D. (1979). Teachers' humor in the college classroom. *Communication Education, 28*, 110–118.

Bryant, J., & Zillmann, D. (1989). Using humor to promote learning in the classroom. In J. H. McGhee (Ed.), *Humor and children's development: A guide to practical applications* (pp. 49–78). New York: Haworth Press.

Cann, A., Cann, A. T., & Jordan, J. A. (2016). Understanding the effects of exposure to humor expressing affiliative and aggressive motivations. *Motivation and Emotion, 40*(2), 258–267.

Cayirdag, N., & Acar, S. (2010). Relationships between style of humor and divergent thinking. *Procedia Social and Behavioral Sciences, 2*(2), 3236–3240.

Civikly, J. (1986). Humor and the enjoyment of college teaching. In J. Civikly (Ed.) *Communicating in college classrooms: New directions for teaching and learning*, (pp. 61–70). San Francisco: Jossey-Bass.

Coleman, J. (1992). All seriousness aside: The laughing-learning connection. *The International Journal of Instructional Media, 19*(3), 269–276.

Coser, R. (1960). Laughter among colleagues. *Psychiatry, 2*, 81–95.

Darwich, L. (2018). New academic year, new beginning: What a teacher does for renewal. *Northwest Journal of Teacher Education, 13*(1), 1–22.

Davis, G. (1999). Barriers to creativity and creative attitudes. In M. A. Runco & S. R. Pritzker (Eds.), *Encyclopedia of creativity* (pp. 165–174). San Diego, CA: Elsevier Academic Press.

Dewey, J. (1894). The theory of emotion. *Psychological Review, 1*, 553–569.

Dewey, J. (1916). *Democracy and education.* Hollywood, FL: Simon and Brown.

Downs, V., Javidi, M., & Nussbaum, J. (1988). An analysis of teachers' verbal communication within the college classroom: Use of humor, self-disclosure, and narratives. *Communication Education, 37*, 127–141.

Evans-Palmer, T. (2009). *The relationship between sense of humor and self-efficacy: An exploration of the beliefs of art teachers* (Doctoral dissertation). University of the Incarnate Word, San Antonio, TX. Available from ProQuest Digital Dissertation. (TX 6-697-683).

Evans-Palmer, T. (2010). The potency of humor and instructional self-efficacy on art teacher stress. *Studies in Art Education, 52*(1), 69–83.

Foley, C. (2014). Why creativity? Articulating and championing a museum's social mission. *Journal of Museum Education, 39*(2), 139–151.

Freud, S. (1928). Humour. *International Journal of Psychoanalysis, 9*, 1–6.

Fry, W. F., & Allen, M. (2017). Humour as a Creative Experience: The Development of a Hollywood Humorist 1. In *Humor and laughter* (pp. 245-258). Routledge.

Frymier, A., & Houser, M. (2000). The teacher-student relationship as an interpersonal relationship. *Communication Education, 49*, 207–219.

Frymier, A., Wanzer, M., & Wojtaszczyk, A. (2008). Assessing students' perceptions of inappropriate and appropriate teacher humor. *Communication Education, 57*, 266–288.

Garner, R. (2006). Humor in pedagogy: How ha-ha can lead to aha! *College Teaching, 54*(1), 177–180.

Glasser, W. (1986). *Control theory in the classroom.* New York, NY: Harper and Row.

Glasser, W. (1997). Choice theory and student success. *The Education Digest, 63*, 16–21.

Gorham, J., & Christophel, D. (1990). The relationship of teachers' use of humor in the classroom to immediacy and student learning. *Communication Education, 39*(1), 46–62.

Gruner, C. (1997). *The game of humor: A comprehensive theory of why we laugh.* New Brunswick, NJ: Transaction Publishers.

Guilford, J. P. (1961). Factorial angles to psychology. *Psychological Review, 68*(1), 1–20. http://dx.doi.org/10.1037/h0045887

Intrator, S., & Kunzman, R. (2007). The person in the profession: Renewing teacher vitality. *Educational Forum, 71*(1), 16–32.

Javidi, M., & Long, L. (1989). Teacher' use of humor, self-disclosure, and narrative activity as a function of experience. *Communication Research Reports, 6*(1), 47–52.

Jennings, P., & Greenberg, M. (2009). The prosocial classroom: Teacher social and emotional competence in relation to student and classroom outcomes. *Review of Educational Research, 79*(1), 491–525.

Kane, T., Suls, J., & Tedeschi, J. (1977). Humor as a tool of social interaction. In A. Chapman & H. Foot (Eds.), *It's a funny thing, humor* (pp. 13–16). Oxford, UK: Pergamon Press.

Koestler, A. (1964). *The act of creation.* New York, NY: Macmillan.

Korobkin, D. (1988). Humor in the classroom: Considerations and strategies. *College Teaching, 36,* 154–158.

Kipper, S., & Todt, D. (2001). Variation of sound parameters affects the evaluation of human laughter. *Behaviour, 138*(9), 1161. Retrieved from http://search.ebscohost.com.libproxy.txstate.edu/login.aspx?direct=true&db=edsjsr&AN=edsjsr.4535881&site=eds-live&scope=site

Korobkin, D. (1988). Humor in the classroom: Considerations and strategies. *College Teaching, 36,* 154–158.

Lippitt, G. (1982). Humor: a laugh a day keeps the incongruities at bay. *Training and Development Journal, 36*(11), 98–100.

Manning, K. (1982). *Lighten up! An analysis of the role of humor as an instructional practice in the urban and/or culturally diverse middle school.* Unpublished doctoral dissertation. Cleveland State University.

Martin, R. (2007). The psychology of humor; An integrative approach. Burlington, MA: Elsevier Academic Press.

Martin, R., Puhlik-Doris, P., Larsen, G., Gray, J., & Weir, K. (2003). Individual differences in uses of humor and their relation to psychological well being: Development of the humor styles questionnaire. *Journal of Research in Personality, 37*(1), 48–75.

Maslach, C. (2003). Job burnout: New directions in research and intervention. *Current Directions in Psychological Science, 12,* 189–192.

McCarron, K., & Savin-Baden, M. (2008). Compering and comparing: Stand-up comedy and pedagogy. *Innovations in Education and Teaching International, 45*(4), 355–363.

McCrae, R., & John, O. (1992). An introduction to the five-factor model and its applications. *Journal of Personality 60*(2), 175–215.

Merolla, A. (2006). Decoding ability and humor production. *Communication Quarterly, 54*(2), 175–190.

Mesmer-Magnus, J., & Glew, D. (2012). A meta-analysis of positive humor in the workplace. *Journal of Managerial Psychology, 27*(2), 155–190.

Morreall, J. (1983). *Taking laughter seriously.* Albany, NY: State University of New York.

Morreall, J. (1997). *Humor works.* Amherst, MA: HRD Press.

Morreall, J. (2009). *Comic relief: A comprehensive philosophy of humor.* Chichester, UK: Wiley-Blackwell.

Murdock, M., & Ganim, R. (1992). Creativity and humor: Integration and incongruity. *Journal of Creative Behavior, 27,* 57–70.

Nesi, H. (2012). Laughter in university lectures. *Journal of English for Academic Purposes, 11*(2), 79-89.

Neuliep, J. (1991). An examination of the content of high school teachers' humor in the classroom and the development of an inductively derived taxonomy of classroom humor. *Communication Education, 40*(4), 343–355.

Opplinger, P., & Zillman, D. (2003). Humor and learning. In J. Bryant, D. Roskos-Ewoldsen & J. Cantor (Eds.), *Communication and emotion: Essays in honor of Dolf Zillman* (pp. 255–273). Mahwah, NJ: Lawrence Erlbaum

O'Quin, K., & Derks, P. (1997). Humor and creativity: A review of the empirical literature. *Creativity research handbook, 1*, 223-252.

O'Quin, K., & Derks, P. (2017). Humor and creativity. Reference module in neuroscience and biobehavioral psychology science direct, EBSCOhost (accessed June 29, 2018).

Oshima K. (2018). Functions of humor in intercultural communication and educational environments. In A. Curtis & R. Sussex (Eds.), *Intercultural communication in Asia: education, language and values* (*Multilingual education, 24*). Cham, Switzerland: Springer.

Palmer, P. (2007). *The courage to teach: Exploring the inner landscape of a teacher's life.* San Francisco, CA: Jossey-Bass.

Pannell, E. (2009, July 30). Bryant teacher of the year uses humor in classes. Arkansas Democrat-Gazette [Electronic versioProvine, R. (1992)]. Contagious laughter: Laughter is a sufficient stimulus for laughs and smiles. *Bulletin of the Psychonomic Society, 30*(1), 1–4.

Perrez, M., Huber G., & Geissler, K. (2001). Psychologie der pädagogischen interaktion. [Psychology of pedagogical interaction]. In A. Krapp & B. Weidenmann (Eds.), *Educational psychology* (pp. 357–413). Weinheim, Germany: Beltz.

Pigford, T. (2001). Improving teacher-student relationships: What's up with that? *Clearing House, 74*(6), 337–339.

Platt, T., Ruch, W., Hofmann, J., & Proyer, R. T. (2012). Extreme fear of being laughed at: Components of gelotophobia. *The Israeli Journal of Humor Research, 1*(1), 86–106.

Pollack, J., & Freda, P. (1997). Humor, learning, and socialization in middle level classrooms. *Clearing House, 70*(4), 176–178.

Pollio, H., & Humphreys, W. (1996). What award-winning lecturers say about their teaching: It's all about connection. *College Teaching 44*(3), 101–106.

Provine, R. (1992). Contagious laughter: Laughter is a sufficient stimulus for laughs and smiles. *Bulletin of the Psychonomic Society, 30*(1), 1–4.

Provine, R. (2000). *Laughter: A scientific investigation.* New York, NY: Penguin.

Robinson, K. (2006). Do schools kill creativity? Retrieved from https://www.ted.com/talks/ken_robinson_says_schools_kill_creativity?utm_campaign=tedspread&utm_medium=referral&utm_source=tedcomshare

Ruch, W. (1998). *Humor research 3: The sense of humor—Explorations of a personality characteristic.* New York, NY: Mouton de Gruyter.

Ruch, W., & Köhler, G. (1999). The measurement of state and trait cheerfulness. In I. Marvielde, I. Deary, F. De Fruyt & F. Ostendorf (Eds.), *Personality, psychology in Europe* (pp. 67–83). Tilburg, the Netherlands: Tilburg University.

Ruch, W., & Proyer, R. (2008). Who is gelotophobic? Assessment criteria for the fear of being laughed at. *Swiss Journal of Psychology, 67*, 19–27. https://doi.org/10.1024/1421-0185.67.1.19.

Scriven, J., & Hefferin, L. (1998). Humor: The "witting" edge in business. *Business Education Forum, 52*(3), 13.

Shade, R. (1996). *License to laugh.* Englewood, CO: Teacher Ideas Press.

Shibinski, K., & Martin, M. (2010). The role of humour in enhancing the classroom climate *Human Kinetics, 15*(5), 27–29.

Sveback, S. (1974). A theory of sense of humor. *Scandinavian Journal of Psychology, 15*, 99–107.

Svebak, S., Martin, R. A., Svebak, S., & Apter, M. (1997). Humor as a form of coping. *Stress and health: A Reversal Theory Perspective*, 173–184.

Tait, G., Lampert, J., Bahr, N., & Bennett, P. (2015). Laughing with the lecturer: the use of humour in shaping university teaching. *Journal of University Teaching & Learning Practice, 12*(3), 7.

Teslow, J. (1995). Humor me: a call for research. *Educational Technology Research and Development, 43*(3), 6–28.

Thorson, J., & Powell, F. (1993). Development and validation of a multidimensional sense of humor scale. *Journal of Clinical Psychology, 49*(1), 13–23.

Todt, D., & Kipper, S. (2001). Variation of sound parameters affects the evaluation of human laughter. *Behaviour, 138*(9), 1161–1178.

Torok, S., McMorris, R., & Lin, W. (2004). Is humor an appreciated teacher tool? Perceptions of professors' teaching styles and use of humor. *College Teaching, 52*(1), 14–20.

Torrance, E. (1970). *Encouraging creativity in the classroom.* Dubuque, IA: Wm. C. Brown Company Publishers.

Walker, B. (2006). Using humor in library instruction. *Reference Services Review*, 34(1), 117–128. Retrieved from http://libproxy.txstate.edu/login?url=https://search-proquest-com.libproxy.txstate.edu/docview/200504821?accountid=5683

Wambach, C., & Brothen, T. (1997). Teacher self-disclosure and student classroom participation revisited. *Teaching of Psychology, 24*, 263–265.

Wanzer, M., & Frymier, A. (1999). The relationship between students' perceptions of instructor humor and students' reports of learning. *Communication Education, 48*, 48–62.

Wanzer, M., Bainbridge Frymier, A., Wojtaszczyk, A. M., & Smith, T. (2006). Appropriate and inappropriate uses of humor by teachers. *Communication education, 55*(2), 178-196.

Wanzer, M., Frymier, A., & Irwin, J. (2010). An explanation of the relationship between instruction humor and student learning: Instructional humor processing theory. *Communication Education, 59*, 1–18.

Weaver, I., Richard, L., & Cotrell, H. (1987). Ten specific techniques for developing humor in the classroom. *Education, 108*(2), 167-180.

Wrench, J., & McCroskey, J. (2001). A temperamental understanding of humor communication and exhilaratability. *Communication Quarterly, 49*(2), 142–159.

Williams, T., Billingsley, B., & Banks, A. (2018). Incidences of student-on-teacher threats and attacks: A comparison of special and general education teachers. *Journal of Special Education Leadership, 31*(1) 39-49.

Wolff, H., Smith, C., & Murray, H. (1934). The psychology of humor. *The Journal of Abnormal and Social Psychology, 28*(4), 341.

Yatvin, J. (2008). 2007 NCTE presidential address: Where ignorant armies clash by night. *Research in Teaching of English, 42*(3), 363–372.

Zillmann, D. (1977). Humor and communication. In A. J. Chapman & H. Foot (Eds.), *It's a funny thing, humor.* Oxford, UK: Pergamon Press.

Zillmann, D., & Bryant, J. (Eds.). (1983). *Uses and effects of humor in educational venues (Vol.2)* pp. 73–93. New York: Springer-Verlag.

Ziv, A. (1983). The influence of humorous atmosphere on divergent thinking. *Contemporary Educational Psychology, 8*(1), 68–75.

Ziv, A. (1984). *Personality and sense of humor.* New York, NY: Springer.

Ziv, A. (1988). Teaching and learning with humor: Experiment and replication. *Journal of Experimental Education, 57,* 5–15.

CHAPTER TWO

What Good Humor Can Do for Art Teachers

Why Good Humor Will Save Your Career

In the same way that athletes' suffering from wear and tear on their bodies are forced to retire early, we teachers prematurely forsake our careers because we are emotionally worn out from teaching. We succumb to job fallout when summer break after summer break fails to revive us enough for a slow and happy slide into retirement. Humor can be our built-in vacation, the renewal we seek *while* on the job. Furthermore, when we employ humor to cope with the hard things teaching flings at us, we become resilient enough to hang in there, to not lose heart serving in the profession we have chosen (Gordon, 2014; Magnuson & Barnett, 2013).

The plan to feel optimistically alive can begin by simply appreciating the funny things happening around us. If you look closely, you will find situations and people very near to you that could bring you joy. The bubbling joy from laughter will strengthen you, it will help you overcome whatever is overwhelming you. And overcomers are winners. Winning means being excellent at what you do. With humor as the second teacher in your classroom, you find you are no longer up-tight about fitting into the teacher-in-charge mold you have grown to inhabit. By relaxing, you grow more flexible and able to improvise instructional processes and procedures that turn out to be quite brilliant!

Humor to Manage Classroom Procedures

Most educators believe classroom management is synonymous with disciplining students. Not so. Effective teachers manage a classroom, much like coaches manage teams and bosses manage employees. Managers manage; they do not discipline the team or the employees. Likewise, good teachers do not discipline a classroom they manage students in the classroom; the behavior of teachers, not the behavior of students sets effective classroom management in motion (Wong, Wong, Rogers, & Brooks, 2012). Teachers who laugh and play generate a physical, cognitive and social flexibility; a requisite presence called "with-it-ness" and the "emotional objectivity" that we all need for effective classroom management (Marzano, Marzano, & Pickering, 2003, p. 66). The "with-it-ness" of good teachers keeps them aware of everything that is going on in the room. The with-it-ness that accompanies humor and play, when joined with a plan for managing the art classroom, motivates students to be responsible for their time, to follow procedures, to be engaged and to achieve (2012). Following the plan to teach joyfully with with-it-ness helps students to be accountable for their own learning and the space in which students learn becomes predictably safe, focused and fun.

How can it be that teacher humor is seldom mentioned in the authoritative studies on classroom management conducted over the last 60 years? (Greenberg, Putman, & Walsh, 2013) If as a student you had a choice, I am sure you would prefer to learn in the classroom of a humor-oriented teacher activating learning into action with wit and mirth in the company of *order*. Your preferred, funny teacher would model good teaching by first setting up classroom systems for organizing, storing, and distributing art materials. They would initiate clever rules, procedures and behavior management devices, while buoyantly enticing student engagement in a bubbling stream of active learning. They would stay afloat in spite of student misbehavior by applying capricious positive humor to classroom interactions (Morton, 2005; Powell & Andersen, 1985).

Five to Thrive Classroom-Based Behavior Strategies

When we were preservice teachers in universities, we learned to structure our classrooms with management components called the *Big Five*: (1) Rules; (2) Routines; (3) Praise; (4) Misbehavior; and (5) Engagement (Greenberg et al., 2013). Although the *Big Five* are embedded in teacher education curriculum, most novice teachers still struggle with student behavior because they did not gain practical field experience designing, implementing, and evaluating interventions with coursework (Moore et al., 2017). Besides, humor is not a component of the *Big*

Five system. My observations as a teacher educator and personal experiences as a K-12 art teacher led to an iteration of the *Big Five* into a list of my own. The *Five to Thrive* are named as such because they effectively reduce teacher exhaustion with productive whimsy. I do not include praise because I assume praise for students is ubiquitously operational in thriving teachers' classrooms. Instead, I add practical *devices* to redirect misbehavior and *consequences* students can expect to experience if they decide to misbehave:

1. *Rules* (to inaugurate behavior expectations)
2. *Consequences* (to equitably deter misbehavior)
3. *Routines* (to guide student activities in the classroom)
4. *Devices* (to redirect misbehavior)
5. *Engagement* (to foster student attention and active learning)

Rules to Inaugurate Behavior Expectations

It is no easy task for one person to take charge of a roomful of kids, turning their personal attention and behaviors toward calculated learning for an hour or more. Teachers manage busloads of bodacious kids every day, more than five or six times a day, in a single room, by their single selves. Whether you are teaching art in an upper echelon suburban haven, an inner city bastion for safe keeping children, or an adult night school, there will be those who see you as "the one to disrupt" simply because you are the authority in the room. For yours and the sake of the compliant students in the class, you will need a plan. That plan is best rolled out with humor on the first class day and should be clearly demonstrated the first few weeks to reinforce behavior, attitudes, and procedures that you expect to see for the rest of the year. "Virtually all research points to the beginning of the year as the 'linchpin' for effective classroom management" (Marzano et al., 2003, p. 92). Introduce rules you will enforce the first class day but limit the rule list. The more rules you have, the more time you will spend addressing and enforcing them. I advise you to "reduce the density of rules for conduct each advancing year in education" (Minor, 2014, p. 15). Keep it simple, keep it real.

For elementary school, I have five rules because I have five fingers (see Figure 2.1). I write LOVE (or RESPECT for upper elementary) on the palm of one hand and explain there is a rule for every finger. To clarify, the thumb most naturally points to yourself, so " I expect you to love and respect yourself. That means you as an artist, your artwork, and any part of you. You must not say, 'I am stupid, I can't draw, or my drawing is ugly.' This is not loving yourself nor is it self-respectful. The pointer finger can point to your classmates; therefore, it represents

Figure 2.1. Rules of Thumb, Fingers and Hand

the idea that loving or respecting them means to honor their ideas, their words, their artwork and most especially, who they are as an artist."

"The middle finger is the tallest one on your hand and represents me, the tallest person in the room. I am asking you to respect me as your teacher (say nothing else about this finger). This means follow my directions, listen when I speak and respect me as the person who carefully considers everything that happens in this room and everyone to whom it happens. The ring finger has a blood vein that connects to your heart so this art-heart connection stands for the art materials you will use. Use them with respect. Wash the brushes carefully, put the caps on markers, organize and store all materials for others to use. The last finger, the pinky finger, although small, has the big job of helping your hand hold onto something. The big but special space where we make art is the art studio, our art classroom. Keeping the tables, floor and counters clean in the art studio gives you and everyone else a clean place to work every time you want to make art here."

Consequences to Equitably Deter Misbehavior

On the other hand, I have five fingers. These represent five consequences for not loving or respecting the aforementioned entities. I explain these as well, ranging in severity from simply talking to the student privately to walking them to the office. One elementary school where I taught was located in a high-crime area of the city, consequently, police arrests, incarceration and court appearances were everyday concepts. This led to an effective misbehavior consequence: the art room jail—a chair off to the side of the room. I would tell my students (smiling of course, to signal that we were playing and pretending), "I can sometimes be the art room cop and may have to make an arrest for breaking art room rules. You will have the right to remain silent—and WILL remain silent—in the art room jail without bars. This means for 5 minutes you can observe but cannot participate in whatever we are doing. You may have an extended stay if you misbehave while in jail." As controversial as this measure sounds, my students wholeheartedly embraced the chair jail because it provided a safety measure for stopping the harmful or hurtful behavior of unruly classmates. It made them feel safe. I will never forget the clever retort of one student while dejectedly serving an extended 5-minute jail sentence. He called out, "I am calling my lawyer!" to which I replied, "There are no lawyers in the art room."

Establishing rules for students at the secondary level calls for more finesse than the five-finger rule presentation. The two rules I rely on the most for middle and high school art classrooms came to be: (1) be respectful and (2) be diligent. Middle students are in the serious business of becoming who they will be as adults. They should be held accountable for their behavior, as adults are. They are responsible for their part of the learning process, therefore, any behavior that impedes instruction and threatens the safety of a harmonious class community is culpable within the bounds of these two behavior expectations. A middle school teacher I know places a mirror on the wall of her classroom with a sign that reads, "Look who is responsible for their grades."

As an incentive to stimulate positive, productive behavior, I awarded Art Heart incentives to exemplary elementary students and DCI Coupons (for diligence, co-operation and interest) to exemplary middle and high school students every 6 weeks. The highly esteemed Art Heart Award was printed on pink paper, rolled into a scroll and tied with red ribbon. DCI coupons were the size of a business card to fit easily into wallets. One recipient in each class accepted the award with high ceremony every 6 weeks. Looking back, I did not play the graduation hit, "Pomp and Circumstance" but I did make sure all of the privileged awardees participated in either high-profile events in the art room (art movies, artist guests or art games) or field trips to local art museums.

Our art museum field trips were frequent and very pleasant to facilitate because only well-behaved students receiving Art Hearts awards and DCI coupons participated. Before the trip, the prototypical students publicly cherished their prized awards and coupons like lottery tickets with winning numbers. Then returned from the trip recounting their experience with glowing superlatives to classmates who coveted the chance to go. Trips were free for students because museum admissions, school buses and driver fees were underwritten by grant funds provided by the art museums we visited. Word spread. Within time, principals happily agreed to cover my classes with substitute teachers and parents eagerly signed permission slips. The special-event field-trip-award system did more to promote good behavior in my art classroom than any extrinsic sticker, stamp, candy or verbal praise I might have doled out.

Routines to Guide Student Activities

Playful humor can set things right even when the dynamics feel like you are in a blender with a classroom of kids. To begin with, activity in an art classroom is easily assigned to designated task areas. If you are following the democratic paradigm in which the teacher directs all instruction, you probably have tables grouped with an assigned title for each group (colors, artists, art elements, principles of design, etc.). Other areas in the room labeled by function (ceramics area, paper cutter area, sink area outfitted with drying rack, storage area, and off-limits teacher area). All materials are amalgamated in four to six identically arranged containers for one-person delivery to groups (which is usually you to curtail excessive movement around the room). This configuration commands you, the material supervisor, to be in charge. The metaphor here is an art room that runs like a restaurant. The teacher is simultaneously the dietician constructing a curricular menu, the chef cooking up appetizing lessons, and the server delivering materials to the table. The students are the customer consumers digesting and internalizing delicious lesson content. Imagine running a restaurant by yourself? This scenario can wear down many a teacher by the end of the day unless little hands and legs are enlisted to help.

I will refrain from detailing all of the serviceable storage container options I procured but I will share the greatest find ever. When the library in our high school underwent a digital transformation from the old Dewey Decimal System, I grabbed the wooden cabinet with thirty-six little drawers used for housing the cards with book call numbers. What a find! In this jewel I placed frequently used objects (like rulers, masking tape, glue sticks, erasers) arranged in alpha order in the drawers. It reduced my responses to students' where-are questions like, "Where can I find a rubber band?" to simply pointing like a traffic cop to the library cabinet and declaring "Under R."

The tips I offer for the democratic classroom over the next few pages came to me when the grinding gears of classroom management screeched to a halt. To get back on track, I assigned one person in each group to be the *Materials Manager*. They were the esteemed individuals appointed to obtain materials needed by their group for the studio process. Consider if you will, their service as a supermarket shopper with curbside delivery. They are charged with picking up ingredients/materials organized in cubicles, cabinets and drawers on one side of the room for their [family] groups on the other. At the close of class, the *Materials Manager* returns the materials to their original storage spot. This model serves operations well for smallish, dense classrooms because a limited number of students are mobile and materials generally stay put.

Another organizational job assignment is *Count Markula*. The *Count* in charge of markers distributes and collects Sharpies planted vertically in a wooden block with drilled holes, one for each marker. When Sharpies are collected, empty holes mean missing markers, and the Count's task is to hunt down all missing markers until all holes are filled. This is important because they simply disappear if not paroled. (Sharpies are an adolescent's tool of choice for writing on bathroom stall walls). There is also the *Brush King or Brush Queen* appointment to maintain cleanliness and order in the court of all things bristly. After scrubbing brushes, they chant "Put the tail in the pail and the hair in the air."

The rotating *Clay Foreman* position supervises all crew assignments for clay days: *Clay Cutter, Canvas Matter, Clay Delivery,* and *Tool Dude*. Canvas mats keep clay off of working surfaces can be shaken out over trash cans and stored in a jiffy. (You can get odd lots of canvas from awning shops for a song.) Clay procedures follow from the clay origination point. The *Clay Cutter* helper cut equitable chunks of clay off of the mother lode that comes in a plastic bag. They place each chunk on a canvas mat, which the *Clay Delivery* conveys to each seated student. Clay tools standing up in handled caddies are easily moved from storage to table by the *Tool Dude*. End-of-class clean-up on clay days concludes with what I call *Car Wash*, a full-on effort in which everyone participates. This experience is not unlike a boot camp drill sergeant's rhythmic chanting to guide the marching of rookie soldiers. I shout out the sound-off phrase, "Car wash, car wash!" Everyone then grabs large squirty bottles of soapy solution, heavy duty car wash sponges and old towels chanting, "Wash those tables, wash them now, if you can't we'll show you how. Car wash, car wash!" It really is a blast.

I also advocate for the *Donation Collection Crew* for orchestrated clean-up of paper scraps on days when collage occurs. Each *Donation Collector* moves through the room asking for scrap paper donations, like ushers walking in between church pews. Student assistants scramble to pick up as many scraps as their hands can hold. The student with the largest handful is first in the line to leave the room. (I cannot explain why this privilege is sought after but I have chosen not to be offended). Truly, there are no students left sitting in a desultory stupor when the game for scraps is on.

If you have adopted the Choice-Based or TAB (teaching for artistic behaviors) exemplar, you have grouped material types into centers or studios that make materials obtainable for students. TAB permits students to intrinsically pursue their ideas with whatever studio paraphernalia they may need (Douglas & Jaquith, 2018). TAB departs from the "do what the teacher does" paradigm by permitting student artists to independently pursue an idea within the art room studio. The teacher is a guide and facilitator of students' artistic practice and not a director, which means there may be five or more different studio experiences happening in a single class. When students enter a TAB art classroom, students sit in a common area to watch a short 5-minute teacher demo, or hear about an artist, an art style, engage in art criticism dialogue or listen to instructions. The rest of class time is spent in free range mode as students conceptualize, explore, investigate, design, and construct personal, meaningful works of art on their own. The teacher facilitates these processes but does very little commandeering. For this paradigm, the heavy lifting of classroom management for teachers at the front end of the school year when furniture is arranged, materials are ordered, labeled, and organized into containers in each of the studio areas.

In a hands-free classroom running smoothly with actively engaged students, the teachers' sense of humor focuses on challenging students to think deeper, engage with materials more bravely and collaborate with their classmates more humanely. For these goals, I address students with humorous prompts, my favorite being, "And then what happened?" Even in university classes I sit next to an immobilized student and ask this question. It is a decontextualized statement that my students understand must be countered by an immediate, novel response of any kind. They are expected to think on their feet and pull an answer from the air. The answer, may of course, not make sense. It forces incongruity, the secret ingredient of creativity and humor, nudging idea innovation into the open. A few responses to the "And then what happened?" query I will always treasure are: "The test was positive," or "It jumped out of the dark and snarled at me," or "It was in her closet one night then under her bed the next," or "The car wouldn't run but it could fly." There will be an endless stream of off-the-wall retorts and each one competing for the most absurd. In every case, however, there is laughter followed by a relaxed mindset and free-flowing ideas.

Devices to Redirect Misbehavior

Sadly, too much of a teacher's day is spent redirecting student misbehavior. It is all so unfun. Teachers spend way too much instruction time redirecting distracting behaviors I classify as *classroom fouls* (students spinning their wheels doing anything unproductive, concentrating their creative intentions outside of art making).

For general inattention, I employ devices such as white board eraser as an instant "remote control" to mute or change a student's channel or use a stapler to call students at their desk: "John, pick up please your teacher is calling." The age-old ploy to enlist the help of restless students who benefit from organizing, sorting, restoring and cleaning usually works if accompanied with effusive praise for the selected student. If they are fidgety because they are seeking attention, special responsibilities provide notoriety.

Every teacher develops a set of tried-and-true responses that incrementally deter misbehavior in their art classroom. I have a few go-to responses for minor misconduct. First, the cosmic teacher locking-eye-glare from across the room can freeze recalcitrant students in their folly. If this does not, the directive to "please step into my private hallway office" may. In the hallway (with the classroom door open to observe classroom activity after you have left the room), I do not rebuke but ask questions. "So, what was going on in there?" or "Is today your birthday?" which, is met with a surprised smile and my reply, "I just thought that was the reason you were acting so special today." At times, a one-on-one confrontation with a more serious tone (minus any humor at all) may be called for if misbehavior by one escalates. I have found that suddenly becoming the unfunny, tersely toned teacher is sobering to a student. Being the object of your unabashed annoyance alone often institutes an about-face behavior switch, but if it does not, you may find yourself reaching for your phone.

Calling parents about their teenager's misbehavior is never a picnic so I adopted an approach that places me in control. A conversation with a perpetrator's parent goes something like this: "Hello, Mrs. Smith, my name is Teri Evans-Palmer, John's art teacher. I have some good news and bad news. Which would you like to hear first? Good news? Ok, you must know that John has developed fearlessly innovative methods for applying paint, a departure from the traditional approach with a brush. The bad news? He was squirting paint on the wall, a surface not designated for student paintings at this time. Our school's discipline plan charges me to contact parents as the fourth step in the five-step procedure. Will you be talking with him this evening to prevent his moving on to step five, an office referral, or would you prefer to speak with him now? He is standing next to me." This approach almost always yields positive student behavior responses not just because I had turned the student over to their parent but also because I called the parent at work where they were probably under the glare of a supervisor.

Incongruous Teacher Responses to Stop Student Distractions

Surprise! Sometimes students disengage from activity in the classroom. Their attention posture can range from the waving hands and bellowing, "Ooooh! Ooooooh!

I know!" of the captivated to the heavily-lidded eyes and peanut butter spine of the unresponsive. We just cannot take it personally. Whatever humor works to interrupt the student disrupting productive teaching and learning is fair game in the classroom, provided it is positive and does not humiliate or harm the student. For instance, I lean hard on incongruity because unexpected responses from a teacher can stymie students. My favorite ridiculously incongruent questions to ask off-task students seem to come out of nowhere but work because they do. The questions, "Where would you like to go on your next vacation?" or "What size shoe do you wear?" are so absurdly out of context to perpetrators they stop what they are doing to decipher the question's meaning. Just as effective to this end are absurd statements like, "I don't like your turkeys." I have heard of a teacher that repeated this statement to a wily student every time he was caught in the act of noncompliance over the course of a year. At the end of the year the student popped into the teacher's classroom and announced, "I sold my turkeys!" to which the teacher responded, "Well, I don't like your chickens either!" I have also whispered excerpts from familiar books and movies to students who cannot follow rules of decorum, "I do not like green eggs and ham. I do not like them Sam I am." If the offending behavior appears again, you follow with, "I do not like green eggs and ham. I do not like them in a box, I do not like them in my socks." You get the picture. Silly yes, but out-of-nowhere responses put you in control.

Absurd metaphors aimed at students behaving badly are another behavior redirection device on which I rely. I approach the student bothering another student with, "I am a marathon runner and I have a rock in my shoe," then walk away. If the disturbing behavior persists, I return saying, "I am running but the rock in my shoe is slowing me down." I return again and again citing progressively more severe statements that end with, "Ok, I have had it with this rock. I am going to sit down, take out the rock and throw it into the ISS pile (in-school suspension)." Even if the disruptor does not clue into the meaning, a peer usually will with, "You're the rock, dude, and you're in trouble."

Thwart Annoying Behavior with Inanimate Objects

A middle school student leaning back and forth on a squeaky chair was enjoying how irritated I was becoming with the strident squeak, so I proceeded to apply indirect discipline. I asked the student (who will be known as John) to carefully get up from the insubordinate chair. I then pulled the chair into a corner and whacked it with a yard stick, admonishing it with "Now chair, you have been to chair training school and know better than to imperil John like that. He may fall!" I then return the chair to John, gently caution him to sit carefully in case the chair repeats its performance. If it does, I remove the chair and John must stand. For the final act I have in my mind to suspend the chair from the ceiling to indicate the disciplinary culmination of in-class suspension for repeated bad performance. Going forward, John does not wish to stand so he forces the chair to comply.

Another example of annoying behavior with an inanimate object is the kid who uses pencils and brushes as drumsticks to play the percussive parts of his favorite song. He is rapping away on the table while you are talking with students across the room. You walk over and begin to dance to his drumbeat. Of course, he ceases because he is embarrassed that one, you are dancing, and two, that you are dancing to *his* music. This is also effective with hummers, strummers and singers.

Students inclined to render X-rated subject matter with rebellious drawing instruments can be indirectly disciplined as well. I approach student artists generating taboo subjects (in public-school environments) by asking them to hand over the offending instrument. I examine it carefully, turning it over and over while saying under my breath, "I do not understand it. This pencil (marker, pastel, etc.) has been my classroom for at least a year and knows better than to draw this way." I assure the artist that I must take measures to stop the activity for their own safety. Then I do it. I break the pencil in half showing obvious disgust, walk over to the trash and fling it into the receptacle. I apologize to the student while handing him an orange crayon, "That should not happen to anyone in my classroom. Shameful pencil. Here is a tool that will not get you into trouble. You can safely draw with it." Crayons behaving badly create amazing encaustics when inserted in old glue guns.

More Annoying Behavior

Students are not permitted to sleep in my art classroom unless I know they are deprived for parental reasons or they are ill. The ones that slip away into slumber land just because they are bored are tired targets for my humor. The irritating authoritarian bell (you know the dome-shaped, flat-bottomed bell that persons in charge use) effectively awakens sleeping students because it is small, portable, and dings really loudly. Or you can blast a trumpet borrowed from the band director down the hall. A teacher I know sings opera at the top of her lungs near the ear of sleepers. Others bark like a St. Bernard, turn on the alarm on their phone, rev up a power tool, etc. Whatever works.

For the many mainstream individual and whole-class misbehaviors, I have developed very specific humor strategies and devices. These are effective for most learners regardless of age. The presentation, of course, should be adjusted for age-appropriate audiences and must comfortably come from a teacher's unique personality.

Classroom Conduct Gauge and Auto Teach. Sometimes the entire class of students pushes back in the act of classroom mutiny, a mobbing phenomenon I encountered while teaching art in a middle school (the one I mentioned earlier, the one in which the principal referred to the art room as the "snake pit"). Mobbing, or the "targeting and subjecting of an individual in an organization to a series of abusive and humiliating behaviors are the characteristic mob perpetrator behaviors" (Duffy & Sperry, 2012, p. 74). The intent of the student mob is to destabilize the teacher victim, in order to neutralize the influence of their authoritative power. If I had paid closer attention, I would have seen the mob effect forming long before it became confrontational.

The first sign of mobbing appeared when students begrudgingly entered the classroom and took their own sweet time settling into a learning posture. I shamefully found myself begging them to let me teach. One class was still not in their seats 15 minutes after the bell rang so I announced, "since you are not ready to be my students, I will wait to be your teacher." Sitting down at my desk I said quietly with measured words, "In the meantime I will be answering emails. Just let me know when you are ready to learn." The first time I did this, 20 minutes passed until I heard a feeble-voiced plea whisper, "We are ready Mrs. Evans-Palmer." I continued typing. Again, a little stronger, "We are ready Mrs. Evans-Palmer." I responded, "Are you sure?" (I really wanted them to beg *me*). Finally, I heard an unenthusiastic plea, "Yeah, we're ready." I went home that night angry that I was angry. In the twilight hours of sleeplessness, I designed a *Classroom Conduct Gauge* out of foam core board that could magically measure the teachability of students in the room. It featured a sliding, arrowed mechanism that moved from the top increment, *ethereal*, to the middle just above the drawn line, *precarious*. Below *precarious* was the veritable bottom line, *egregious*.

I unveiled the *Gauge* the next day with a spiel directing students to obtain their materials and settle into their seats within 5 minutes at the start of class (see Figure 2.2). The *Gauge*'s sliding arrow mechanism would be set at *ethereal* when they entered and would slide southward from there. If after 5 minutes classroom behavior provoked the arrow to drop below the *precarious* line, the instructional delivery method to follow would be *Auto Teach*, indicating probationary punitive status. The rationale for *Auto Teach* is that when students are not available for instruction, they will not be taught by a teacher but will teach themselves. For example, they will not be painting with brushes and juicy color but will read and write about painting. And that is all they will do. They will breathe, blink, sit and write. They cannot talk or be excused from the room for any reason. If *Auto Teach* is violated by a student during the imposed period, all students are automatically assigned for *Auto Teach* on the subsequent scheduled class. After three days of

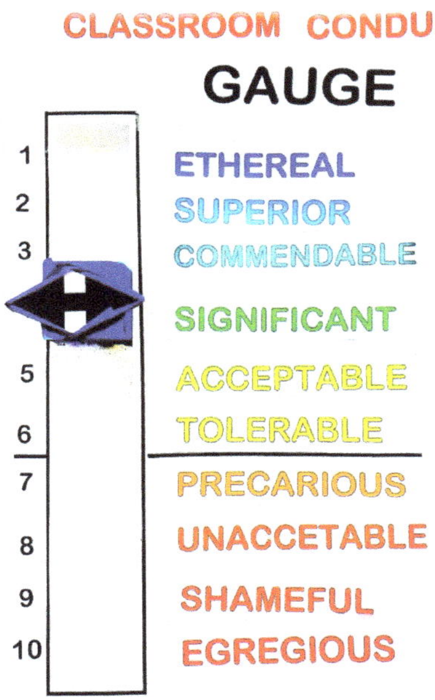

CLASSROOM CONDUCT GAUGE

1	ETHEREAL
2	SUPERIOR
3	COMMENDABLE
4	SIGNIFICANT
5	ACCEPTABLE
6	TOLERABLE
7	PRECARIOUS
8	UNACCETABLE
9	SHAMEFUL
10	EGREGIOUS

Figure 2.2. Classroom Conduct Gauge

restrictive behavior for a class of students, peer pressure came into play to overturn *Auto Teach*. Thereafter, students entered art class with one eye on the *Gauge* whispering, "Hurry up, we're going down!"

The Eye Can Enabler. I do not permit my students at any time to utter the phrase, "I can't (insert any artistic endeavor here)." Ever. I find support for this mandate from Genesis 1:3 when "God said, 'Let there be light,' and there was light." If words hold the power to speak something into existence, then I believe words hold equal power to keep something from becoming. When a student says, "I can't draw," they are speaking failure into their art making, failure that blocks artistic self-efficacy, and they truly do fail.

At one point, spoken failure had become so prevalent in my art classes I had to do something. I covered a large Rock Star beverage can with magazine photos of eyes, then sealed the photos on the can's surface by slathering a mixture of equal parts white glue to water (see Figure 2.3). The can would be placed (by me initially then later by students themselves) in front of the soul proclaiming self-failure. Eyes of all colors staring at you are powerfully definitive. I still use the *Eye Can* with twenty-somethings in college classes and it is still one of my favorite instructional resources.

Figure 2.3. The Eye Can Enabler

External interruptions. So, you have won everyone's attention, launched a lesson, and are just winding down instructions for students to begin studio work when Johnny B. Late arrives 15 minutes after the bell. Late arrivals are *so* unnerving. I have borrowed procedures from adult venues to accommodate late comers while preserving the integrity of instruction. From nightclubs, I have adopted the door *Bouncer* concept. Most classroom doors have a window. I lock the door after the bell rings, attach the class roster to a clipboard labeled *Guess List* at the top, and hand it to the *Bouncer* (usually a student who would benefit from being in charge of something). Their instructions are to watch the door window and only let students in the class who belong in the class. Instruct them to sign the *Guess List* and record their late arrival time. Aha! Documentation accomplished for tardy students! Now you can proceed uninterrupted.

You would agree that the first few minutes of instruction is delicate. Student attention hangs by a tenuous cord swinging back and forth from engagement to disinterest in secondary school classes. Any nanoscopic movement or fluttering sound can sever the cord. Blaring PA squawks can sever the cord. Student helpers sent by office personnel can sever the cord. Like clockwork, office helpers come unannounced the first 10 minutes of the period to escort students out of my art classes for standardized test tutoring. I imagine the dispatching administrator wrongfully assumed that removing a student from the chaotic melee of an art class meant relief for the teacher. This is not the case in my art classes where every moment of instruction is precious. I therefore boldly deflected interruptions from the office by posting a small note on the locked door:

> Instruction in art class during the first ten minutes of the period is perilously fragile. The teacher is setting up a learning environment conducive to the highest order of thinking, so please do not knock now but return in five minutes. Thank you, The Management.

Essential visits to the bathroom will happen but how and when they happen are up to you, the teacher. Requests to use the bathroom are especially tiresome in middle school. They want to visit the boys and girls room for any number of inane reasons like checking to see if their hair-do has not evolved into a hair-don't, texting their friends, running lots of water, gazing into the mirror, dancing on the tile floor, writing on the stall walls, etc., etc. Maybe they need the time alone to synthesize the amazing information imparted in art class? Fat chance. Preadolescents like being excused to leave the room as a means to test the boundaries of probity and to find ways to misbehave out of sight. Be sure they do not take a Sharpie with them! Writing bathroom passes is tiresome, so I endowed my classes with two neon-strapped safety vests labeled, "Student from Mrs. Evans-Palmer's Art Class Making a Rest Stop." Over time, fashionable students reluctant to don the potty vests would postpone visits to the bathroom during my class. I heard of a middle school teacher who appropriated toilet lids to use as potty passes, one for boys and one for girls. And then I didn't. I imagine an adult in authority intervened because of potential parental litigation.

Engagement Strategies to Foster Student Attention and Active Learning

Overcoming learning inertia is a chronic challenge to all teachers but overcoming student laziness and reluctance to work is especially exasperating. Teachers find they spend almost as much time outwitting students who are trying *not* to learn as they spend planning for their learning. My determination to dislodge immobile students from complacency triggered the creation of devices that do just that.

The Magic Wand Motivator. A 2-year teaching stint with the Department of Defense Dependents Schools (DoDDs) took me overseas to Germany where wine festivals along the Rhine River festooned the fall calendar. I observed stoic

Germans transform into giddy merrymakers in the streets of villages where grapes were crushed after harvest. Celebrants toted brightly colored, plastic toy hammers to surreptitiously bop unsuspecting revelers on the head. The surprise of being bopped, along with the honking sound it produced on the head of the *boppee*, provoked instantaneous laughter. I brought the *Happy Hammer* with me when I returned to the States and quickly consolidated it into classroom protocol. Students were just as amused as the Germans when their enlightened responses to my questions were rewarded with a celebratory *Hammer* bop. It was a success until one student stopped me in the hall shouting, "Ms. Evans-Palmer, hit me, hit me!" You know where I am going with this, so you should not be surprised that I substituted the *Hammer* with the innocuous *Magic Wand*.

I procured the *Magic Wand* from a local toy store (which was really a bubble bopper) and came outfitted with a bubble blowing circle wand at one end and moisture sensor rings at the other. When the rings comes into contact with moisture, one of three entrancing electronic sounds are emitted (see Figure 2.4). I introduced the enchanted pink and yellow plastic *Wand* to my students with deadpan delivery as follows:

> Scientists are still studying the phenomenon of the *Magic Wand*. You see, when you respond to a question with insight, you do not win a red corvette, $200 or a two-week trip to the Caribbean, instead, you win the opportunity to touch the *Magic Wand*. A jolt from the *Wand* sends a powerful electrical charge into the body through the hand and surges down to your feet and back up to your brain to stimulate your cerebral cortex. The result: four hours of unconventionally innovative ideas. Your eyes will be glassy and you may have difficulty walking straight but your imaginative capacity will be at peak performance. Ok, are we ready to try it out?

The *Wands'* 24 inches of battery-powered magic revved up interest at every age level in whatever topic we were discussing. The incongruity of the ridiculous *Wand* joined with my no-nonsense tone provoked interest (as would any inanimate object elevated to magical status), intensified student attention and activated learning. (It is quite possibly the most effective engagement tool in my toolbox.) At any rate, the *Wand* possessed misbehavior mojo because everyone wanted positive praise. A student stealing a touch would hear, "No, Mary, you cannot touch the *Wand* unless your response to my question tells me you are thinking deeply."

The Magic Pencil Prompter. Another highly suggestive device for students who lack drawing self-efficacy is the index finger of the drawing hand. Here is how the *Magic Pencil* plays out in a classroom scenario: a student is near tears because they are unable to draw on paper what is in their mind. Let's say a first-grader wants to draw a rhinoceros. You ask them if they have tried drawing with their *Magic Pencil?* Assuredly, they have not because they didn't know they had one. You

Figure 2.4. The Magic Wand Motivator

hold up your right hand with an extended index finger and demonstrate how to sharpen it, since it is new and has never been used. Any movement with the *Magic Pencil* elicits a sound, therefore inserting it into the enclosed left hand's "sharpener" makes a grinding sound. A smile pops up on the students' face and they are ready to follow you. You ask them what shape the rhino's head is—a good place to start. Most likely they will reply, "a circle" or "an oval." You are facing the student and mirroring anything they do with their *Pencil*, encouraging them to make a sound as the *Pencil* makes magical unseen marks in the air. The circular head may sound like, "zzzzzzzzzzzzshhhhpop!" (The pop indicates that space has been enclosed.)

You let them take the lead, prompting them to make shape after shape until they are satisfied with the air drawing of their rhinoceros. Now, the good part. You gently place a real, graphite-and-wood pencil in their hand, guide it to the paper on the table and tell them they have successfully draw a rhino in the air and can now draw one on the paper. You smile warmly (after all, you are consummately amused at this point) and walk away. The walking away part is essential, because if you do not, the student will balk just so they can bask longer in the warmth of your assuring attention. As you look back over your shoulder you announce, "Good job! I will return for a visit when you have finished that amazing drawing!"

Warming up Cold Pencils. To achieve the same drawing outcome as the *Magic Pencil*, warming up a cold *real* pencil is recommended for students who don't want to draw, not students who do not think they can draw. I approach a comatose student, pick up their pencil and command, "No wonder you are not drawing, your pencil is cold!" They look bewildered as if in a dense fog. Rolling the cold pencil between my hands quickly you can be sure the pencil becomes warm. At this point, I talk to high school students about machines in their home equipped with a priming or choke function to activate ignition and explain pencils are no different. I then hand the pencil back to the immobilized student and ask them, "Warm, right?" They nod. I assure them they will now be able to draw as their pencil has been properly primed. Understandably, it is not the warm pencil that enables their drawing, the pencil is simply a prop, a means to motivate. It is the teacher-student interaction that supports students' drawing efficacy. It is proof that "the strongest unique predictor of middle and secondary students' self-beliefs about their own creativity" is positive teacher feedback (Kaufman & Sternberg, 2010, p. 458).

My Response To Lazy Students Asking, "Hey Teacher, Is This Good Enough?" Believe it or not, not every student will be as engaged in art making as you expect them to be. Revelation! These students are intent on breeding mediocrity with works of art that just get them by. You have set a bar for their work with carefully articulated parameters. These have been presented, posted and published on the classroom board and on digital media. Yet, inevitably, there are those who must ask, "Is this [drawing] good enough?" To this, I want to reply (but don't), "Good enough for what? To frame in gold and hang over the sofa? To post on the fridge with a souvenir magnet? To use as a reference iteration of an improved drawing that will follow?" Instead, I offer the assessment with a broadly genuine smile, "Let me look at it carefully ... hmmmm, how provocative, compelling, and a clever manipulation of media!" Stymied, the inquiring student stands transfixed, sifting the superlative statement over in their mind trying to understand my meaning. To be sure, I have found that students benefit most from genuine adult interest in their artwork and not a grocery list of options that help them move toward realism (Watts, 2010). You may challenge them with, "I am thinking it could be even more amazing than it is now, perhaps with greater contrast, heightened emphasis or repeated shapes? What do you think?"

My Response to Gifted Students Eager to Accelerate Your Teaching Speed. Last but not least, are the cerebrally gifted students. You the know type. They took private lessons in Paris last summer, their aunt teaches design at RISD Rhode Island School of Design, or worse, their father is an art professor at a local university. Extremely intelligent students may arbitrate your attention because they feel superior, are bored, or just need to be challenged. Let's face it, time moves at a glacial pace in public schools, especially in art rooms where the teacher orchestrates all learning precious moment by precious moment. The art classroom in this case is like a tour bus; you are the driver but you cannot pull out of the parking lot to head to the theme park until all students are in their seats. To a compliant, bright student who is ready to begin as soon as the bell rings, the wait for your attention is interminable. Ok, these students might be right on both accounts. But I've learned that it is best to bring them aboard by using humor, providing a class that is not boring, and showing respect for their intelligence. No matter how high the student's IQ intelligence quotient, you still know more about art than they do. Like or not, they have entrusted the business of their learning to you. And learn they will if your conversational tone is one you would have while talking to a colleague. You might say something like this to a GT student, "Have you ever wondered what life would be like if humans had the option to fly as well as walk? What changes to our environment would you expect to see? I am really curious about this question and have been pondering it over for some time now. Could you help me out by making a few sketches showing interventions in our world if flying were an option?" When a teacher's approach is horizontal (person to person) and not vertical (teacher to student), gifted students often respond with adultlike verisimilitude, adopting precocious statements like, "Hmmm, I understand your quandary. Let me give it some thought." And they do.

The Big Word Club. I flinch at anything interrupting the trajectory of a lesson but relish interruptions brought on by the utterance of exquisitely complex, big words. I borrowed the *Big Word Club* idea from a master teacher friend, Linda Heier, who captured intellectually rigorous words by recording them with a marker on a large foam bat she called *The Big Word Club*. When a new word surfaces in classroom dialogue, everyone rushes to look up the meaning of the word (see Figure 2.5). Words written on the club are then inculcated into our everyday speech from that moment on. Of course, every *Big Word Club* needs a president so I appoint an officer of the bat for each class to decorously record words.

For example, one day my students and I were discussing negative comments people often make about groups of people. I nonchalantly offered, "There really is no excuse for civilized people to use pejoratives in respectful conversations." They stared and blinked at me and one said, "Someone look up pejorative and someone get the *Big Word Club*!" After a flurry of activity, pejorative was written on the foam bat. You would be surprised at the significant contribution this small gesture has made to the meaningful acquisition of new vocabulary! The *Club* has even become a hit at the university level where I often hear students exclaim, "Get the club, I've got a word!"

Humor to Relieve Stress and Anxiety

A recent study on coping strategies revealed what teachers rely on to manage stress (Moore, 2013). Humor [and laughter] ranked second below the first coping strategy, spiritual or religious beliefs. I do believe God has a sense of humor as we

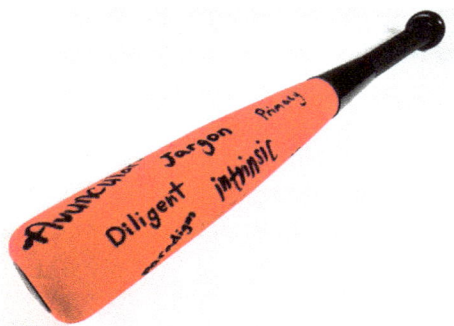

Figure 2.5. The Big Word Club

are created in his image and it is God-given joy that is my greatest help in the classroom. I am encouraged by the counsel that reads, "Do not grieve, for the joy of the Lord is your strength" Nehemiah 8:10 (New International Version). Joy, laughter and humor in general come soon enough to rescue teachers but are usually not the first response to an anxious situation. Controlling anger and fear take up positions on the front line.

You know your grasp at control has left the building when you are engulfed in debilitating helplessness. Long bouts of helplessness wear down teacher resilience like long stretches of road wears down the soles of our sneakers. When a teacher "feels uncertain about having control over subjectively important tasks, the focus becomes anticipated failure" (Bieg, Grassinger, & Dresel, 2017, p. 25). Then anxiety creeps in. When this is how you feel, you may need the help of other teachers to rescue you off of the island. Perhaps gather up a few of your best teacher friends and plan a Laughter Hour, time (which may or may not include adult beverages) set aside for sharing funny stories that happened in the classroom. These almost always offer encouragement of the life-saving kind.

Raising Resilience: When Bad Things Happen to Good Teachers

I was bitten in the right hand by a Western Diamondback Rattlesnake in mid-July outside my home in south Texas. No, it was not funny, it was excruciatingly painful. The surging venom felt like thousands of tiny knives slashing into my right hand. (Just wait, the humor is here in this momentous event). While two EMT paramedics worked on my vitals, one was calling the hospital ER to procure antivenom. He had asked my age and was telling a hospital tech that "an elderly woman" would soon arrive. My response (because I am NOT elderly) was, "Really? Do I look elderly to you? See that stone wall outside? I built that in a few months with these very hands!" Flustered but amused, they loaded me into the ambulance. As we took off, I asked, "Aren't you going to turn on the flashing lights and siren?" The driver smiled then retorted, "Oh you're fine. It is just a snake bite. We have a 2-hour window to get antivenom in your blood before the bite is fatal." Happy to hear we could make the hospital destination in time I was really hoping we would have some fun getting there. After all, I may not have another opportunity to ride in an ambulance again.

I make my point with an out-of-classroom experience but nevertheless I stress that we must as humans in life find humor in the darkest of times. Humor provides us with a resilient rubber cushion that emotionally sustains us from the impact of adversity. Cancer patients during treatment wholeheartedly confirmed that humor not only helped them navigate through times of deep depression, but also helped them to survive:

> Humor helped them stay grounded, feel normal, and find joy in life even when things seemed dire. For some, the ability to laugh gave them hope and encouraged them to persevere and focus on those moments. (Golembeski, 2020)

Although teaching may not be life and death to many, teacher resilience offers teachers the same capacity to adapt and thrive through times of challenge in the classroom. One tense situation that happened while teaching middle school clearly stands out as a challenge to me. My bare-bones budget left me with limited resources and I asked students to kindly share their watercolors with a buddy. Abruptly, an angry, pint-sized 8th-grader stood up in the classroom bellowing, "I am NOT sharing my paints with anyone! I am sick and tired of you teachers telling us what you want us to do! What about what WE want?" Time stopped. I moved to the window to gather my thoughts. I stood staring out the window wondering to myself how ludicrous it would be to argue with a 13-year-old. Students stared. I waited. After a yawning 3-minute stretch of time, the demanding student wilted into her chair. I mused to myself out loud, "Wow, the color of the clouds are really magnificent today. They are transparent, yet saturated with gray, violet, deep blue that is edged with a pinkish orange. Could we mix colors like that with our paints? Let's give it a try." Turning to the students I said with artificial enthusiasm, "Ok, let's begin." When the horse of the gun-ho teacher-leader is shot from underneath them, they fall to the ground. In this case, I was able to get up, dust myself off and step over the dead horse. Incongruity, not humor, rallied my resilience in this case but humor does a lot to perpetuate perseverance. Responding in an unexpected way to brush off a student's verbal attack comes more easily when you are used to applying incongruencies to elicit laughter.

While I have grown to rely on out-of-the-blue responses to disengage student antagonism and alter the emotional tone of tense student-teacher interaction, other factors in the teaching environment can dismantle the core belief that I can teach well. Managing student misbehavior, in the context of a burdensome high-stakes testing environment challenges all public-school teachers, but art teachers in particular, are called to work through discipline-inherent issues that assault their emotional, physical, and psychological well-being (Schonfeld, 2001). Here's the deal. Art teachers deliver instruction to students in a single class who are broadly different as A is to Z in regard to their social, cognitive, and skill abilities. They teach in an environment that demands social sharing, which can intensify student behavior issues. Match these with large classes, a shrinking materials budget, ubiquitous helicopter parents and a schedule-squeezed curriculum in a high-anxiety standardized testing work environment and you can understand the factors that frustrate art teachers' efforts to set up learning environments conducive to creativity.

One way teachers cope with negative circumstances is to exploit self-deprecating or self-disparaging humor. Show me a teacher willing to laugh at themselves (and never at students), one who vulnerably offers up their lives for the sake of their students, and I will show a classroom where mistakes are shared and experimentation is encouraged. Humor of this type moves teachers toward psychological well-being because they are able to amuse others while accepting their own imperfections (Martin et al., 2003). It is humbling. It is self-sacrificing and it takes a teacher who has become comfortable with failure to model the life skill of failure-recovery to students.

I explain this with a scenario to give you an idea of this concept in the classroom. One particular day I was demonstrating to high school students how to cut an opening in a mat. Students were drawing self-portraits on the white side of matboard scraps and had brought them to be matted where I was leading the demo. (I remember I was wearing jeans with a faulty zipper.) I picked up what I thought was a mat board scrap and carefully cut the opening with the color-side up. Facing the students, I held it up to show students the finished mat when I observed looks of twisted horror on all of their faces! I had cut a hole in a student's portrait AND my zipper was down! Yikes, a double-header mistake and everyone was looking at me. Searching for a way to offer a heartfelt apology for my matboard transgression, I humbly offered, "I have been exposed" then stepped quickly into the kiln room to recover. Admittedly discomforting, my mistake provided a teachable moment for students. The kind student whose portrait into which I had cut the hole graciously turned it into a bas relief sculpture, raising up the cut out features for emphasis, a brilliant catch! Flexibility and forgiveness can produce genius.

At another time I was introducing linear perspective to middle school students when I unintentionally drew a converging parallel line some inches away from the vanishing point. A student pointed out my mistake to the class in a most patronizing manner. At this juncture, I had several options: save my ego or save the moment. I chose to admit to the error with levity with "Oops, that line was heading off to vanish in a parallel world." Laughter's safety net usually makes for a soft landing. If you are like me, your first priority is to be an excellent human, then an excellent teacher. Humility knocks instructional accuracy off of its throne every time, reminding me that I do not have to be cool, that is a teenager's job.

A teacher's ability to enjoy a joke at his or her expense models learning as a reality process of trial and error: stumble and recovery. It may be difficult for students to acknowledge ignorance while simultaneously trusting in the ability to learn. To learn you must be able to say, "I can do it." When we model humor as a means to laugh and forgive our mistakes, we release students to do likewise, to become lost in the learning process. Poking fun at our own frailties can show students that being in the "one-down" position of the learner does not interfere with our teaching confidence. In the same way, admitting what they do not know can students be open to learning what they need to know (Freda & Csikszentmihalyi, 1995).

Humor Helps with External, Adverse Impingements

Lunchtime had ended at the high school where I was teaching and I was blithely strolling to the art room with a few students. That is when I heard the explosion. A water bottle bomb filled with liquid chemicals planted in the trash can about five feet away from us exploded and propelled down the hallway, missing several disarmed humans by inches. We thought the worst was over when it happened again! A second bomb followed the path of the first. In shock, I scooped up the inert contents with a paper towel then rushed to the office. I could find only one assistant principal present sitting at a computer in the office's open area. I stood next to him like a stone statue until I gained his attention. He looked over his shoulder at the bomb contents while continuing to type. Raising his eyebrows, he asked, "Whatcha got there?" I described the threatening event, clearly emphasizing the narrow escape of life and limb. He asked, "So no one was hurt?" I told him, "No, fortunately." Satisfied with my response, he returned to his typing. I left deeply discouraged by the blasé response to near fatality.

Try as I might I could find little humor in the bomb scenario at the time. Months later, however, I was able to laugh at the administrator's response as I related the event to other teachers. Together, we concocted a stream of the most horrible situations imaginable that would have surely shaken the yawning administrator off of his stool. Bloody paper cutter limb detachments, facial injuries from a kiln explosion, and third-degree hand burns from a hot glue gun were just a few. Even the sad incongruity of a near death experience passed off as a bothersome interruption can be laughable after passing time distances us from the primary threat. Whatever gets us through the day. In stressful life-and-death situations, we often use black humor to vent feelings, elicit social support, ensure us distance from and response to a traumatic event that may reoccur (Rowe & Regehr, 2010).

A year after the bottle bomb explosion, the Columbine, Colorado school shooting took place. Feeling the impact of the violence, many schools such as ours moved into preventive action. The hallways in our high school were outside, wide open to encroaching visitors on all sides of the campus. The principal initiated a feeble crisis plan for teachers to follow, none of which would achieve the goal to stop a shooter from wounding or killing students. The plan included tactics like announcing password warnings on the PA system and placing color-coded, safety-level paper indicators in classroom windows. On my own, I activated an art room safety plan that commanded students to run into the concrete-blocked kiln room, locking the hollow metal door behind them. I visited the main office after a drill one day and could not believe my eyes. The office doors had been replaced with heavy, Titanic-level galvanized steel doors that locked on the inside, sealing the secured office with a definitive "thud!" Feeling snarky, I announced "Well my goodness it feels like Fort Knox in here! Yep, just like Fort Knox!" Office workers and an assistant principal shot me a look-that-could-kill but I left knowing I had made a point in some small way. They knew we knew that the unassailable breach of office personnel took priority over the safety of faculty and students. The principal left his position not long after the incident. I can still picture him driving away in his shiny red Corvette.

Threats and Attacks on Teachers

It is no joke that attacks in schools, including student-on-teacher threats, are on the rise. I recently learned that public schools near the university where I teach have reached a point of heightened anxiety because teachers are being trained in professional development sessions to effectively pack bleeding wounds (C. Bandy, personal communication, Hays CISD, September 2019). Violence in schools, "intentional use of physical force or emotional abuse against an employee, which results in physical or emotional injury and consequences" is our reality (Gerberich et al., 2014, p. 294). The more teachers experience physical threats on their jobs, the more teachers teeter on the edge of decision to exit the profession (Leithwood & McAdie, 2007).

We are riding a worldwide wave of an emotionally troubled generation greater than previous generations. Kids in our schools are exiled from feelings, lonely, depressed, more angry and unruly, more nervous and prone to worry, more impulsive and aggressive (Goleman, 1995). The teachers that work with emotionally exiled students must have human capacities to be successful.

We have hope. We are hopeful that we can nurture relationships with our students that undergird peace and dissuade violence. We are hopeful educational leaders will eradicate pervasive threats on teachers, to "create safer schools, and provide needed support to students who act out" (Williams et al., 2018, p. 45). We hope administrators will listen to teachers to learn about the context in which problems with students occur so they, in turn, can develop plans of action to de-escalate aggressive behaviors. We hope administrators encourage self-care to help teachers understand that their health, their longevity in teaching, and the academic and behavioral outcomes of their students are influenced by emotional capacities that enable them to listen with empathy and respond with sensitivity. Let's face it, the emotional burden of teaching is heavy.

Humor Minimizes Our Perception of Threats and Attacks

Humor is a unique phenomenon capable of minimizing emotional heavy-lifting. When we perceive danger as in physical or emotional threats, our body releases the hormone norepinephrine to prepare us to fight or flee (Morreall, 2009). Norepinephrine equips us for these responses by raising our heart rate, adding oxygen to our muscles so we can be more alert and have more energy. If we cannot escape the attack and are hurt, we feel sadness from the injury that is akin to losing something of value. The negative emotion of sadness we feel serves to immobilize us, therefore reducing the chance of injuring ourselves further. The biological function of positive laughter disables the negative response of fight or flight. "When we are afraid or angry, we are ready to run or attack—we're engaged. When we are amused, we may fall down and wet our pants—we're disengaged" (Morreall, 2009, p. 31). A sudden shifting from negative feelings when threatened to positive amusement disengagement when laughing is accomplished by humor.

I experienced disengagement from danger while teaching in an alternative high school where my students were a mixed assortment of socially delinquent, physically handicapped, emotionally disturbed, and briefly incarcerated students. The art classroom was located in a building over 1,000 feet across campus from the administrative forces that offered security in emergencies. Essentially, I was left to my own resources. To add to this situation, I was an racial minority, second year teacher just a few years older than most of the adult students aging out of general high school. Students were angry and aggressive. They figured I was a sitting target and aimed for my demise at every opportunity. The wildest situations I have ever experienced happened at this school and included: students bursting into class singing and dancing, a few running to the cabinets and taking spray paint, one held a knife at my throat and one ran through the room with a loaded gun, (far worse than running with scissors). Most came to class as high as kites. I was a feather in a hurricane taking control with humor. Laughter at the time seemed to be diametrically opposed to serious danger but served me as a weapon stronger than any other. Truly, joy was my strength. I brought in music of the calming kind and played it nonstop in my classroom. I locked the door and employed classroom "bouncers" to usher in students who belonged in the class and keep out trespassers who did not. I turned "lock out" times into "singing commercials" for students that wanted to make unsolicited but friendly performances during classes. I laughed with students, played with students and, in between, taught art.

Did I mention that the majority of students smoked marijuana between classes? I knew who they were. The glassy-eyed students moving in slow motion with their eyes locked on a pencil for 20 minutes were sure giveaways. I spoke quietly to these students, capitalizing on their drug-induced paranoia with statements like, "I know what you have been doing." Being high became so ubiquitous that I ran an intervention initiative entitled, *Make Your Mark,* a mural program that permitted students to "tag" the walls in the building with their paintings. To accomplish this, students were given a license to paint (literally—a painting license) by passing a color theory test and submitting a sketch for approval. I often returned the sketch to them if it was not acceptable content. If accepted, they were excused from class assignments to paint on their mural (just outside the classroom). If they came to class high at any time during the painting installation of their mural, I would roll over it with white latex paint and assign the space to another. This initiative was successful for one reason and one reason only: they wanted to paint their art on the walls for everyone to see. This motivation gave me control. Humor gave me sanity and the walls were soon covered with the most amazing, sober-inspired paintings imaginable.

Humor Maximizes Internal Emotional Health

Teachers are among the throngs of professional workers in the industry of service; front persons leaders of customer service to students, if you will. We must appear professional at all times, even when we do not feel like it. We align our inner feelings and outer emotional expressions with the standard expected of customer service professionals. This is what we call emotional labor. One strategy that teachers use to carry on emotional labor in the classroom is to suppress their "true feelings and express emotions that are fake but desirable. They engage in *surface acting* or *deep acting* to perform the emotions that are expected to express" (Brotheridge, 2006; Brotheridge & Lee, 2003). We hide negative feelings because we believe we are supposed to be positive at all times. When teachers hide or suppress negative emotions it means they are probably not enjoying teaching. Sadly, over time, we pay an emotional price for suppressing our true feelings and that price is detachment, burnout and turn out. We leave teaching because we no longer love teaching.

Let me take you to a time in my life when this happened to me. I was a seasoned teacher when I accepted a position at a middle school (the one with the snake pit art room). Stoked with my props, my humor and my experience, I thought a school where kids wore uniforms must be better than a tough high school. Same contents in smaller cartons, right? Well I was wrong. All of my years of experience and my cheery disposition did not prepare me for the wall I would hit with pre-adolescents. Day after day, I would pull out my tools to poke at the giants of bad behavior through a chain of crowded classes with no break in between. One morning, I felt an overwhelming helplessness rather like being in a shipwreck, after a string of bad behavior onslaughts. So, I pressed the emergency button in the classroom. We were told to save The Button until a true emergency merited an administrator coming to the rescue. I pressed it hard. The assistant principal, a spunky 32-year-old who greeted me each morning with a lilting "and how are we doing today?" opened the door. Today, I would have responded with, "I don't know how we are doing, but I am having a tough time." Anyway, when she arrived, I had intended to step through the door with a breezy, "Could you please take my class for a few minutes?" but, what came out was, "I am taking the rest of the day off. No, I am taking the rest of the week off and I am going to look for another job."

My exit that day was not irresponsible, it was essential. I drove to a nearby cemetery and cried for 2 hours. It was an ideal place to cry because I felt certain no one would interfere with a crying person in a cemetery. At the heart of my despair was the realization that I was a teacher, was born a teacher, excelled as a teacher and now, I hated teaching. I am a praying person, so I prayed first, then made an appointment with a kindhearted career counselor who asked me what my dream job was. I told her I had always hoped to teach in a university. She advised me to write it on a Post-It Note and stick it on my bathroom mirror. I looked at it each day until I made an appointment at a nearby university. The short ending to the longer story is that I am a teacher teaching in my dream job. I am not ashamed to say hitting a wall in one job caused me to find a path to another. (You would be interested to know that the position I left at the middle school was filled by a new grateful graduate from the university I entered).

Humor to Build Confidence in Your Teaching (Self-Efficacy)

What gives us confidence in our ability to teach well has been the subject of extensive research for the past 30 years. It has shown us that *what teachers' believe* about their ability to perform a teaching task (self-efficacy) is actually more powerful than their *ability to perform* the task (Bandura, 1997; Pajares, 2002). Self-efficacy, not self-esteem or self-worth, is more powerful than any instructional method or approach with which we may use to teach. Our perception of our effectiveness not only influences our present teaching and classroom management performance but also predicts what our performance will be (Pajares, 2002; Rimm-Kaufman & Sawyer, 2004; Toumaki & Podell, 2005; Tschannen-Moran & Hoy, 2002).

If we possess a high sense of efficacy, we work harder and persist longer than teachers with lower self-efficacy because we believe we can teach any student when given the right resources (Tschannen-Moran & Woolfolk Hoy, 2001). Efficacious teachers are enthusiastic, they show strong commitment to the profession (Coladarci, 1992), they look for problem-solving strategies and are more likely to stay in teaching than their lower-efficacy colleagues (Tschannen-Moran & Woolfolk Hoy, 2006). They manage students in their classroom with positive,

Table 2.1. Definition of Self-Efficacy Terms

Term	Definition
Affective Processes	Processes regulating emotional states and elicitation of emotional reactions.
Cognitive Processes	The thinking processes involved in the acquisition, organization, and use of information.
Personal Self-Efficacy	The conviction that one can successfully execute the behavior required to produce an outcome.
Outcome Expectation	The degree to which teachers believe the environment could be controlled and a given behavior will lead to an expected outcome.
Self-Regulation	Exercise of influence over one's own motivation, thought processes, emotional states and patterns of behavior.
Teaching self-efficacy	Teachers' belief in their capability to organize and execute courses of action required to successfully accomplish a specific teaching task in a particular context.[a]

[a] Tschannen-Moran, M., & Hoy, A. W. (2001). Teacher efficacy: Capturing an elusive construct. *Teaching and teacher education*, *17*(7), 783–805.

preventative behavior strategies as opposed to the negative, reactive strategies of low-efficacy teachers who see more student misbehavior in their classrooms and send more referrals to administrators (Ashley, 2009).

Just as a teacher's high self-efficacy beliefs power them forward to excellence, the negative perceptions of others can demolish that power. I can remember a season in my career when my new assignment to the department raised the ire of two colleagues on the faculty. My colleagues in question were cruelly critical of my performance in the classroom. My ways were not their ways and I felt their searing scrutiny. One colleague even stepped into my classroom and corrected a point I was making during a presentation in front of my students. Ghastly behavior! Teachers behaving badly! It was during this season that I began to question my ability to teach, although I had earned the respect of students and administrators in previous job assignments. Even with my prior successes to shore up my confidence, perceptions of my capabilities unraveled. I felt myself spiraling downward. Laughing with students gave me some buoyancy and over time, I recovered. Thankfully, a group of loving peers helped me to believe again in my good teaching. My point: peer criticism at any age is spitefully counterproductive.

The findings of the study I conducted with art teachers supported what I had experienced with my peers: that instructional self-efficacy is influenced by social humor. I determined levels of stress influenced the positive relationship between sense of self-efficacy and perceptions of humor (Evans-Palmer, 2009). I found statistical significance supporting the notion that unchecked, persistent stress reduces a teachers' ability to cope and downgrades belief in their capability to engage students and deliver instruction effectively. Plainly stated, the outcome of my analyses asserted when art teachers experience high levels of stress, belief in their ability to teach well takes a plunge no matter what age or how many years they have been teaching.

I also discovered that instruction, a function of social behavior, is strongly linked to the use of social humor, the kind of humor teachers use to activate effective instruction. Unfortunately, I found that highly stressed teachers under the influence of a forcefully negative emotional state are unable to reach for humor as a coping mechanism. They simply cannot laugh because they want to cry. It would take a room full of stressed teachers to pull them back from the edge. Supported as a member of a team, teachers could be encouraged to develop a robust sense of self-efficacy if they were helping one another to be adept at humor to cope with adverse conditions that thwart classroom instruction (Tschannen-Moran & Woolfolk Hoy, 2002).

I was encouraged to read how prisoners of war, held captive together for 7 years, helped each other survive life-threatening danger by laughing a lot. When asked about their experience, the prisoners explained that laughing about the funny side of bad things helped them to pull together and be stronger through all of the torment (Henman, 2001). One difference between being held prisoner in a camp with other prisoners and teaching art is that art teachers work alone in their classrooms. Art teachers, especially the new ones, need the same emotional resilience that prisoners require to shift their perspectives from saddened to sunny. Although humor may not be the answer for every issue they face, the altered outlook and the positive feedback they gain from humor builds morale and teaching confidence in such a way, they are able to solve problems more effectively (Nasiri & Mafakheri, 2015).

Smiling, laughing and being playful fills our resilience reservoirs with joy. The reservoir we pull from in trying times (Tait, 2008). We need joy to rise above our self-doubt, to minimize our exhaustion, to neutralize our negative attitudes we may feel toward our students, and to overcome our feelings of inadequacy (Reglin & Reitzammer, 1998). As a seasoned teacher and a fan of Seinfeld, I must tell you I try to see the humor in everything (even if it is about nothing). Call me crazy, but I am convinced that laughing in the face of adversity is not a tired old adage, it is a fresh new way to teach strong.

Table 2.2. A Few Humor Strategies

Elementary	Secondary
Magic Pencil Air Sketch *to overcome fear of failure.* Invite students to use their pointing finger to sketch in the air. Every mark in the air is accompanied by a sound. Once the air drawing is completed, hand them a drawing tool. Smile while telling them their drawing will look even better on paper.	**Metaphors** *to indirectly correct misbehavior* Correct misbehavior by telling them a story using an appropriate metaphor. Not to be a direct address of the unwanted behavior but a simile, an analogy, a vivid parallel description that brings images to mind.
Magic Wand *to engage; heighten attention* Obtain a toy wand. Memorize a sales spiel claiming the magic powers of the wand. Use to reward student responses with the promise of a magic impartation from the wand that will enlighten ideas for the next 4 hours. Powerfully suggestive.	**Classroom Conduct Gauge** *to halt whole-class misbehavior (essentially time out probation)* Draw a thermometer on the board or use a gauge you've constructed to "measure" the extent of "teachability" of the class. Indicate levels of their receptiveness to learning. When behavior does not merit being taught, students are placed on "auto-teach" to teach themselves with written assignments.

Table 2.2. *Continued*

Elementary	Secondary
Eraser Mute/Delete *to gain attention* Use the chalk or white board eraser to pretend you are calling a student, muting classroom noise or deleting an unwanted object from the classroom.	**Disciplining Inanimate Objects** *to indirectly discipline a student's misbehavior* If a student is using an object to distract your teaching, ask if you may have the object (pencil, comb, make up, tapping brush, squeaking chair, etc.), then tell the object they have been to __(object)_-training school and should know better than to behave that way. Replace the object with a quieter, more juvenile object and continue teaching.
Code Glue *to revive "dying" works of art with two bottles of white glue as defibrillator on a crash cart.* Place a bottle of glue in each hand and lay on top of nonresponsive artwork. React as if an electrical charge has surged through the bottles. Hand the revived work to the student artist with a smile and tell them it is ready for its operation in which the student is the physician.	
	License to Paint *to ensure material readiness* Students meet two requirements to earn a Painting License: a painting performance test and written assessment. If passing, they receive a license that looks like a drivers' license entitling them to paint. Consequence for reckless painting incidents can be teacher citation or revoked license.
Eye Can *to overcome fear of failure and discourage persistent "I can't" statements* Introduce the Eye Can as a classroom "failure inhibiter," claiming it can correct their inability to succeed. Invite students to place the Can in front of discouraged peers.	**Count Markula** *to ensure marker return* Assign a student to be the Count, hand them a block with Sharpie-sized holes, each with a number. Their job: collect a marker from each student to fill the holes at the end of class.
Cold Pencil *to overcome student drawing inertia* Approach student reluctant and tell them they are not able to draw because their pencil is "cold." Roll the pencil between your hands to "prime" the pencil. Hand warmed pencil back to student, smile and walk away. Check back later and continue encouraging.	**Group Hug** *to comfort emotional student* Speak tenderly to the emotional student requiring attention. Ask them if they would like the entire class to encircle them in a group hug. They will say "no" but you have shown them the support they need.
Willie the Worm *to exemplify line and shape* One-yard, personal "pet" piece of heavy yarn.	

Bibliography

Ashley, S. (2009). *Self-efficacy beliefs of elementary general education teachers in inclusive classrooms and the role of professional development* (Dissertations, Theses, and Masters Projects). Paper 1539618704. https://dx.doi.org/doi:10.25774/w4-a2mg-gh30

Bandura, A. (1997). *Self-efficacy: The exercise of control.* New York, NY: W. H. Freeman.

Bieg, S., Grassinger, R., & Dresel, M. (2017). Humor as a magic bullet? Associations of different teacher humor types with student emotions. *Learning and Individual Differences, 56*(2107), 24–33.

Brophy, J. (1996). *Teaching problem students.* New York, NY: Guilford.

Brotheridge, C. (2006). A review of emotional labour and its nomological network: Practical and research implications. *Ergonomia, 28*(4), 295–309.

Brotheridge, C., & Lee, R. (2003). Development and validation of the emotional labour scale. *Journal of Occupational and Organizational Psychology, 76*(3), 365–379.

Coladarci, T. (1992). Teachers' sense of efficacy and commitment to teaching. *The Journal of experimental education, 60*(4), 323-337.

Douglas, K., & Jaquith, D. (2018). *Engaging learners through artmaking: Choice-based art education in the classroom (TAB).* New York, NY: Teachers College Press.

Duffy, M., & Sperry, L. (2012). *Mobbing: causes, consequences, and solutions.* Oxford, UK: University Oxford Press.

Evans-Palmer, T. (2009). *The relationship between sense of humor and self-efficacy: An exploration of the beliefs of art teachers* (Doctoral dissertation). University of the Incarnate Word, , San Antonio, TX. Available from ProQuest Digital Dissertation. (TX 6-697-683).

Freda, P., & Csikszentmihalyi, M. (1995). *The influence of teachers.* Boston: Houghton-Mifflin.

Gerberich, S., Nachreiner, N., Ryan, A., Church, T., McGovern, P., Geisser, M., & Pinder, E. (2014). Case-control study of student-perpetrated physical violence against educators. *Annals of Epidemiology, 24*(5), 325–332. http://doi.org/10.1016/j.annepidem.2014.02.006

Greenberg, J., Putman, H., & Walsh, K. (2013). Training our future teachers: Classroom management. *National Council on Teacher Quality.* Retrieved from http://www.nctq.org/dmsStage/Future_Teachers_Classroom_Management_NCTQReport

Golembeski, J. (2020). *Designing humor—utilizing humor, wit, and play as a strategy to address serious issues* (Thesis). San Marcos, TX: Texas State University.

Goleman, D. (1996). Emotional intelligence. Why it can matter more than IQ. *Learning, 24*(6), 49-50.

Gordon, M. (2014). Friendship, intimacy and humor. *Educational Philosophy and Theory, 46*(2), 162–174.

Henman, L. (2001). Humor as a coping mechanism: Lessons from POWs. *Humor: International Journal of Humor Research, 14*(1), 83–94.

Kaufman, J., & Sternberg, R. (Eds.). (2010). *The Cambridge handbook of creativity.* Cambridge, UK: Cambridge University Press. Retrieved from http://www.ebrary.com.

Leithwood, K., & McAdie, P. (2007). Teacher working conditions that matter. *Education Canada*, 47(2), 42–45.

Magnuson, C., & Barnett, L. (2013). The playful advantage: How playfulness enhances coping with stress. *Leisure Sciences*, 35(2), 129–144.

Martin, R., Puhlik-Doris, P., Larsen, G., Gray, J., & Weir, K. (2003). Individual differences in uses of humor and their relation to psychological well-being: Development of the Humor Styles Questionnaire. *Journal of Research in Personality*, 37(1), 48–75.

Marzano, R., Marzano, J., & Pickering, D. (2003). *Classroom management that works: Research-based strategies for every teacher*. Alexandria, VA: Association for Supervision and Curriculum Development.

Minor, D. (2014). The captain of the ship: Classroom management. In N. López-Burton & D. Minor (Eds.), *On being a language teacher: A personal and practical guide to success* (pp. 178–201). New Haven, CT: Yale University Press. http://www.jstor.org.libproxy.txstate.edu/stable/j.ctt13x1swk.14

Moore, J. (2013). Resilience and at-risk children and youth. *National Center for Homeless Education*.

Moore, T., Wehby, J., Oliver, R., Chow, J., Gordon, J., & Mahany, L. (2017). Teachers' reported knowledge and implementation of research-based classroom and behavior management strategies. *Remedial and Special Education*, 38(4), 222–232.

Morreall, J. (2009). *Comic relief: A comprehensive philosophy of humor*. Hoboken, NJ: Wiley-Blackwell.

Morton, M. (2005) Practicing praxis: mentoring teachers in a low-income school through collaborative action research and transformative pedagogy, *Mentoring & Tutoring: Partnership in Learning*, 13(1), 53–72, http://doi.org/10.1080/13611260500040278.

Nasiri, F., & Mafakheri, F. (2015). Higher education lecturing and humor: From perspectives to strategies. *Higher Education Studies*, 5(5), 26–31.

Pajares, F. (2002). Overview of social cognitive theory and self-efficacy. http://www.emory.edu/EDUCATION/mfp/eff.html

Powell, J., & Andersen, L. (1985). Humor and teaching in higher education. *Studies in Higher Education*, 10(1), 79–90.

Reglin, G., & Reitzammer, A. (1998). Dealing with the stress of teachers. *Education*, 118(4), 590–596.

Rimm-Kaufman, S., & Sawyer, B. (2004). Primary-grade teachers' self-efficacy beliefs, attitudes toward teaching, and discipline and teaching practice priorities in relation to the Responsive Classroom approach. *The Elementary School Journal*, 104(4), 321–341.

Rowe, A., & Regehr, C. (2010) Whatever gets you through today: An examination of cynical humor among emergency service professionals. *Journal of Loss and Trauma*, 15(5), 448–464. http://doi.org/10.1080/15325024.2010.507561

Schonfeld, I. (2001). Stress in first-year women teachers: The context of social support and coping. *Genetic, Social, and General Psychology Monographs*, 127, 133–168.

Tait, M. (2008). Resilience as a contributor to novice teacher success, commitment, and retention. *Teacher Education Quarterly*, 35(4), 57–75.

Tait, G., Lampert, J., Bahr, N., & Bennett, P. (2015). Laughing with the lecturer: the use of humour in shaping university teaching. *Journal of University Teaching & Learning Practice, 12*(3), 7.

Tournaki, N., & Podell, D. (2005). The impact of student characteristics and teacher efficacy on teachers' predictions of student success. *Teaching and Teacher Education, 21*, 299–314.

Tschannen-Moran, M., & Woolfolk Hoy, A. (2001). Teacher efficacy: Capturing an elusive construct. *Teacher and Teacher Education, 17*, 783–805.

Tschannen-Moran, M., & Woolfolk Hoy, A. (2002). The influence of resources and support on teachers' efficacy beliefs. *Review of Educational Research, 68*, 202–248.

Tschannen-Moran, M., & Woolfolk Hoy, A. (2006). The differential antecedents of the self-efficacy beliefs of novice and experienced teachers. *Teaching and Teacher Education, 23*(6), 944–956.

Watts, R. (2010). Responding to children's drawings. *Education 3–13, 38*(2), 137–153.

Watts, R. (2005). Making art in primary school. *International Journal of Art & Design Education, 24*(3), 243–253.

Wong, H., Wong, R., Rogers, K., & Brooks, A. (2012). Managing your classroom for success. *Science and Children, 49*(10), 60–64.

CHAPTER THREE

Humor Connects Teachers with Students

Connections in classrooms are crucial. Ask a teacher what we should do to deter violence in our schools and you will get a simple but wise answer: keep kids connected. Teachers have made observing children their profession and we know positive messages are crucial to connecting with kids, especially those who are emotionally out of step, those who feel alienated by themselves or by others. Dysfunction begins with disconnection. When kids are consumed by feelings of loneliness, they eventually resort to being noticed by any means. Fortuitously, teachers have the power to make kids feel included, valued and worth knowing. The care we give to individual students has an exponential effect on the collective whole because "kids are more likely to care about others if they know they are cared about" themselves (Kohn, 1996, p. 111). Hanging out in your classroom are loosely knit students who will over time, be either woven into a richly diverse tapestry or unravel into frayed knots (or afraid nots!) The odds of a class becoming one in holy *classimony* are in your favor if you promote harmony as the teacher. Your inner capacities and identity, your intuition, emotional intelligence and humor harmoniously draws students together into a group that feels connected to each other. Classroom personas mirror a teacher's persona; the organization collectively adopts the identity of its leader. "Community is an outward, visible sign of an inward, invisible grace, the flowing of personal identity and integrity into the classroom" (Palmer, 2007, p. 93). How does this happen?

For learners to want to learn together, they must be motivated to mutually honor each other. This concept crystalized when I visited an Italian school for 3-, 4- and 5-year-old children, whose curriculum flies under the banner, "one teaches everyone and everyone teaches one." Learners are not only learners but also knowers united in relationships that benefit mutuality in a space; art is made together in one endeavor and individually, in many endeavors. The artwork of children covers the walls and halls of the school, leaving little doubt that making art is the center of all learning (a second motto murmured among teachers was "Here we make little Gucci's"). The director of the school inaugurates acceptance among classmates by acknowledging the unique contribution each student makes to the vitality of the whole. In this community of practice, allegiances are made; good habits are formed and everyone in that space is eager for the main event: learning.

Teachers are the main motivators essential to helping students connect with one another. As it happens, motivation and emotion share the same Latin root, *motere* meaning *to move*. We are all motivated to achieve goals that make us feel good and loved by others (Goleman, 2011).

"Emotions are paramount to learning and student outcomes within the classroom" (Brackett, Reyes, Rivers, Elbertson, & Salovey, 2011, p. 34). Every day, teachers reach into their emotional repository to animate leadership in a way that has yet to be regarded with credibility by educational leaders. The education citadel historically prefers to focus on training brains over dealing with the messy functions of the heart largely because logical thinking is easier to measure and produces discrete data. (Don't we just love data?) Generally, academic culture honors only two sources of knowledge: empirical observation and logical reasoning. But we do not live on science alone. To survive and thrive, we rely on the knowledge embedded in our feelings. After all, "science itself begins with hunches, intuitions, and bodily knowledge that lie behind testable hypotheses" (Palmer, 2007, p. 208).

Our Intuition

Many of us are called to teach by way of our hearts. Head over heart, reason over response is how most of us roll. We collect behavior data throughout the day from our students through hunches, voice inflections, body language cues, and invisible emotional vibes. We call this valid data collection method, *intuition*, the capacity to attain knowledge or cognition without rational thought. The inner voice of intuition tells us what we are feeling deep below the strata of reason, flowing most likely from our gut, to communicate our feelings into *knowings* that we cannot explain. Literature supported by researchers from the medical community, Mayer and Holzer respectively, explain this phenomenon much better than I am able. Mayer as cited in Gordon (2017) argues:

> "The gut," Dr. Mayer says, "converses with the brain like no other organ. When people talk about going with their gut feelings on an important decision, what they're referring to is an intuitive knowledge based on the close relationship between our emotions and the sensations and feelings in the gastrointestinal (GI) tract." (Abstract)

In agreement with this idea, Holzer (2017) adds:

> Brain imaging techniques have revealed that part of the subconscious information that flows from internal organs is also fed into the corticolimbic system where it is very likely to influence thinking, emotions, and mood. This process is embodied in the term "interoception," and it is emerging that - via the process of interoception - signals from the gut and other internal organs exert an influence on our "feelings" (emotion, cognition, and mood). (Abstract)

The enactment of our *knowings* into actions inexplicably connects us to students. Is there something to be gained from this connection? Most definitely.

When teachers step into the performance limelight as the instructional force in the room, they take their personal selves with them. The source of emotional competence, the personal capacity that powerfully equips us to teach well, comes from our feelings. You see, our binary brain operates with two separate systems processing independently; the intuition of System 1 operates very effectively apart from the logic and reason of System 2 (Kahneman, 2011). Intuition naïvely enables us to make connections quickly, mechanizing impulsive, unconscious, expedited, metaphorical, investigative and exploratory processes, while logic and reason of System 2 (generally associated with thinking) activates conscious, controlled, sequential, numerical, deliberate, methodically slower processes (Andrei, 2012). All too often intuitive System 1 succeeds in solving problems long before System 2 can work through the facts. The most effective teaching resources to which we have access are intuition and emotion, which abide in System 2. Helen Keller, born deaf, blind and mute, led a rich life in an unseen world by relying only on internal capacities to perceive the external. Her secret? She confesses, "The best and most beautiful things in the world cannot be seen or even touched. They must be felt with the heart" (Goodreads, 2019).

Our Emotional Intelligence

Teacher intuition empowers us to collect emotional data from interactions with students while we are teaching. At the same time, a complex emotional radar system is collecting vital emotional information to guide what we will say or do next. The radar system, one of the "soft skills" on our teaching tool belt, is *emotional intelligence* (EI or EQ, not IQ), which gives us the extraordinarily sensitive capacity to perceive and absorb individual emotional nuances of student moods from their body gestures (Goleman, 1995; Martin, 2007). The EI capacities of teachers socially enable hunches, instincts, and the gut feelings of System 1, to help us capture emotional data from classroom situations, then rapidly process the data, and finally assess and respond to the situation, all without regard to System 2's slower cognitive processes (Mayer, Salovey, & Caruso, 2000).

The speed at which this chain reaction occurs is known as *immediacy*, the capacity to quickly connect with students, a capability fueled by knowledge embedded in intuitive feelings. Intuition working efficiently with immediacy, "animates learning and leadership" (Palmer, 2007, p. 208). Students think teachers are immediate when they use a variety of verbal and nonverbal behaviors to shorten the physical and psychological distance between themselves. Budding relationships, the ability to "get students" are the result of this immediate connection. (Richmond, Lane, & McCroskey, 2006).

Teachers are able to understand their own feelings and have empathy for the feelings of their students through the insula node working with the somatosensory cortex, both situated on the brain's right side (Goleman, 2011). We have been told most of our careers about the right-brain creativity payoff for artists. Now, we have a reason to value right-brain functions working for teachers to run EI rather like undercover intel working the room. With EI, we observe and read interactions for emotional clues, then use the emotional intel to monitor our thinking and actions (Arendt, 2006; Mayer & Salovey, 1993). If we are among the teachers who believe in our ability to help students learn with the right resources, our emotional intelligence is optimized by this belief.

Self-Awareness and Self-Monitoring

Many times, every day the emotional information we gather alters our actions to make us better teachers (Goleman, 1995). Although the *self-awareness* aspect of EI equips us with an extraordinary sensitivity to students' feelings, the *self-monitoring* aspect helps us act upon that emotional information (Arendt, 2006; Goleman, 2011; Mayer & Salovey, 1993). An example of emotional sensitivity and self-monitoring working together as a process might be better explained with a scenario from my teaching life. I was showing young children how to hand build clay pinch pots while crouched in a corner with my back to the classroom. Watching a child awkwardly manipulate clay, I suddenly sensed something was not right elsewhere. I could feel it from across the room. I stood, turned and walked toward the source of the feeling only to discover a despondent child sobbing. Her pot was a misshapen ball of sodden clay. I grabbed some clay of my own and formed a ball. I showed her how to insert her thumb into the ball, then rotate the ball while pinching the outside. I did this slowly, very gently, kneeling next to her and speaking softly. I encouraged her with a broad smile and the statement, "See, you can do this. I just know you can!" Handing her my ball of clay, I watched her face transform to joy. Within 5 minutes she was humming to herself and working away.

Now, I am no emotionally intelligent guru. Most of the time I do not know where I parked my car when I leave a shopping area (which calls for car-awareness not self-awareness), but I have learned to feel my way around a classroom. The pinch pot example is merely a snapshot of a teacher seeking emotional information from students cues and acting on the emotional data that self-awareness tracked down. Much of emotional intelligence is inherent, but I would argue much is acquired through experience as well. We can learn to be more sensitive to the emotions of others and we grow neural cells to help us achieve this. The mythical belief that we are born with a colossal amount of brain cells which slowly dissipate until we die, is a lie (Goleman, 2011). Instead, the brain continually reshapes itself to accommodate whatever new thing we are trying to learn.

If you desire to heighten rapport and establish deeper emotional connections with your students, you might want to adopt three simple behaviors that achieve this goal (Tickle-Degnon & Rosenthal, 1990). The first behavior is to be completely tuned into each student. Give them your full attention without distraction of any kind. Second, be in synch non-verbally. If you were to observe two people connecting really well at a distance without hearing what they are saying, their movements would look like they were rehearsed, like a play. Oscillator neurons in our brains automatically regulate how our body moves in relationship to another person's body. Hence, synchronous movements that occur when people are connected generate an association, a familiarity, a comfort to be in that person's presence. It is almost like looking into a mirror. Third, be positive. Interpersonal chemistry emanating from pleasurable feelings shared with others establishes a bond that tethers us to another. Good feelings create the ultimate tie that binds. Practicing these behaviors will place students within your reach who are generally unreachable.

Developing Emotional Intelligence Capabilities

Art teachers celebrate even the smallest transformations making art brings about in the lives of youth. Admit it, your heart inflates when you see students achieving something. My goal for preservice teachers in my classes is to allow them to experience their "teacher selves" before they step into a room with their name on the door. I allow these soon-to-be teachers to experience their unrecognized capacity for EI during classes dedicated to student presentations. It is a pleasure to watch students present gobs of good knowledge while smoothly handling "planted" misbehavior archetypes with which their peers have improvised to interrupt them. As I expected, the soft skill tools of emotional intelligence and intuition help presenters effortlessly glide through misbehaviors without missing a beat.

After the incident, they confess that they did not think about what to do, they just did it. When I ask, "How did you know to resolve the incident as you did?" They cannot tell me. Essentially, they realize they can rely on the data input from their intuition and emotional intelligence, their dispositional secret weapons and standard equipment for managing students with ease. I follow Parker Palmer's recommendation to teacher educators: lead disciplined group inquiry as a means to help new teachers personalize the phenomenon of EI response and raise their self-efficacy perceptions (Goleman, 2011).

We would all agree that being emotionally intelligent teachers has it benefits. Here is one more: emotionally intelligent teachers are likeable. Students favor them because they are intuitive, honest, accessible, sincere, relaxed, optimistic, resilient. enthusiastic and caring instructors who will do anything to help their students learn. Being likeable is especially strategic for teachers as leaders of learning in the classroom, but please know that one does not have attained EI excellence to embrace its benefits. We can cultivate EI likeability by following a few quality communication guidelines (Hoenigman Meyer, 2018):

1. Talk less … smile more.
2. Look intently at a speaking student and ask questions to dig deeper for understanding.
3. Take a step back and try to objectively hear what they are saying.
4. Check your ego. We are adults, we've got it going on, our students are finding their way.

In as much as a teacher's likeability is attributed to emotional intelligence, it is also associated with their humor style, or mode of humor that we demonstrate on a day-to-day basis (Martin et al., 2003). Humor styles are adapted by personality types; highly humorous teachers who effortlessly generate fun in their classes possess social skills that come from extroverted, positive, and cheerful personality traits (Martin, 2007; Merolla, 2006). Humor conceptualized as humor appreciation, however, does not require an extroverted personality, assuming that everyone appreciates humor to some degree (Thorson & Powell, 1993). The difference here is that actively generating humor is a different behavior than passively enjoying or appreciating humor. With the help of emotional intelligence's barometer for gauging what humor works and when, teachers of any age or level of experience, either extroverted or introverted, can pull off funniness:

> The more you understand and can control your own emotions, the more you can relax. The higher your level of emotional intelligence, the more you will take chances and laugh at more diverse types of humor. As children grow, and mature, their sense of humor also develops. Moreover, as people increase their level of factual knowledge, their development of symbolic, logical and abstract reasoning skills, as well as their humor production, also increases. There is a theoretical connection between your emotional intelligence and your age, gender, intelligence and sense of humor. (Jonas, 2004, p. 81)

The capabilities to produce humor and self-monitor work together. Social humor serves teachers as a pedagogical resource to engage and illuminate, but it also helps them believe in their own good teaching (Evans-Palmer, 2009). There is a strong connection to making something funny and altering your behavior after the funny bit either flies or flops. Stand-up comedians use this connection to deliver and edit their material. Teachers use social humor in their instruction to engage students, then adjust their behavior as they receive student response feedback from the engagement (Kelley & Gorham, 1988). It is the same. For teachers, the self-efficacy benefit of social humor interacting with self-monitoring comes from interaction raising their belief in their teaching skill. In other words, their ability to "read the room" gauges the receptivity of their students so they can fine-tune humor into their instruction for maximum. This effect, in turn, raises their teaching confidence. It would seem that the concepts of emotional intelligence, self-efficacy and sense of humor are like separate cars in a teaching train, but no one is quite sure which one is pulling the train.

What we do know is that humor helps with heavy lifting because it does not operate alone. When humor enters the classroom, it also brings laughter, emotional pleasure, relief, relaxation, and a feeling of fun. If fun is a frequent factor in learning with a specific teacher, students come to expect any learning experience with that teacher to be fun (Martin, 2007). You see, the more positive emotion students invest in something, the more of that thing they will receive (D. Ivan Young as cited in Nuttt & Hardman, 2019). Comedians are teachers of sort who use both emotional intelligence and self-monitoring during their stand-up sessions. Masters of emotion, connecting with people is central to their profession:

> Comedians surround themselves with humor and devote their careers to observing, analyzing, creating, practicing, and performing humor. They think about new material every day, write jokes for their act, perform on stage with clear feedback from audiences, and watch other comedians, with whom they discuss their work. Comedians must be sensitive to audience reaction and tune their act accordingly. (Greengross, Martin, & Miller, 2012, p. 79)

Think about it, comedians with successful careers are professional observers of human behavior. They remain acutely aware of the humor in their own lives and in the ordinary things we all do. They process their observation by spinning them into funny monologues. When they deliver their "material," they are quick to pick up cues that register as acceptance or rejection, then adjust their delivery to accommodate the audience.

Like confident comedians, humor-oriented teachers create and deliver humor while operating in the same soft skill sensitivity modes as comedians. They observe their students to gather and analyze emotional information, then self-monitor their thinking and actions in response to the emotional receptivity of students (Arendt, 2006; Bell, McGhee, & Duffey, 1986; Martin & Ford, 2018; Mayer & Salovey, 1993). The ease in which they deliver stand-up comedy instruction is facilitated by their emotional intelligence, self-awareness and teaching self-efficacy.

Historically and hysterically, humor and laughter have been socially magnetizing humans long before we ever used words to communicate (Martin, 2007). Victor Borge said it nicely: "Laughter is the shortest distance between two people" (Sullivan, 1992). Like making art, humor transcends spoken words. Like art, humor communicates messages deliciously rich with sensory elements. The noninvasive, nonmanipulative, nonverbal behaviors of positive humor constructively charges interactions in classrooms (Shor & Freire, 1987). We know it is virtually impossible to feel alienated when we are sharing laughter with our peers (Sim, 2015). Relationships rarely sour in spaces where humor keeps social relationships positive (Taupin, 2018). Heavy doses of laughter keep everyone in the art classroom connected and engaged in learning together. How does a teacher make a united community happen with humor? Read on.

We have enjoyed the cohesion effect attributed to humor for as long as humans have been laughing together. One of the behaviors on our social skills toolbelt, humor acts as a powerful adhesive joining people in positive social interactions (Rao, Beidel, & Murray, 2008). Laughter unites us with a tangible bond and distances us from rigorous constraints. You remember the *laughter-demic*, the exceedingly bizarre outbreak of contagious laughter reported at a Tanzanian girls school? If only researchers had tracked down the triggering source of this event, we would joyously replicate it in our classrooms. We would bottle it or can it and spray it around the room to bring on gales of contagious, infectious and cohesive laughter. Brandishing humor is this way would give us a settling sense of efficacy, of silky ease and controlled advantage in the work we do.

Our Physicality

Call me insecure, but I find myself inordinately in need of an immediate connection with students from the time they enter the classroom to the time they ooze out the door. A strategy I use to make a first impression connection in the first class is to stand at the door and shake hands with every student that enters. I look them right in the eye, smile, and extend my hand. I must tell you that being a smallish, not imposing-looking female standing at 5'3 could be a detriment for me in dealings with football players and gargantuan-sized students. I deliver a strong, hard-squeeze handshake accompanied with a strong gaze and sunny smile to counteract perceptions of size to strength ratio. These behaviors quickly communicate the words you do not have to speak: "I am so glad to meet you. Now, I may look small but I am in charge here. I eat rocks for breakfast so consider yourself on notice!" This haptic connection between teacher and students embodies a physical connection between teacher and students on one hand, and on the other, it reels in their attention. (Shaking hands with students is notably one of the few ways we can legitimately touch them without fear of litigation). If shaking hands feeds the germaphobe within you, go with fist or elbow bumps for less precarious options.

The human touch is a teaser for provoking learning that happens when our bodies and brains are engaged simultaneously (Strean, 2011). Humor, like the human touch, shakes our bodies awake for full engagement in learning. Positive and pleasurable affiliative humor is "related to extraversion, cheerfulness, self-esteem, intimacy, relationship satisfaction, and predominantly positive moods and emotions" (Martin et al., 2003, p. 53). Affiliative humor helps teachers ease interpersonal tensions and establish a closeness that advances into mutually respected relationships with their students (Lefcourt, 2001). Turning negative emotions around feels to some students like they have moved from a dark place into the light if the humor teachers use is positive and appropriate.

Types of Teacher Humor

Appropriate teacher humor dialogue is multidimensional and appears in four types to achieve either positive connection and deeper learning responses or negative alienation and intimidation responses:

1. Affiliative humor with *no* connection to the content
2. Affiliative humor *with* connection to the content
3. Self-disparaging humor focusing on a teacher's weakness
4. Aggressive humor that denigrates or ridicules students.

Positive affiliative humor enhances, expands, explains, and exemplifies as opposed to the negative, aggressive humor type, that negatively ridicules, harms, alienates and angers students. Of the four types, affiliative, feel-good, content-related humor is one of the most effective methods a teacher can use to construct social relationships and support learning of key concepts in the classroom. Friendly humor, with a thematic connection to the topic, not only motivates and satisfies social and motivational functions, but also brings the cognitive functions of teaching into play (Bieg & Dresel, 2018; Klauer, 1985). Teacher humor related to course material is positively associated with student enjoyment, their intrinsic motivation for the subject matter and their use of elaboration strategies. The most frequently used humor teachers present (60% of all content-related humor) appears as media/external objects (19%), jokes (14%), examples (14%), and stories (13%). Appropriate humor related to course material makes content more relevant to students and easier to process; if teachers wish to upgrade student motivation and ability to process cognitively, appropriate humor related to course material should facilitate learning (Martin & Ford, 2018).

Inversely, teacher humor type four is the least effective in achieving learning and unity because aggressive, dysfunctional humor rife with negatively charged emotional messages break down unity in the classroom and have a debilitating effect on student engagement. Examples for this type of verbally aggressive, offensive humor attacks students' self-concept by disparaging them on the basis of intelligence, gender orientation, personal opinion, appearance or religion (Infante, Riddle, Horvath, & Tumlin, 1992). Teachers tend to use aggressively hostile, sarcastic humor to tease and ridicule students engaged in undesirable behavior. Humor may work to correct bad behavior, but it does so at the expense of student rapport. Targeted students for aggressive humor and those in the room watching the humor correction feel powerfully intimidated (Martin, 2007). Seriously, if you were a disparaged, annoyed student feeling like a target for a teacher's sharp wit, would you be able to focus on conversation content? I suggest we do not use this type of humor. Students simply will not enjoy aggressive teacher humor nor are they intrinsically motivated to learn (Bieg & Dresel, 2018; Frymier, 2008; Wanzer, Frymier, & Irwin, 2010).

Affiliative humor unrelated to content, teacher humor type one, shows up in dialogue as anecdotal side stories and incoherent jokes. Not surprisingly, this type of humor tends to sidetrack students from the very material the teacher is trying to elucidate (Frymier et al., 2008; Martin et al., 2003). Being amused in our own minds may be a way to leave the room without taking our body but it is not a way to make what we are teaching accessible to students.

Self-disparaging humor, teacher humor type three, contains self-deprecating humorous comments and embarrassing stories aimed at a teacher's weaknesses and their personal characteristics, poking fun at their mistakes and making fun of their lack of ability. Students identify teacher attempts at self-disparaging humor to be both an appropriate and inappropriate form of humor. Research that creates positive rapport with students or negative affect with student learning or group unity.

It is interesting to note that teachers who use humor in instruction vary with respect to gender and level of education. For instance, male teachers at the secondary and post-secondary level use humor in their classrooms slightly more frequently and differently than females. Males were reported to tell more funny stories and jokes not related to the subject than females, who leaned toward telling anecdotal, spontaneous stories related to the subject (Bryant et al., 1980). College professors are at the top of list of teachers who use humor most frequently at seven attempts per class when compared to high school and middle school teachers make an average of only two attempts (Javidi, Downs, & Nussbaum, 1988; Neuliep, 1991).

Humor-Enhancing Dialogue

Since most people love to laugh, it should be no surprise to learn dialogue with students in your classes is enhanced by humor. Humor, the matrix of dialogue, sparks deepened, mutual trust between the dialoguers (Nouri & Sajjadi, 2014). That is to say humor helps make the learning moment "real," a quality replacing the artificiality of school experiences with humor-birthed "human moments" (Shor & Freire, 1987). A human moment is when we "authentically connect to another human to such a degree that the learning at that moment feels real" (Shih, 2018, p. 234). The alluring take away from using humor to launch real learning moments is this: lighthearted students laughing with each other retain lesson content to a greater degree than those who are isolated, anxious, and intimidated (Opplinger & Zillman, 2003).

What does humor look like in is humor in classroom dialogue? According to humor psychologist, Rod Martin, teacher humor in dialogue is:

> Anything that people say or do that is perceived as funny and tends to make others laugh, as well as the mental processes that go into both creating and perceiving such an amusing stimulus, and also the affective response involved in the enjoyment of it. (2007, p. 5)

Students enter a classroom with anticipated expectations for dialogue that is either congruently normal as expected or incongruently funny as unexpected. Students respond in one of three ways to teachers' humorous messages intended to elaborate a topic in an unexpected, incongruous way. Our target response is most likely the first, in which students recognize the message to be funny because it's incongruency is both resolved and interpreted to makes sense to the student. A second possible response would be that the message's incongruity is recognized but not resolved. When this happens, the message confuses students. They may recognize that the teacher was making a joke with an incongruity but they missed it and could not attain resolution. In the third response, students do not recognize the incongruity nor do they perceive any humor at all, with the whole attempt at humor flying right over their heads.

The effect of dialogic teacher humor on students unfolds like a line of people carefully walking on a tight rope across a deep canyon to get to the other side. They are concentrating on carefully putting one foot in front of the other to keep their balance so they will not fall off the rope, when suddenly, a bird flies by with a note in its mouth that reads, "the canyon is only a foot deep and filled with gummy bears." The unexpected event is curiously disruptive, but also informative. One person realizes that this is funny and falls off, landing in the shallow bed of bears. Another follows until they have all collapsed in a heap of laughter. The point I am making is in order for students to perceive that something a teacher says is funny, the so-called funny thing must be recognized as an incongruity to the expected context, then resolved as funny when it has been decoded as funny content. The bird flying by with a note is an unexpected incongruity to the line of expected context of people walking on a rope to cross a canyon. The note bearing the information about the gummy bears in the shallow canyon is decoded and resolved as funny because it suddenly shifts the context of the situation.

However, if the note in the bird's mouth reads, "Canyons are formed over millions of years from rushing river waters wearing away the land." Students would not think this was funny because it is not incongruous to the context of the canyon crossing situation. The fact is, we already knew this about canyons. Nor would they think a note reading, "Hoping on one foot on a tightrope exercises the balance the inner ear achieves when not walking on solid ground because the incongruity is too absurd or complex for the recipient to comprehend. When this happens, they will not get the joke or possibly not even recognize that a joke was intended" (Wanzer et al., 2010, p. 4). No recognition, no resolution, no interpretation—not funny. In sum, a clever teacher says something funny to introduce a new idea that adds meaning to the content they are delivering.

Student Response to Your Humor

Humor's Positive Effect on Student Emotions

As we learned from the Tanzanian girls school event, emotions are contagious (Goleman, 2011). We can spread the joy just as easily as we can spread the dread. Contagion of emotions is attributed to "mirror neurons" in the brain that activate in us exactly what we see in others. Essentially, we mirror their emotions, their movements, or their intentions. Mirror neurons function like a neural WIFI to connect our brain with another brain. Brain-to-brain connections could explain why emotions are contagious. There have been experiments where two strangers enter a lab, fill out a mood checklist, sit in silence looking at each for 2 minutes. They then fill out the same checklist. The person of the two who is the most emotionally expressive is able to convey their emotions to the other in two silent minutes (2011). This emotional contagion, the subtext present in every interaction with others, is automatic, instant and unconscious. The question here is how does this play out in a classroom? If the emotional sender is the most powerful person in the room (we are rooting for the teacher to wear this name badge), then the teacher sets the emotional state for the entire group. Studies indicate that when a positive and cheerful leader [teacher] influences their students to feel positive, the collective positivity heightens their performance. If students are given negative performance feedback in a very warm, positive, and upbeat tone, they came out of there feeling pretty good about the interaction. If they were given positive feedback in a very cold, critical, judgmental tone, they came out feeling negative, even with positive feedback.

In spite of your cheerful influence, there will be a handful of students in your art classes that enter hating art. (Inconceivable, right? It is as farfetched to us art teachers as hating food is to chefs.) Strange as it is, they come to a place of hating art because they want to avoid the stranglehold expectancy placed on them to produce realistic artwork, or because they do not like the feeling of their hands in gooey materials, or possibly because they want to avoid contentiously sharing art materials with others, or even worse, because they do not like listening to the teacher prattle on about this artist and that technique. Any of these reasons make art repugnant to them. Here's where humor comes in.

Patrick, a high school freshman in my Art 1 class was one of them. Patrick was taking art to earn the required fine arts credit to graduate. He sat like a gargoyle along the room's perimeter, never participating in class activities without my prodding. He appeared to be transparently not enamored with art, with art class, or with me. I decided to climb into his world to find a way to make his time in art class at least enjoyable. I chatted casually with Patrick about his life at home hoping to unearth info bits with which to entice. Digging paid off. As the official DJ who takes no requests, I frequently play unobtrusive, innocuously instrumental music in the art room during studio activity to serve as background support for working hands and busy minds. I asked Patrick what kind of music he liked to listen to and he replied, "Motown, because my parents play it all the time at home." (If you are not familiar with the Detroit music label, they brought us the great soul sounds of Temptations, Michael Jackson, Diana Ross, etc.).

Not long after Patrick's "hate art" confession, I planned to model watercolor techniques in a guided practice with students. I set up two sets of paper and materials at the front of the room and cued up, "My Girl" by the Temptations. When Patrick entered, I sang out across the room with the music, "Hey Patrick, I've got sunshine on a rainy day and when it's cold outside ...." He jumped in with "you've got the month of May?" Seamlessly, I handed him a paintbrush, pointed to the paints, and together, we improvised a watercolor mixing choreography that stirred up delight for the rest of the class. Our footwork needed work but still, the performance was magical. Patrick's favorite music, laughter and play connected Patrick to art and me to Patrick. For as long as he was sitting in my art classroom, Patrick was motivated to make art while humming to Motown hits. Although I lean toward music without lyrics so students are not sidetracked from thinking about art to decipher music, when Patrick was in the room Motown lyrics were essential to his good mood.

Engagement and Interest

If teachers want rapport with students, humor offers a vein of gold in the ore of student behavior. Humor entices interest, provides a focus for attention, motivates to learn, engages with the subject, with the teacher and with each other (Axelson & Flick, 2011). Among the dimensions of student engagement researchers have identified, the range of engagement on a learning continuum is the lowest at superficially attending and rockets upward to sustained immersion. You can always tell a student is actively engaged because their eyes are locked on the speaker and their body is alertly leaning forward. The student who is not engaged may be looking away, looking at something else or looking at the phone in their lap glowing with the movie Saws III.

Shake students into engagement! Leverage their maximum attention with unpredictable, unexpected, humorous behaviors, like voice fluctuations, animated gestures that arouse emotions and funny stories that relate to the subject. Speak to an imaginary student in an empty chair. Hop onto a desk and conduct class from a higher position. Assume a precarious balance on one leg. Stand really close to a disengaged maverick but act like you are not. Speak with an affected Texas twang or British inflection. Whisper into a student's ear using a megaphone or paper towel roll. Sing out, shout out, rap out or dance about. You are a privileged performer in a room with a captive audience and your performance is free. (I have been known to tell students entering the art room that, "Today's instruction, normally $29.99 per hour, is free today!"). You may have to leave your dignity at the door but the payoff is students will watch your every move, placing you in control of your teaching. Remember, you do not have to be perceived as cool—that is what they expect of each other. No, you are beyond cool. As an adult, you do not need peer approval from kids, you need students' attention so you can effectively do your job.

Quite simply, student attention is prolonged in the classrooms of humorous teachers much longer than in those who offer dry, deliberate and uneventful delivery (Martin, 2007). Fast-paced instructional humor delivered in short spurts captures and holds the attention of particularly young children in primary grades (Martin & Ford, 2018; Wakshlag, Day, & Zillmann, 1981), while witty puns, metaphors, word plays and relevant humor is more suited to older teens. Even with college students, the more an instructor uses intellectual humor within a course, the more students are interested in the material and intellectually stimulated by the instructor (Freitas, 2018). Students engaged with positive humor will perceive a teacher to be confidently and competently in control, which could be because humor-oriented teachers *look* like they are in control. Humor helps teachers to be relaxed, flexible, and more willing to try new ideas to enhance student receptivity.

Learning

In elementary through secondary art classrooms, teachers are making learning happen by delivering the good stuff with levity. Although, most research significantly supports the effect teacher humor has on inciting students' cognitive and affective learning, the jury is still out on research agreement that humor conclusively effects student performance (Martin & Ford, 2018). One college study found no effect of instructor humor on students' performance with evidence that pointed to instructional humor making no difference in student learning of new information (Houser, Cowan, & West, 2007). In the pro humor camp, one study found that instructors' use of related humor was associated with learning because it enhanced students' motivation by being relevant and increasing students' ability to process information in clarifying the content (Wanzer et al., 2010). When asked about teacher humor, students answered they learned more from teachers "who got them excited and involved in the learning process, challenged them to be the best students they could be, showed them hard work is worth it, and helped them think deeply and critically about concepts" (Bolkan & Goodboy, 2010, p. 103). Then, of course, there is value to humor's mitigating effect on stress that reduces learning by decreasing the brain's capabilities to learn and remember (Kaufeldt, 2009; Korobkin, 1988).

A device I use to reduce performance stress for students engaged in artwork critiques is the Post-It Note Valentine delivery. It begins with students laying their artwork in progress to completion out on the tabletops. Each student is given three small Post-It Notes and encouraged to "shop" the room for three deserving works of art they would like to commend for excellent visual quality. The notes are anonymous but must contain a phrase related to elements of art or principles of design. Such notes might read, "Dynamic, undulating lines cause movement!" or "Compelling emphasis on the focal point shape." Each note must address the aspect of the artwork that contributes to overall unity and viewer interest using attributing art language. Notes are attached to the sides or bottom of the esteemed artwork and left for the artist returning to read them after the 5-minute viewing period. Students evaluating the work of their peers alleviates pressure to speak to their peers. Student artists benefitting from authentic comments enjoy accolades that will guide their artwork to successful completion. The Post-It Valentine Delivery is called such because it feels as emotionally positive to send and receive "love" notes as it does to send and receive Valentines.

Memory and Recall

Truly, laughing while learning pays off for students because they can retrieve informational bits that have been embedded into their long term memory with humor more easily than information not associated with humor (Opplinger & Zillman, 2003; Teslow, 1995). In addition, lab experiments on humor and memory indicate "information presented in a humorous manner is remembered better than information presented in a serious way when both occur in the same context" (Martin, 2007, p. 360). Misfit concepts not normally linked together are a primary component of humor-saturated communication and study after educational research study, found humor enhances student memory (Derks et al., 1998; Martin & Ford, 2018; Schmidt, 1994, 2002; Schmidt & Williams, 2001). There is "consistent evidence that humorous information is recalled better than non-humorous information when both are presented in the same context" (Martin & Ford, 2018, p. 352).

The flip side of humor's enhancing effect on memory is that information accompanied with humor can displace the recall of non-humorous material presented at the same time. For example, a visual meme to help students remember that analogous colors "sit" in cars next to each other on the color Ferris wheel may help students' recall the meme but their recall of other color schemes might be diminished. Research is yet to be conclusive but we do know that we remember events in our lives connected to a strong emotion, therefore, a nugget of information delivered with humor can be easily retrieved because humor gives us emotional access to that memory.

Humor keeps on helping us remember even as we age. A study determining the effects of humor on short term memory of people aged 69–71 years found that humor improved their learning ability by 38.5%, improved delayed recall by 43.6%, and increased visual recognition by 12.6% (Bains et al., 2015). Now that's comforting to know. Help spread the good news: continuing to laugh to the end of our lives may stave off the effects of dementia!

Humor Reaches Out to Students with Diverse Identities and Challenges

Our American society is superdiverse: its diversity is diverse (Vertovec, 2007). While being superdiverse may be framed as a strength, it also presents a monolithic challenge to which teachers must respond. Maintaining emotional positivity while attending to student idiosyncrasies within a learning space requires a depth of humanity. But the payoff is worth it! Humanized learning interactions seek to understand and value the amalgamation of human *belongings* that play a part in the forming of each student's identity. These *belongings* include "age, gender, and/or sexuality, socioeconomic class, exceptionality (giftedness, differently abled, health), geographic location, language, ethnicity, race, religion" and other ideologies (Freedman & Stuhr, 2004, p. 817).

Yes, teaching in this present society demands that we model esteem for student identities as if they were our own. Perhaps we should also model the grace our society so desperately needs to relax our hypersensitive response to messages we perceive to malign our identities? Do we hope to soberly isolate identity distinctions in our classrooms or convivially celebrate identity varieties? If our desire is for celebrating in one accord, then humor can serve us as a way to embrace and acclaim contradictions, incongruities and ambiguities inherent to interpersonal relationships (Mulkay, 1988).

Teachers who laugh at themselves and laugh with (never at) students, reduce much of the tension that inherently resides in highly interactive art classrooms with highly diverse student populations. I have experienced it myself and know it to be true. Although it might not be possible every day (come on, we are human), we can aim for bringing joy with us into our classrooms. The presence of a relaxed and happy teacher creates a calm that settles like a soft, quieting cloud over a learning space. Your good mood influences all of the students around you. It supersedes language, activates acceptance and positively charges a community to make connections that cross borders. Positive feelings emanating from laughter prime members of a space for discourse which is free to develop contexts for creative and critical inquiry (Freedman & Stuhr, 2004). Furthermore, collaborative inquiry driven by cultural awareness fosters new ideas—powerful determiners of studio production. I like to think that humor functions like a social glue adhering potentially dissenting individuals together into a united group with a common goal.

Inclusive optimism spawned by humorous teachers blurs the borderlines of social distinctions with the help of love, humility, hope, acceptance and critical thinking collaborations. As a mechanism of human connectedness, humor dismantles the factious effects of prejudice, discrimination and stereotypical marginalizing in our schools. Humor is not partial to anyone but beneficial to everyone. Humor-rich face-to-face communication relaxes students to the extent that they are socially vulnerable, socially respectful and socially engaged. In sum, humor illustrates, encourages creativity, reduces anxiety, promotes critical thinking skills, keeping every student engaged with each other, with the subject and with you, the teacher (Bryant & Zillman, 1989; Coleman, 1992; Ziv, 1983; Torok, McMorris, & Lin, 2004).

Culture

Students in your classroom identify with specific cultures upholding social norms that influence their perception of your humor. Western societies, e.g., distinguish good humor as that which resolves incongruity on the high end of the humor spectrum, while nonsensical, unresolved absurdity resides on the low end. Germans, e.g., seem to have a stronger affinity for nonsense than do individuals from other cultures. Student preference for one or the other correlates with dimensions of their nationality as well as personality (Ruch, Attardo, & Raskin, 1993). It is undeniable that humor serves a purpose in society and is effective in many interpersonal, social interactions (Martin, 2007). One unique social function of humor is that it allows individuals to claim or disclaim responsibility for their actions (Kane, Suls, & Tedeschi as cited in Martin). Why, then do we engage in humorous activities as a society? There is at least one motivation behind every behavior (Ziv, 1984). Research has reached one conclusion, however. Most students find humor to be inappropriate if it singles out or disparages others (Frymier, Wanzer, & Wojtaszczyk, 2008; Jonas, 2004).

Gender

My goal to be a culturally responsive teacher who upholds students' individuality and cultural competencies with anti-oppressive, humanizing practices can actually be met with the help of humor. Art teachers have the potential to help every student impact the formation of a community larger than themselves (Freire, 1970). I know being a joyful teacher keeps me grounded in a place of acceptance where everyone is invited and valued equitably, without fear of displacement. One approach I initiate to establish safety for students negotiating their gender is roll call. As the first class begins, I pick up a clipboard with the roster and hand it to each student to initial by their name. I inquire of each in a whisper if they have a preferred nick name or pronoun as a precaution to not "out" anyone. Then, one by one I call last names. When I reach a name without an initial, I ask, "Ok, it appears that Magnusen is not here. Would anyone like to be Magnusen for today? It may prove to be a worthy experience …." Plus, there are always the names that you just have to play with, like Art ("What a great name, did you know it is my favorite?") or Justin ("Now are you just in time or just in case?")

In line with this approach is the Living Painting improvisation in which I project a painting with grouped subjects on a large white board and ask for volunteers to make the painting come alive in front of the image. Students select the subject to which they identify and adopt the same position. This simple, lighthearted exercise frees up students to claim their gender in the context of artworks, although sometimes a shortage of gender-specific subjects requires any available person to sit in. Becoming the painting also allows knowledge of the work of art to be enhanced by body position. Of course, we zap photos of the scenario, such as the ones in Figure 3.1.

Autism

Serenely safe learning spaces are essential for students on the Autism spectrum who approach social engagements with anxiety (Taupin, 2018; Torok et al., 2004). One way to invite humor that decreases social anxiety for children in a therapeutically creative way is improvisational comedy (Phillips Sheesley, Pfeffer, & Barish, 2016). For kids diagnosed with Autism, theatrical improv displaces the social anxiety they feel with social communication skills (Ansaldo & Hopf, 2016). "What improv really does is create a safe and fun and authentic environment, where mistakes really don't matter" (Balonon-Rosen, 2017, p. 1). An improv activity capitalizing on the improv notion of "yes, and" (accept and build) confronts kids with another's idea from which to build from. In this activity, kids pick sentences out of an envelope, then at-random, choose a card with an emotion. They read the sentence expressing

Figure 3.1. Laocoön and his Sons Sculpture Comes to Life

the emotion. The kids usually can guess the emotion with the help of the whole group. For example, one child announces, "It's over!" after reading the sentence and waiting for the other children to guess the emotion. "Umm, sad," someone says. "No," says Ira. "Scared." "No." "Happy?" "Yes!" The teacher jumps in to help with a question posed to the class, "What would have helped Ira to show happiness more obviously?" A student not diagnosed with autism excitedly yells, "Yay! It's over!" while jumping up and down. Although expressing their own emotions does not come naturally to kids with autism, humorous improv can help them find ways to show emotions through the eyes of others as they act out characters (2017).

Perfectionism

Students shelter a variety of beliefs about their achievement capability. On the high end of the attainment spectrum are those who want the highest grade and will sacrifice everything else in their lives to attain it. Along with these are the perfectionists who focus on what they can do better, not what they have already done well (Goleman, 2011). High-achievers, the relentless learners, the perfectionists, are those who love to be on top and will need frequent feedback from you about their performance. Competing with themselves, they are always trying to do better.

Helping these high-achievers not take themselves too seriously may be the best gift you can give them as a teacher. One device I use in elementary art classroom is to set up an imaginary defibrillator to revive "dying" works of art. When a tearful child perfectionist sadly approaches me with their "sick" artwork, I grab two bottles of white glue, one in each hand, lay them down on the artwork and pretend an electrical jolt has passed through them. Yelling, "Art attack, code glue!" the student and I together revive the work. This procedure usually snaps students out of their state of self-inflicted degradation and if it does not, I resort to surgical consultation. As the doctor, I discuss diagnosis for the artwork with the artist. We consult about viable corrective procedures to alleviate pain such as the all too familiar *mistakectomy*, removal of the mistake, or *artotomy*, removal (and possibly replacement) of the inflicted artwork.

A colleague shared with me that she endorsed students celebrating their distressing failures. I was not able to spin failure as dramatically as she but her failure flip meant a student who had made a misjudgment that flopped would jump up and assume the Olympic gymnast horse dismount. You know the one, your arms are spread in the air and your feet are spread on the ground while you announce, "I failed!" The class is instructed to applaud and cheer at that point and everyone gleefully returns to their work. She believed that permitting students to make failures a frequent and common occurrence in studio art making lessened its negative impact on students.

To some, failure can be debilitating. I remember asking a discouraged overachiever, "Do you want to be your own best friend or your own worst enemy?" She looked vexed, so I described a scenario in which she was outside the door waiting to attack herself and beat herself up. She was shocked but understood. She could visualize herself thrashing herself with berating judgments and harsh criticism for not performing perfectly. She accepted my scenario, smiling and settled. I committed a similar performance perception hijack to a grad student obsessed with completing a perfect thesis. She wandered hither and thither, improving and revising her final draft until her writing hit a wall. I asked her, "Ok, so what makes a good thesis good?" Stymied, she could not identify the criteria minutiae tying her to the ground like the Lilliputians did to giant Gulliver. I then offered a phrase I had heard many times while writing my dissertation, "A good thesis is one that is finished."

Perfection is not required in art making. Perfection is imposed on students by teachers who expect perfect art products. While observing a student teacher in an elementary school, I noticed small baskets filled with various-sized circular lids on each table. I watched while students traced the lids to draw circles in their artwork during the lesson. Later, during our conference together, I asked the student teacher why lids were used to draw circles? She replied, "The cooperating teacher (CT) does not want them to draw freehand circles because they are so messy. Lids help kids make perfect circles." Ok, I understood that the ringmaster CT had a thing about artwork representing student products of perfection, but I encouraged my student to respectfully offer kids the option to draw their own circles anyway. As I left the art room it dawned on me why a palpable sense of desperation immobilized the kids: they were perched precariously on the precipice of perfection.

Every earthbound plane with a smoking engine has an escape hatch. It is not necessary to go down with the ship. Instead, buckle on the parachute stowed in the overhead humor bin and jump into the unknown with a resolve to defy gravity. Humor in teaching allows both students and teachers to take risks while remaining vulnerable to potential failure and exposure:

> To learn you must be able to say, "I can do it." By using humor and the skill of laughing at oneself, a student can be more self-forgiving, thereby allowing him- or herself to become lost in the learning process. A difficult part of the student role is to acknowledge ignorance while simultaneously trusting in the ability to learn. By poking fun at their own frailties, teachers can show students that being in the "one-down" position of the learner does not interfere with self-esteem. Only by admitting what they do not know can students be open to learning what they need to know. (Pollack & Freda, 1997, p. 177)

Anger

Every art teacher has come face to face with an angry student. Perhaps this happens daily. Kids actually have many reasons to be dissatisfied with their lot in life but bringing it into the art room and flinging it at the art teacher simply will not do. We should heed the advice of well-known comedians handling angry hecklers in the audience during their monologue (Patrick, 2014). For example, one comedian decided to take on the role of a Heckle Therapist to help hecklers who yelled negative commentaries. When a person said something offensive, the comedian did not assume a defensive position, but instead offered sympathy to help the heckler with their problem. He would say "You seem so upset and I know that's not what you wanted to have happen tonight. Let's talk about your problem." The audience would laugh, the heckler was confused that he was being helped and not herded out. Despite the heckler, the comedian remained in control. On another occasion, a comedian walked onto the stage in mustard-colored high tops and an angry heckler yelled "I hate your shoes!" Biding his time, he thought to understand what the heckler said and replied with linear composure, "You are very, very fortunate, because these shoes will not be performing [today]." He did not hear from the shoe hater a second time. Yet another comedian when noticing an audience member not facing him nor paying attention, immediately abandoned his planned material and began an entertaining conversation with the bored person's back. By stepping aside to engage the bored person, the comedian maintained control of the conversation and was able to return to his material at any point he chose.

I have a slew of impromptu humor devices to lighten up a darkened, angry countenance. Do you remember the movie Castaway, in which lonely and marooned Tom Hanks was so desperate for companionship that he conversed with a beached volleyball? When sullen, surly students make a point of not looking *at* or listening *to* me, I draw the Wilson Happy Face on the board behind me and turn to discuss life with him. If no one was listening to me up to then, they certainly were after a few minutes of my chatting with a face on the board. Come on, you have just got to step up to the plate and swing for a homer! The rest of the class is hoping you will. When a student is antagonistic, humor diffuses hostility largely because the majority of students in your class want to continue to feel the pleasure that rapport brings when they feel connected by mirth.

Sometimes when I perceive that the attitude of an entire class is sour, I make up a story about the class and tell it out loud. I may begin with, "Once upon a time, there was a group of unhappy fifth graders in a small boat full of holes. Water poured in and the ship began to sink. It was unfortunate because it happened to be sinking in shark-infested waters. They could see their demise ending badly when suddenly, a very large cruise ship appeared on the horizon ...." This story has many versions depending on the class or mood, but usually ends with a teacher-like hero saving the day.

John F. Kennedy once said, "There are three things which are real: God, human folly, and laughter. The first two are beyond our comprehension. So, we must do what we can with the third" (Hunsaker, 1988). Helping students learn are what we are about. Helping them learn while laughing not only motivates them more but also helps them retain information easier than when they feel anxious and threatened (Opplinger & Zillman, 2003). We know humor heads off negative emotions because we have felt anxiety slip away when we laugh (Martin & Lefcourt, 1983).

Humor Engages Students with Art

To engage students calls on your mood to do so and students' mood to be engaged. Managing your mood is a given. Teachers are expected to leave behind personal baggage when we enter our classrooms. However, for students, it is something we must aim for as these yet completed adults are still grappling with keeping their emotions in check. Many bring with them tension from relationships, anxiety from performance expectations, and resistance to adult authority. They may be hungry, sad, angry, feel alienated, rejected or delightfully popular. Truly each class each day is a mixed bag of many flavors and your job is to determine how you will perform to spellbind the collective student community into engagement with art. What word is hiding in the word heart? Why, art of course. Teaching is not for the faint hearted, the courage to teach comes from a determination to do whatever we can do to dissolve impediments for learning.

The anticipated heart-to-heart affiliation teachers expect to have with their students is primarily what draws them to the teaching profession (Manning, 1982). As we previously discussed, conclusive research validates individuals with a sense of humor are competent to promote positive social interactions with others. Similarly, humor creates connections between teachers and their students through a shared understanding and common psychological bond (Garner, 2006). When people laugh together, they are linked united in human rapport. Rapport is a function of this connection and the uniqueness of appropriate humor encourages a tight bond, improves communication, and encourages cooperation among those that laugh together (Berk, 2003). Ultimately, students may never feel comfortable enough to share new ideas and insights if rapport with the teachers is not established first (Freda & Csikszentmihalyi, 1995).

Teacher humor related to content as a thematic connection seriously promotes cognitive functions toward instructional clarity (Bieg & Dresel, 2018; Klauer, 1985). With our brains generating 10,000 stem cells every day and half of them migrating to where they are needed in the brain for new learning, humor helps determine a destination (Goleman, 2011). Humor makes learning stick. In other words, new learning takes place with more ease and is recalled more readily when associated with something that amuses us than with a serious presentation (Opplinger & Zillman, 2003; Teslow, 1995).

Several humor facilitation factors can accentuate student learning outcomes in our art classrooms. Factor #1: Mirth associated with the learning experience arouses students' emotions positively, sustaining their attention so they can better focus on what is being taught (Opplinger, 2003). Factor #2: Relevant, concept-related humor, instances in instruction where dominating ideas are manipulated by humor foster superior student learning (Zilman & Bryant, 1983).

I have joined with researchers advocating for playful metaphors to make learning new concepts appropriately relevant to specific age levels. In fact, "metaphor and humor are two vital devices to express thoughts" (Kuan-Chen, 2018). Let me explain with a snapshot from my elementary school days. One day, I fired up my pitch to present the concept of complementary colors in regard to their location on the color wheel. My audience: a restless company of distracted third graders yawning and staring at me with that, "go ahead— make our day" look. (Not a good look. This cue calls for a quick plan to reel in attention).

So, I began with a story describing the houses of color arranged in a neighborhood circle (also called a cul de sac). Complementary color houses are situated across from each other in the circle. I explained that one morning, cheery Yellowman came out of his cute, yellow house to get into his shiny, yellow car. Quiet Violetman, spied his exit from across the color cul de sac and called out to him, "Hey, Yellowman, you are looking very sunny this morning!" Yellowman chirped back, "Thanks, for the compliment Violet guy!" Although they remained friends, they did not mingle much to avoid grayed down versions of themselves. This metaphor, accompanied with white board sketches, led seamlessly into a line of student raised questions investigating the personality of colors and their location in the color neighborhood. I mean, seriously, you could grow this metaphor to something short of a reality show. You could add analogous neighbors living side by side; warm colored-neighbors who liked to BBQ together, the cooler-colored neighbors who lived on the shady side of the street, etc.

Metaphors magically make facts stick because they manifest images in the mind. We are teaching visual learners to "see," so why not help them remember with visual anchors that elaborate content? Visual images conjured up to serve as proxy word pictures standing in for more complex data easily embed into our memories, especially if they are placed there with pleasurable emotions. Humorous metaphors help deliver content messages that not only express a teacher's unique ideas but also clarify the meaning of these ideas (Tsai, 2018). Think of bringing a guest to the party of an old friend. You are the vivacious emotion, bringing along a new idea to introduce to the host. After the party winds down, the host may not remember the new guest but they will certainly recall their association with you, the positive emotion. The linkage with emotions sorts new knowledge into the frequent flyer party list.

The Big Picture about Teaching with Humor

There is little wonder why humor is rated as one of the most desirable characteristics of effective teachers (Fortson & Brown, 1998; Martin, 2007). It is just plain fun to be able to laugh a lot during a working day. I know this because I just paid $200 for a ticket to see Seinfeld in a local venue. Doubtful that he could make me laugh for 90 minutes (the length of the show), I was more than willing to put him to the test. My unspoken confession is that I expected to laugh. (By the way, I did laugh the entire 90 minutes). When students know that a teacher employs humor in their classes, they look forward to being in that class, to learning, to bask in the presence of an adult who is truly joyful. They expect to find pleasure in your class. Surprise! Students esteem joyful, funny teachers more highly than those who rarely smile and rarely laugh (Bryant, Brown, Parks, & Zillmann et al., 1983).

Student performance, the ultimate goal for instruction, teeters on the effectiveness of one individual: you, the teacher. You are free to choose the type of teacher you want to be. You can be a teacher who operates with an instructionally driven set of gears moving when you throw on the switch. You are the factory foreperson watching over a top-down learning mechanization, stopping the learning machine only to fix glitches. If this is you then students in your classroom enter knowing what to do and when to do it. This environment does not allow serendipity to function in which happenstance unpredictably transforms your classroom from a factory to a scientific laboratory where surprise is always a host residing over the unconventional, the authentic creations, yes and even emerging Frankensteins.

On the other hand, you can be the teacher who releases your directorship for a more organic operating system, one in which you are a co-learner flourishing along with your students. Rather than directing, you guide with a sense of fun, releasing your students to embark on a mutually enjoyable experience both you and your students seek to repeat (Martin, 2007). Students are enticed to engage with the subject because they no longer have to be persuaded or ordered to engage, they *want* to engage. A sense of fun thrives in places where humor lives.

Bibliography

Andrei, S. (2012). Psychologists at the gate: A review of Daniel Kahneman's "Thinking, Fast and Slow." *Journal of Economic Literature, 4,* 1080.

Ansaldo, J., & Kopf, R. (2016). Camp yes and: An improv camp for teens and teachers. *The Reporter, 21*(6). Retrieved from https://www.iidc.indiana.edu/pages/camp-yes-and-animprov-camp-for-teens-with-asd-and-teachers

Arendt, L. (2006). *Leaders' use of positive humor: Effects on followers' self-efficacy and creative performance* (Unpublished doctoral dissertation). The University of Wisconsin-Milwaukee, Milwaukee, WI.

Axelson, R., & Flick, A. (2011). Defining student engagement. *Change, 43*, 38–43. https://dx.doi.org/doi:10.1080/00091383.2011.533096

Bains, G., Berk, L., Lohman, E., Daher, N., Petrofsky, J., Schwab, E., & Deshpande, P. (2015). Humor's effect on short-term memory in healthy and diabetic older adults. *Alternative Therapy Health Medicine, 21*(3), 16–25.

Balonon-Rosen, P. (2017, February 13). Using improv to help kids with Autism show and read emotion. Retrieved from https://www.npr.org/sections/ed/2017/02/13/508978540/using-improv-to-helpkids-with-autism-show-and-read-emotion

Bandura, A. (1997). *Self-efficacy: The exercise of control.* New York, NY: W. H. Freeman.

Bell, N., McGhee, P., & Duffey, N. (1986). Interpersonal competence, social assertiveness and the development of humour. *British Journal of Developmental Psychology, 4*(1), 51–55.

Berk, R. (2003). *Professors are from Mars, students are from Snickers.* Sterling, VA: Stylus Publishing.

Bieg, S., & Dresel, M. (2018). Relevance of perceived teacher humor types for instruction and student learning. *Social Psychology of Education, 21*(4), 805–825. https://doi-org.libproxy.txstate.edu/10.1007/s11218-018-9428-z

Bolkan, S., & Goodboy, A. K. (2010). Transformational leadership in the classroom: The development and validation of the student intellectual stimulation scale. *Communication Reports, 23*(2), 91–105.

Brackett, M., Reyes, M., Rivers, S., Elbertson, N., & Salovey, P. (2011). Classroom emotional climate, teacher affiliation, and student conduct. *The Journal of Classroom Interaction,* (1), 27–36.

Bryant, J., Comisky, P., Crane, J., & Zillmann, D. (1980). Relationship between college teachers' use of humor in the classroom and students' evaluations of their teachers. *Journal of Educational Psychology, 72*(4), 511–519.

Bryant, J., Brown, D., Parks, S., & Zillmann, D. (1983). Children's imitation of a ridiculed model. *Human Communication Research 10*(2), 243–255.

Bryant, J., & Zillmann, D. (1989). Using humor to promote learning in the classroom. In J. H. McGhee (Ed.), *Humor and children's development: A guide to practical applications* (pp. 49–78). New York: Haworth Press.

Coleman, J. (1992). All seriousness aside: The laughing-learning connection. *The International Journal of Instructional Media, 19*(3), 269–276

Derks, P., Gardner, J. B., & Agarwal, R. (1998). Recall of innocent and tendentious humorous material, *Humor: International Journal of Humor Research,* 11(1), 5-19.

Evans-Palmer, T. (2009). *The relationship between sense of humor and self-efficacy: An exploration of the beliefs of art teachers* (Doctoral dissertation). University of the Incarnate Word, San Antonio, TX. Available from ProQuest Digital Dissertation. (TX 6697-683).

Evans-Palmer, T. (2015). Humor and self-efficacy traits that support the emotional well-being of educators. *Journal of Research in Innovative Teaching, March*, 21–34.

Freda, P., & Csikszentmihalyi, M. (1995). *The influence of teachers*. Boston, MA: Houghton-Mifflin.

Freedman, K, & Stuhr, P. (2004).Curriculum change for the 21st century: Visual culture in art education. In E.Eisner and M. Day (Eds.), *Handbook of research and policy in art educa-tion* (pp.815-828). Mahwah, NJ: Lawrence Erlbaum Associates

Freitas, T. (2018). *Student perceptions of instructor humor as a predictor of student intellectual stimulation, academic interest and engagement* (Thesis). University of the Pacific, Stockton, CA. https://scholarlycommons.pacific.edu/uop_etds/3117

Fortson, S., & Brown, W. (1998). Best and worst university instructors: The opinions of graduate students. *College Student Journal, 32*(4), 572–576.

Frymier, A., Wanzer, M., & Wojtaszczyk, A. (2008). Assessing students' perceptions of inappropriate and appropriate teacher humor. *Communication Education, 57*, 266–288.

Garner, R. (2006). Humor in pedagogy: How ha-ha can lead to aha! *College Teaching, 51*(1), 177–180.

Goleman, D. (1995). *Emotional intelligence*. New York, NY: Bantam Books.

Goleman, D. (2011). *The brain and emotional intelligence: New insights*. More Than Sound. Retrieved from: https://learning.oreilly.com/library/view/the-brain-and/9781934441152/?ar

Goodreads (2019). *Emotion quotes*. Retrieved from https://www.goodreads.com/quotes/tag/emotions

Gordon, D. (2017). *Understanding the constant dialogue that goes on between our gut and our brain*. UCLA Newsroom. Retrieved from http://newsroom.ucla.edu/stories/understanding-the-constant-dialogue-that-goes-on-between-our-gut-and-our-brain

Greengross, G., Martin, R., & Miller, G. (2012). Personality traits, intelligence, humor styles, and humor production ability of professional stand-up comedians compared to college students. *Psychology of Aesthetics, Creativity, and the Arts, 6*(1), 74.

Hoenigman Meyer, E. (2018, May 7). The secret to likeability [*Career News*]. https://www.higheredjobs.com/Articles/articleDisplay.cfm?ID=1621&utm_source=05_16_2018&utm_medium=email&utm_campaign=InsiderUpdate

Holzer P. (2017) Interoception and gut feelings: Unconscious body signals' impact on brain function, behavior and belief processes (Abstract). In H. F. Angel., L. Oviedo, R. Paloutzian, A. Runehov, & R. Seitz (Eds.), *Processes of believing: The acquisition, maintenance, and change in creditions. new approaches to the scientific study of religion, Vol. 1*. Cham, Switzerland: Springer.

Houser, M. L., Cowan, R. L., & West, D. A. (2007). Investigating a new education frontier: Instructor communication behavior in CD-ROM Texts—Do traditionally positive behaviors translate into this new environment? *Communication Quarterly, 55*(1), 19–38.

Hunsaker, J. S. (1988). It's no joke: Using humor in the classroom. *The Clearing House, 61*(6), 285–286.

Infante, D., Riddle, B., Horvath, C., & Tumlin, S. (1992). Verbal aggressiveness: Messages and reasons. *Communication Quarterly, 40*, 116–126.

Javidi, M., Downs, V., & Nussbaum, J. (1988). A comparative analysis of teachers' use of dramatic style behaviors at higher and secondary educational levels. *Communication Education, 37*, 278–288.

Jonas, P. (2004). *Secrets of connecting leadership and learning with humor.* Lanham, MD: Scarecrow Education.

Kahneman, D. (2011). *Thinking, fast and slow.* New York, NY: Macmillan.

Kaufeldt, M. (2009). *Begin with the brain: Orchestrating the learner-centered classroom.* Thousand Oaks, CA: Sage.

Klauer, K. (1985). Framework for a theory of teaching. *Teaching and Teacher Education, 1,* 5–17.

Kohn, A. (1996). The trouble with character education. *Yearbook-National Society for The Study of Education, 96,* 154–162.

Korobkin, D. (1988). Humor in the classroom: Considerations and strategies. *College Teaching, 36,* 154–158.

Kuan-Chen, Tsai. (2018). An empirical examination of the relationships among creativity, the evaluation of creative products, and cognitive style among Chinese undergraduates. *International Journal of Cognitive Research in Science, Engineering and Education, 6*(1), 53.

Lefcourt, H. (2001). *Humor: The psychology of living buoyantly.* Hingham, MA: Kluwer Academic.

Manning, K. (1982). *Lighten up! An analysis of the role of humor as an instructional practice in the urban and/or culturally diverse middle school* (Unpublished doctoral dissertation). Cleveland State University, Cleveland, OH.

Martin, R. (2007). *The psychology of humor; An integrative approach.* Burlington, MA: Elsevier Academic Press.

Martin, R., & Ford, T. (2018). *The psychology of humor: An integrative approach.* New York, NY: Academic Press.

Martin, R., & Lefcourt, H. (1983). Sense of humor as a moderator of the relation between stressors and moods. *Journal of Personality and Social Psychology, 45,* 1313–1324.

Martin, R., Puhlik-Doris, P., Larsen, G., Gray, J., & Weir, K. (2003). Individual differences in uses of humor and their relation to psychological wellbeing: Development of the humor styles questionnaire. *Journal of Research in Personality, 37*(1), 48–75.

Mayer, E. (2011). Gut feelings: the emerging biology of gut–brain communication (Abstract). *Nature Reviews Neuroscience, 12*(8), 453, Retrieved from https://www.nature.com/articles/nrn3071

Mayer, J., & Salovey, P. (1993). The intelligence of emotional intelligence. *Intelligence, 17,* 433–442.

Mayer, J. D., Salovey, P., & Caruso, D. R. (2000). *Emotional intelligence as zeitgeist, as personality, and as a mental ability.* In R. Bar-On & J. D. A. Parker (Eds.), *The handbook of emotional intelligence: Theory, development, assessment, and application at home, school, and in the workplace* (p. 92–117). Jossey-Bass.

Merolla, A. (2006). Decoding ability and humor production. *Communication Quarterly, 54*(2), 175–190.

Mulkay, M. J. (1988). *On humor: Its nature and its place in modern society.* Cambridge, UK: Polity Press.

Neuliep, J. (1991). An examination of the content of high school teachers' humor in the classroom and the development of an inductively derived taxonomy of classroom humor. *Communication Education*, *40*(4), 343–355.

Nouri, A., & Sajjadi, S. M. (2014). Emancipatory Pedagogy in Practice: Aims, Principles and Curriculum Orientation. *The International Journal of Critical Pedagogy*, *5*(2), 76-87.

Nutt, L., & Hardman, L. (2019). *Complete the agenda in higher education: challenge beliefs about student success*. Lanham, MD: Rowman & Littlefield.

Opplinger, P., & Zillman, D. (2003). Humor and learning. In J. Bryant, D. Roskos-Ewoldsen & J. Cantor (Eds.), *Communication and emotion: Essays in honor of Dolf Zillman* (pp. 255–273). Mahwah, NJ: Lawrence Erlbaum

Palmer, P. (2007). *The courage to teach: Exploring the inner landscape of a teacher's life*. San Francisco, CA: Jossey-Bass.

Patrick, C. (2014). 11 Ways to handle a heckler. Retrieved from http://mentalfloss.com/article/54496/11-ways-handle-heckler

Phillips Sheesley, A., Pfeffer, M., & Barish, B. (2016). Comedic improv therapy for the treatment of social anxiety disorder. *Journal of Creativity in Mental Health*, *11*(2), 157–169.

Rao, P., Beidel, D., & Murray, M. (2008). Social skills interventions for children with Asperger's Syndrome or High-Functioning Autism: A review and recommendations. *Journal of Autism and Developmental Disorders*, *38*, 353–361. http://dx.doi.org/10.1007/s10803-007-0402-4

Richmond, V. P., Lane, D. R., & McCroskey, J. C. (2006). Teacher immediacy and the teacher-student relationship. In T. P. Mottet, V. P. Richmond, & J. C. McCroskey (Eds.). Handbook of instructional communication: Rhetorical and relational perspectives (Ch. 8). (pp. 167–193). Boston, MA: Allyn &Bacon

Ruch, W., Attardo, S., & Raskin, V. (1993). Toward an empirical verification of the General Theory of Verbal Humor. *International Journal of Humor Research*, *6*(2), 123–136.

Schmidt, S. R. (1994). Effects of humor on sentence memory. Journal of Experimental Psychology: Learning, Memory & Cognition, 20(4), 953-967.

Schmidt, S. R. (2002). The humour effect: Differential processing and privileged retrieval. Memory, 10(2), 127-138.

Schmidt, S. R. & Williams, A. R. (2001). Memory for humorous cartoons. Memory & Cognition, 29(2), 305-311.

Shor, I., & Freire, P. (1987). What is the "dialogical method" of teaching? *Journal of Education*, *169*(3), 11–31.

Shih, Y. H. (2018). Rethinking Paulo Freire's dialogic pedagogy and its implications for teachers' teaching. *Journal of Education and Learning*, *7*(4), 130-235.

Sim, I. (2015). Humor intervention program for children with chronic diseases. *Applied Nursing Research*, *28*(4), 404–412.

Strean, W. (2011). Creating student engagement? HMM: Teaching and learning with humor, music and movement. *Creative Education*, *2*(3), 189–192.

Sullivan, R. (1992). Students learn more when they're having fun. *Vocational Education Journal*, *67*(3), 36–3.8

Taupin, A. (2018). *Humor: A bridge to social skills for individuals with high-functioning autism.* Chester, PA: Widener University.

Teslow, J. (1995). Humor me: A call for research. *Educational Technology Research and Development, 43*(3), 6–28.

Thorson, J., & Powell, F. (1993). Development and validation of a multidimensional sense of humor scale. *Journal of Clinical Psychology, 49*(1), 13–23.

Tickle-Degnon, L., & Rosenthal, R. (1990). The nature of rapport and its nonverbal correlates. *Psychological Inquiry 1*(4), 285–293.

Torok, S., McMorris, R., & Lin, W. (2004). Is humor an appreciated teacher tool? Perceptions of professors' teaching styles and use of humor. *College Teaching, 52*(1), 14–20.

Tsai, K. (2018). Evaluation of creative products, and cognitive style among Chinese undergraduates. *International Journal of Cognitive Research in Science, Engineering and Education, 6*(1), 53–60.

Vertovec, S. (2007). Super-diversity and its implications. *Ethnic and Racial Studies, 30*(6), 1024–1054.

Wakshlag, J., Day, K., & Zillmann, D. (1981). Selective exposure to educational television programs as a function of differently paced humorous inserts. *Journal of Educational Psychology, 73*(1), 27.

Wanzer, M., Frymier, A., & Irwin, J. (2010). An explanation of the relationship between instruction humor and student learning: Instructional humor processing theory. *Communication Education, 59*, 1–18.

Ziv, A. (1983). The influence of humorous atmosphere on divergent thinking. *Contemporary Educational Psychology, 8*(1), 68–75.

CHAPTER FOUR

Humor Invites Play, Divergent Thinking and Creativity

Some years ago, in the early 90s, I was teaching art in an elementary school within a city zone that housed residents of low socioeconomic and high-crime demographics. A week of bad weather and standardized testing supervision without play had made kids wiggly, jiggly, jumpy, bumpy, itchy and twitchy. As I escorted a second-grade class into my art room, I could sense they were ready for something haptic and manipulative, something they could control, so I gave them each a ball of clay as big as they could handle. My only instructions to them were, "Play with the clay and invent something new we do not have but need in order to make our lives easier." (Now mind you, this was in the era of pagers worn on the belt—before portable cell phones were inspired). When we reached the point for students to share their life-improving inventions, one boy was eager to show me his clay gun. "Miss, this gun will help you clean your teeth! Really. Want to see? A little man sits on a brush inside the gun here, and when you shoot him into your mouth, he brushes your teeth!" Surprised, I considered this to be a truly innovative, clever invention one might pitch to Waterpik. The next student to show his piece was 7-year-old Abel, now proudly holding up his clay object. "It's a pager with a phone on the back. When they page you, you flip it over to use the phone to call the person who paged you. If you need to look something up, you open it up to use the computer." Wow! Who would have known that the iPhone was invented by a 7-year-old in the early 1990s, long before its appearance in Steve Jobs' think tank?

The clay activity with second graders required little research, a second of planning and 5 minutes of instruction. The rest was up to the kids. I simply gave them the material and permission to play. Freedom to playfully invent allows new ideas to crystallize significantly into tangible forms. The kids were thinking about new ways to live and went for it. They were not hampered by voices in their head saying, "Well now THAT won't work!" Those voices come from people around us and the crowd grows larger as we grow older. Children's best creative endeavors happen in learning spaces where adults are not controlling learning with the mindset that learning must be serious work. It isn't fun because work is the hard stuff, we must all do to earn time to play. We work to produce results and products, to earn our living. Teachers nudge students along with phrases like, "Finish your work!" or praise them when they finish, with "Good job!" Think of all the associations teachers make with work and productive learning: "Get back to work! Mind your own business. Good job, good work!" We even call work we do when we make art, *artwork*, right? These phrases definitely are not associated with play!

Play

Just exactly what is play? The kind of play we associate with learning is a "positive mood state in which the learner is more inclined to behave in a spontaneous and flexible way" (Bateson, Bateson, & Martin, 2013, p. 100). Playing people are in a state of psychological and physical well-being that makes them sensitive to conditions around them, similar to emotional intelligence (Held & Spinka, 2011). Playing people do not seem to need external rewards to keep on playing, but they stop playing when they are stressed, anxious, hungry or ill (2013). The more we have been deprived of play, the more we will play when we have an opportunity, to make up for the time we were not playing.

I am pretty sure most teachers work hard at playing and having fun when they are far from the classroom. I just bet they laugh more outside the classroom than inside, maybe even more than the norm for adults who average 18 times a day (Martin & Kuiper, 1999). I know a busload of art teachers who revel in imaginative play in their own lives and cannot help but bring the playfully oriented person they are into their classrooms. Understand that the very play that invites wildly imaginative thoughts is regulated by their identity, an identity that transforms into a teacher when they enter the classroom. These fun teachers shake students out of the serious box of convention by inviting them to play.

Playful humor and creativity come from the same family, sharing look-alike behaviors. To make up something funny, to generate humor requires creativity in itself, and spontaneous play holds the strongest theoretical connection to humor and creativity (Murdock & Ganim, 1992). For example, one teacher I know playfully engages her students by mimicking game show hosts. What kid wouldn't want to be included in a game show art class? You can be sure that the content presented in those tv-formatted art classes became memorably potent because students were learning while playing.

Another art teacher I know uses her hands as portable puppets named Frida and Lida, who frequently talk to each other at any given time. Another pulls out a jar containing her pet caterpillar, Crayola, a fuzzy fat string she has wired to flip around wildly when students demonstrate achievement. Still another teacher breaks into glorious operatic songs with lyrics she improvises from textbook themes or lyrics out of their intended context. When asking students to stand back to look at their work during a critique, she will launch into the song, "From a Distance" by Bette Midler. Okay, it is cheesy, but certainly fun for us and for students. Whatever fun comes from us naturally opens up possibilities for students to join us physically and mentally in play.

We cannot cease from playing even when we are irritated. I knew a teacher who was being pushed over the edge by her class of students behaving badly. She stood quietly in front of the room looking at kids through her thumb and index finger. She pretended to pinch their heads while simultaneously making spurting sounds with each pinch. The students stopped, stared and asked her what she was doing. She replied, "I am upset with your behavior, so I am squishing your heads."

When I have been at a loss for action and words, I have picked up white board erasers and used them like remote controls to "mute" loquacious students. As mentioned before, I use two bottles of Elmer's glue to revive "dying" works of art as art attack defibrillators on a crash cart. I have pitched squishy balls to students during discussions to incite their participation. I have even lapsed into a foreign accent, a scheme that serves me well on Mondays when everyone is overcoming the slow-motion inertia of the weekend. It is the height of play for me, although I understand it may not be for everyone. My accent "attacks" come on suddenly, like a cold—and that is the delight of it. I can maintain an accent to carry on ordinary classroom procedures for about 10 minutes after which it dissolves into something unrecognizable.

Yes, creative play is highly valued by students and teachers alike. I question the status of seriousness over playfulness in education, although I am not the first to do so. In 1910, our education forefather, John Dewey, contended, "teaching is an art; therefore, the teacher is an artist and the ideal mental attitude of the teacher to work combines the playful and the serious" (Skilbeck, 2017, Abstract). In my mind playfulness, invention, divergent thinking and humor are interrelated. Playfulness is really not as antithetical to productive work as you think. Just watch unsupervised children and you will see that they are serious about playing to learn. They cannot help themselves. Try and stop them from wondering, wishing, exploring, pretending, imagining, trying, failing, and trying again. Listen to their play and you will hear giggling and shrieks of laughter. If they are not guided into a serious "work" mindset, something wonderfully unexpected happens while they laugh and play: they make up something new. Play is essential to social rightness. When children can't play, they grow up socially dysfunctional. A study in Texas revealed a common factor among 90% of sociopathic murderers: they were deprived of childhood play (Brown, 1998). Yikes! A good reason to keep recess in schools and play in our classrooms.

I imagine that shifting into playful creativity mode for children feels a lot like running naked in the wind—alone. First of all, they are running. Faster than the speed of walking, racing toward something they are excited about gets them there quick. Second, they are naked. I am not especially fond of being naked out in the world but children often are. They "get naked" when they simply do not care what others think of their nakedness. They are unhampered, unhindered and authentic. They have abandoned crowd-imposed ideas on how to behave by shedding their clothes, the factor identifying them with a civilized group. And lastly, they are alone in the wind. The space and time when we excuse ourselves from asking permission is what we call being "alone in the zone." If we are lucky, we can sometimes visit the zone as adults but children own time share properties there. Being in the zone is when we are engaged in creative activities we love, those that fill us with joy, with energy and flinty focus. Creating a zone in our art classrooms is what we all hope to replicate. We would love for our learning spaces to be zones where Creativity runs naked with Play and Laughter, into the wind of change, bringing innovation to life.

Torrance (1972) identified three aspects of creativity we see in children: *fluency*, *flexibility* and *originality*. Fluency refers to generative frequency. Children can be very *fluent* with their art making. Why draw one drawing when the effusive search for shape and form can be explored with 20 drawings? In other words, the more drawings I make, the more I learn about what I am drawing. *Flexibility* refers to the capacity to generate ideas from various categories. A child will ask, why just draw people? Why not paint them or make them with clay, with stitchery, photography and sculpture? Flexible searching to capture form with a variety of materials is rather like pursuing speed, let's say, on several playground equipment apparatus. Speed feels differently on a swing, a merry-go-round and a slide. Finally, originality refers to the novelty of an idea that departs from convention. *Original* ideas are those we have not seen before. A child's original rendition of a house may depart from the familiar schema of a square with a triangle roof and rectangle windows, to draw one that floats in the air on clouds with ropes reaching to the ground. Fluency, flexibility and originality come from play, something artists have been doing for a long time. M.C. Escher fooled around with incontestable certitudes and found pleasure in rendering staircases spatially as combinations of two- and three-dimensions while messing with gravity (Bateson, 2014). Picasso thoroughly enjoyed playing while making art. He filmed himself painting on glass while someone watched from the other side; sketching a goat, embellishing it, adding and taking away shapes until the final drawing was utterly unrecognizable (2014). Needless to say, the viewer was confused but Picasso got to play.

It All Adds Up: Interconnectedness of Play, Humor and Creativity

Let's look at the idea of being in a good mood to better understand the interactive effect of play on creativity and innovation. How do we get into a good mood? Humor puts us there. Humor and play both happen in safe environments, both require social interactions, both make us positive and sensitive to conditions around us, both are intrinsically motivated and do not require external rewards (Bateson, 2014). Like play, humor generates unconventional combinations of creative thoughts that rattle traditions. Creative growth comes through analogy, through seeing things connect rather than only seeing how they might be different.

Essentially, the interconnection is an infinity knot: playfulness activates humor and humor activates playfulness and the result is amazing innovation and creativity! What does the relationship between a joyful, playful mood kindling creativity look like in our everyday lives?

Go Bananas! An Example of Play, Humor and Creativity

Here is one example. I play and laugh often. Playing and laughing and talking to strangers in the grocery store makes the banal chore of gathering food from various shelves across the store much more fun. One day, I was rolling past the checkout line and noticed a self-important store associate directing a miry mass of shoppers to assigned cashiers. I approached the harried person with, "Might I suggest you use two bananas to help direct traffic? You can hold them like the airport officials hold flashlights to send planes down the runway." The look he gave me is one I see often but I tell you, after 10 minutes when I rolled by again, he was gleefully pointing bananas at smiling people! Approaching him, I added, "Oh, I forgot to tell you if traffic gets too heavy, you can call for help on your banana-phone." I did not look back later to see if he was making a banana call but I just bet he was. Playing placed me in a positive mood, which enlightened a creative thought about ordinary bananas.

I have used bananas a number of times in my art classes to spike creative thinking. I challenged students to invent sustainable, biodegradable fast-food packaging with aesthetic appeal to the masses. Time passed and even collective brainstorming did not net a viable model. So, I held up a banana. "Just look to natural foods like fruits and nuts to see the greatest food-keeping system known to man. The peels or shells keep the contents fresh for a long time. See how easy it is to peel down one strip of the banana peel? Couldn't we make a package that peels as easily and keeps the food fresh?" Wheels turned and ideas flowed.

On another day, high school art students were wondering what components comprise oil paint. We talked about the color property of pigment that has been ground into an oil base, called the vehicle or binder. I challenged them to go home and make paint from substances in their home; they simply needed a pigment to add color and a binder to adhere the color to a ground, or canvas. Each student brought in their "paint" to add to our paint buffet and everyone proceeded to paint with the home samples. Results ranged from dry gelatin powder (Jell-O) + olive oil; runny mustard + fireplace ashes; lipstick + creamy peanut butter, and smooshed eye shadow + baby oil. My all-time favorite though, was ketchup blended into banana pulp. It was creamy when applied and dried to a wonderful luster!

Shifting our perspective with a playful approach is not only a side effect of humor, but also a requisite skill for creating something novel. The capacity for generating something funny or something unique both call upon our ability to connect two completely different concepts.

Useless New Inventions: A Playful Activity for Emerging Artists

A fun concept I have adopted to ease emerging artists into a creative endeavor the first time they enter the classroom is re-inventing things we use into new things. It also is a great way to offset what I call *graphiphobia*, fear of drawing realistically, a crippling perception that stunts creative growth in any area. (Please tell me *why* every adultish students new to art class think they will be expected to draw an object as accurately as possible on the first day of class?)

I take them by the hand with an activity called "Useless New Inventions" after reading Tina Seelig's book, *Ingenius* (2012). Introduced in Japan as *chindōgu (Patton & Bannerot, 2002)* This silly activity connects and combines objects that seem unrelated, allowing students to generate a slew of wonderfully unusual inventions. It feels like a fun game because it is. First, I load up a canvas bag with all kinds of everyday objects—toilet paper cardboard rolls, door stops, potato mashers, wine stoppers, unique hair accessories, tools from the garage, and outrageous objects I procured from late night tv commercials. Then, students partner up and select an item from the bag, joining their creative resources to accomplish the four-step creative improv challenge:

1. Forget the traditional use for the object and think of a new use. It can (and probably should) be silly and improbable.
2. Give the object a name.
3. Decide who would use this object in the new way you have invented. (Targeted market)
4. Act out a commercial enticing your market to want it.

An amazing amount of ingenious devices are born during the "Useless New Inventions" activity (see Figure 4.1). Most are silly and many bring paroxysms of laughter as students present. For example, there was the thoughtful Netti-Spaghetti Strainer, a zippered mesh laundry bag originally intended for washing unmentionables in the washer. It was announced as "perfect for the pasta-loving consumer with laundromat issues. Simply fill with cooked pasta, rinse and drain! Today, rinse your pasta, tomorrow wash your panties!" There was the wooden doorstop reconceptualized as the Houdini Hamster Driving Ramp, sending hamsters airborne after accelerating off the ramp; also in the line up, was a spin on the circular hair bun sponge touted as the Ever Present Elbow Rester, and finally, the Tail Wagger Egg Beater, a multifunctional device harnessing the power of a wagging tail to beat eggs. The activity fulfilled my objective for the game: to help students recall the fun they felt as children playing, pretending and inventing. They need to play to counteracts creative paralysis so they can run naked in the wind!

Playful Inventing and Divergent Thinking

The majority of innovations we value as a society are products invented to solve a problem or meet a need. The problem precipitates inventing something new. From light bulbs to Post-It Notes, many new products had their beginning from someone thinking off of the grid or thinking divergently. You knew Thomas Edison conquered darkness with his brilliant light bulb invention, but did you know he made 9,999 attempts at finding the longest lasting filament before he happened onto carbon? Optimistic Edison did not see these prior iterations of his bulb as failures, but as "9,999 ways NOT to make one" (Ramirez, 2015). Edison

114 | THE ART OF TEACHING WITH HUMOR: CRAFTING LAUGHTER

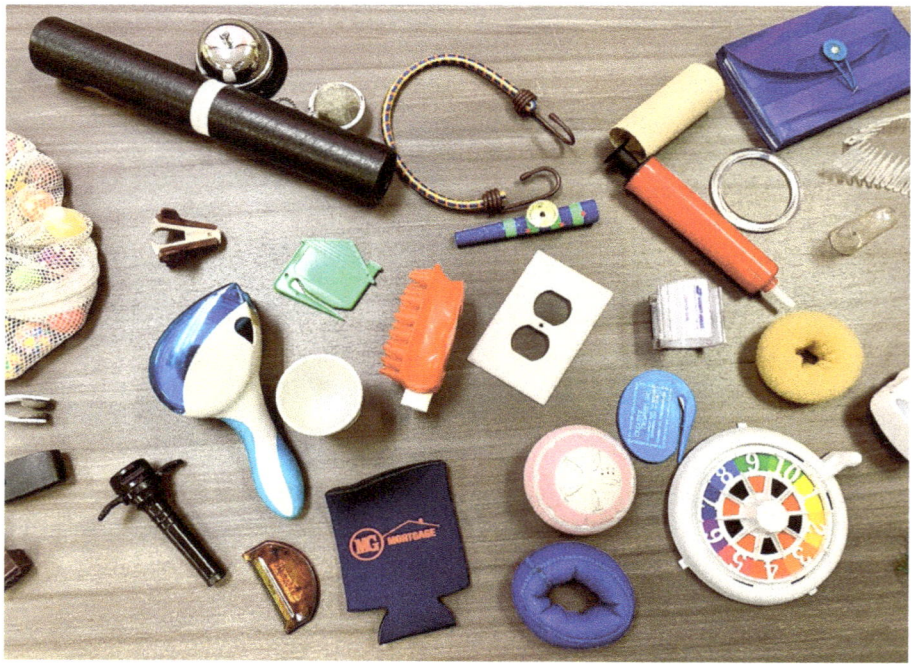

Figure 4.1. Useless New Inventions Everyday Objects

was a *diverger*, a generator of many ideas to find the best fit, as opposed to a *converger*, one focuses on finding a single solution. If you ask a *converger*, what they would do with a fork, e.g., they would tell you to eat with it. An appropriate, logical response (although not very creative). The *diverger*, on the other hand, would give you a list of fork uses: a musical instrument, a whisk substitute, a device for applying texture to a painting, a paper sorter, backscratcher and so forth. Finding solutions to problems with creative, divergent thinking involves pulling a topic apart, examining all the parts and quickly generating a surplus of ideas related to the topic. We use both processes thinking divergently to generate solutions and convergently to select and develop them (Brophy, 2001).

Brain Thunder

To expedite whole-class divergent thinking, I rely on *Brain Thunder*, a brainstorming exercise to generate a superfluity of uncensored ideas quickly. Unlike brainstorming, brain thunder begins with lightening (or enlightening), 2 minutes of eyes-closed, silent thinking to consider the topic, and is followed by a thunderous 2-minute round of students simultaneously yelling out unrestrained ideas while I will write

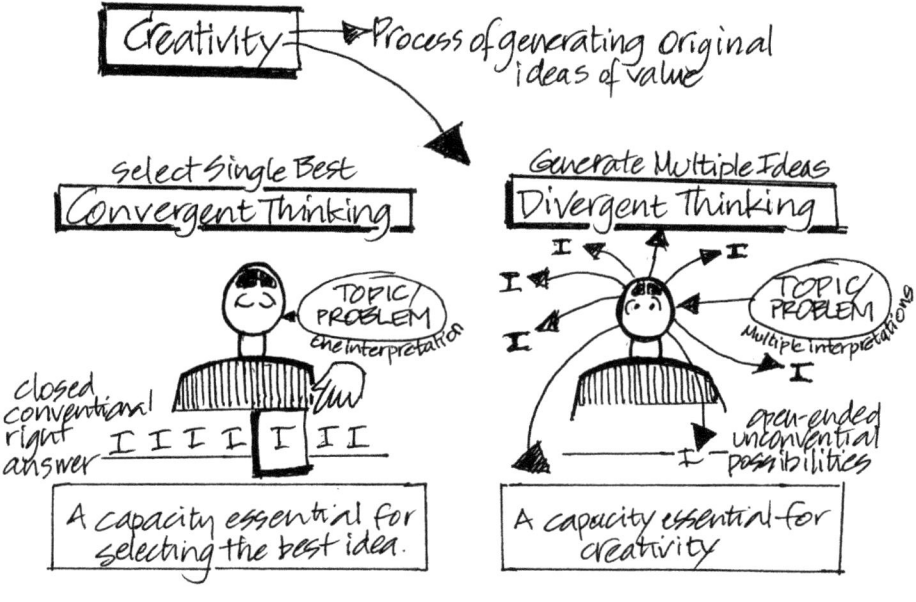

Figure 4.2. Divergent vs. Convergent Thinking

them on the board as fast as humanly possible. Every idea is recorded without judgment. After generating the stormed ideas, we collectively select, consider, tweak and discard ideas until a consensus is reached for one. I have observed single students voluntarily brain thundering with a few friends to search for conceptual ideas from drastically different perspectives. Spontaneous, free-flowing, random, disorganized and playful divergent thinking is absolutely essential to artists and studio art making.

On the slow end of the divergent thinking continuum is musing, a fertile state of wondering without time constraints. Although someone musing may appear to be sitting and staring, most likely they are focused on speculating, selecting, and appraising. The genius of Einstein was rooted in his ability to ponder and let the mind go out to play with entertaining ideas. The practice of mind play musing for artists is like a road trip just for the fun of it. They pull their vehicle off of the pulsing highway to think while the engine idles. They truly are going somewhere—following a mental map to a fantasy destination. Powerful envisioning pushes imagination propels artists forward with powerful purpose. With the help of convergent thinking, they are able to enact their visions in a practical, organized way.

Fearless divergent thinking opens us to wonder "what if?" and "why not?" by connecting the unconnected, a skill we can use to make something new from two unrelated ideas (see Figure 4.2). Incongruity, the core of both creativity and humor and a necessary tool for problem solving, is brought to life with humor. "Being able to connect and combine nonobvious [incongruent] ideas and objects is essential for innovation and a key part of the creative thinking process" (Seelig, 2012, p. 34). Word and image metaphors have helped well-known innovators mentally connect unrelated but parallel concepts:

> Isaac Newton paralleled a falling apple to gravity's pull on the moon. Johannes Kepler connected the mechanism of a clock to the motion of the planets. Even Einstein found a relationship between railroad trains and the motion of light in his special theory of relativity. (Ramirez, 2015)

Linking Thinking

An open-ended activity I call *Linking Thinking* develops students' ability to make connections with random objects. If introduced prior to studio art making, it can optimize students' unique connections with materials, content or approach to traditional processes. I present two word lists, side by side, then challenge students to determine connections with one word from each list:

> List 1: *bicycle, kite, fire, spaghetti, kitten, boot, mountain, triangle, crowd, gum, scissors, circle*

> List 2: *football, paper, dog, cage, nursery rhymes, bald head, flashlight, sky diver, cave, apple*

Connections are not judged but must be explained. For example, a connection between spaghetti and football might be explained with the drawn play paths on tv screens are lines that look like spaghetti. Or, fires and flashlights both produce light in dark places. Or even, round bicycle tires imitate the curve of a bald man's head.

The esteemed position of "inventor" brings to mind a heroic mastermind imbued with special talents, magically materializing innovations that save the day. We adopt this stereotype from schools and museums where inventors are introduced to children as an elite class of uniquely intelligent humans, but they really are regular people like you and me. They just started early. How children play and how inventors conceive new ideas are remarkably comparable. The creative invention process in which inventors engage duplicates children's play process because inventors began using the process as children. Like children at play, inventors persist and strive until a satisfactory end is achieved. Like children, inventors are inspired by the world around them: nature, built environments, learning by mistakes, and most importantly, open-ended play.

A Method for Teaching Successful Inventing

Case in point, inventor B. Edward Shlesinger, Jr. who began inventing early in life, reflected, "if children could be taught to play a musical instrument, they could be taught to invent" underscoring the notion that the invention process taught at an early age continues through life (1982, p. 214). Shlesinger initiated "The Art of Successful Inventing," a course he offered to all ages of learners but found that elementary school-aged children were the most receptive, the most uninhibited and possessed the greatest surplus of imagination needed to produce new ideas and inventions. He began his course by telling children he could make inventors out of them, which they readily believed and accepted as truth. Inventing, (making up something never made before) is easy as pie for kids. Needless to say, they were eager for instruction on how to go about doing this.

Shlesinger exploits three aspects of children's creativity to make first graders into inventors with his course. The first aspect is how to quickly *link incongruous concepts together* to produce solutions to invention problems. This is an easy one because linking incongruities resides at the very core of humor and invention and occurs naturally in the process of play. The second aspect, *imagination*, allows children like Able to consider any solution as possible, especially solutions that overstep reality. The third, *observation* occurs naturally in children as they are new to the earth and have a short time to figure out how everything works and why. They are always observing to make sense of the world, to read clues hidden in physical science, in human interaction, etc. However, children are not able to anticipate or predict what will happen because most things are new to them. Consequently, they frequently mix things and surprisingly find themselves with unconventional results. The primary goal of Shlesinger's instruction is not just inventing but learning the step-by-step thought process that leads to invention. He presents a challenge to guide students through each of the six steps: introduction, identification, foundation, data, imagination, and limitations. Essentially the steps lead learners to identify social needs where problems exist and solve the problems by searching and editing solutions. "If children can recognize problems, they can invent" (p. 217). Our plan as innovation educators should be to teach invention early so children develop the habit of solving complex problems with authentic inventions and continue in that habit through adulthood.

Teaching Divergent Thinkers

We could easily replace the prevailing scientific method with creative thinking and invention as core parts of education outside of art education. Even as art educators, we may not want to approach students' studio art making as "projects" or "assignments" but as challenges to solve problems. Framing assignments as challenges, permits students to be engaged with their artwork as an open-ended long term supposition and not a prescribed, temporal "project." In addition, if we presented the challenge in the context of a thing which they are most passionate about (a medium, a tool, an idea), prompting them to explore, innovate, push the boundaries and do something new with that thing, they will want to create.

The way to go is giving students the mental tools to find answers to their questions and not the answers is the way to go (Azzam, 2009, p. 4). We should not expect them to reach an end, a desired statistic in the right bracket. "The regime of standardized testing has led us all to believe that if you can't count it, it doesn't count." We know this is not true. How about we ask them to stop at some point in the process so we, the teachers and they, the artists, can assess growth together? We would not be comparing artist to artist, but artist to themselves, evaluating the extent to which the artist investigated, persisted, and applied alternatives to develop solution to the problem challenge.

PTDS: A Factor Hindering Successful Inventing

Far from the place of play is a hampering place where others unintentionally impose judgments on the work of young artists. As I mentioned earlier, the majority of students entering your middle or high school art room will exhibit symptoms of a condition I call "PTDS," Post-Traumatic Drawing Syndrome. PTDS, instigated by the judgmental adult, parent or peer is a devastating public indictment of a child's innocent rendition of an object. The indictment usually manifests as a broadcasted criticism such as, "Horses don't look like that!" or "People don't have arms that short," or "Why can't you draw like Andrew? His people look real!" Many times, regrettably unforgettable classroom teachers issues statements of this caliber. (Please note, if you are reading this book you are most likely not guilty of this offense, nor are you the teacher described below).

> Dragon teachers, following the lead of their namesakes, inflict injury on their students by subtle and often thoughtless blows that sting and leave scars that can last a lifetime. Blows from the Dragon teachers cause students to avoid not only the Dragon but the Dragon's lair—in this case, the art classroom. (Smith-Shank, 2014, p. 151)

PTDS child victims of dragon assault carry their visceral angst to make art look real into youth hood. Realism as a standard of achievement of high art is deeply rooted in Western thought and is still alive and living well in our school communities. Regrettably, PTDS victimization is widespread and many develop into adulthood believing the assassinating criticism of their creative potential. It does not only effect drawing abilities but also diminishes the perception of any potential they may have to be creative. They suffer from what I call low artistic self-efficacy, the "I believe I am not creative" syndrome. Sir Kenneth Robinson, author of *Out of Our Minds: Learning to Be Creative* says, "A big part of being creative is looking for new ways of doing things within whatever activity you're involved in" (Azzam, 2009).

Sadly, children from the 6th grade to college students walk into art rooms muttering aplogetic introductions like, "Hi, my name is Mary and I can't draw so please do not expect anything creative from me this semester," or, "Hi, I'm Clayton and I am not an artist, my people look like stick figures." These poor students are PTDS survivors whose tainted perceptions of their artistic efficacy trip a default mechanism that undermines their success in producing anything creative. Since representational drawing is usually the trauma trigger, I look for ways to help them overcome *graphiphobia* with joyful success in creating something. Traditional drawing would not do the trick. I had to think of something.

Analog Abstract Drawings: Nonthreatening First Drawing Challenge

Years ago, I attended a workshop led by Betty Edwards, author of several books about drawing from the right side of the brain (2013). She led participants in sketching preliminary compositions of intangible concepts, such as problems, people, places, and emotions. Her one rule: you can use shapes, lines, value, contrast, unity and balance but you cannot draw anything we recognize. I remember how easily we were able to express an idea from heart to paper without the left-brain voice negotiating likeness. Our drawings were of the analog or analogue type that involve an "artist's hand moving across the paper to leave traces of thoughts and feelings unveiling fragments of the subconscious in the form of visible marks" (Garrels, 2005, p. 16).

The Dead Fly Story

The Analog Abstract Drawing exercise is the first drawing assignment I introduce to emerging artists (including PTDS learners) and begins by telling them a funny story I made up to demonstrate composition as well as relax any anxiety they may be feeling. The story is entitled, "The Dead Fly Story." I draw out the story on a white board or large tablet as my storytelling unfolds: "Once upon a time, a blank canvas was hanging in an art museum. Visitors would walk up to it, examine it, but quickly move to another work of art because the blank canvas had nothing interesting to hold their attention. One day, a pesky fly flew into the gallery and committed fly-i-cide right there on the blank canvas. There it lay, sort of in the middle, an amalgamated center of interest composed of busted up fly parts and dried fly goo. Well, the museum curator got wind of the violated canvas with the distasteful focal point and hired an abstract artist to camouflage the dead fly detritus with a composition of their choosing. The artist would receive $50,000. upon completion. As the artist began the composition by emphasizing the fly focal point then leading viewers' eye out to the edges of the canvas. The thrill of earning so much money to paint whatever the artist wanted guided all parts of the composition. Lines undulated with excitement, colors were explosively happy, repeating shapes danced in jubilant procession to and from the focal point. The artist took care to arrange all of the small parts of the painting together to create a feeling of unity. When finished, the artist titled the delightful painting, *Successful Composition Number 1.*"

After the Dead Fly Story chalk talk, we look at a few projected works of art to identify the focal point and all of the formal elements the artist included in the work. This leads to deconstruction of the artwork to interpret possible meanings hidden in certain shapes of certain colors placed in certain areas of the work. Then, I encourage students to give the work a new title asking them to explain what they see that makes them think of the title. Monet's *Haystacks* was re-titled "Sunrise Cupcakes" and Picasso's *Three Musicians* became "Chunky-Colored Blue Men Group." All the talking and looking and laughing primes students for beginning their own graphite drawing in their sketchbooks.

Thumbnail Sketches of Four Themes

I verbally guide students through an initial drawing process with the goal to generate four preliminary thumbnail sketches of concepts relevant to every human: (1) *A Problem I Have,* (2) *A Person I Know Well,* (3) *A Place I Like to Go* and (4) *A Feeling I Have.* Students draw four format shapes (squares or rectangles) freehand and write one of the title prompts underneath each of the four formats. Beginning with the first, *A Problem I Have,* I instruct students to, "close your eyes and think of an overwhelming problem in your life with which you are currently facing. Consider yourself in the midst of the problem. What shape are you? Are you small and helpless or large and brave? You are the focal point in this first and each of the four compositions. Draw your shape self somewhere in the format area. Where you place yourself in your problem will express more about how the problem is affecting you. What other parts of your problem can you identify? Think about whether they are lines or shapes. Are these parts weighing you down, depressing you or controlling you? Are there more than one of these factors in your problem? If so, then be sure to add them to your composition as a repeating pattern. Fill up the entire format area with your problem, making sure to touch all four sides. When you finish drawing every part, go back to your shape self at the focal point and decide if you are light against a dark background or dark against a light background. Then begin to add value by shading. Continue adding value throughout the rest of your composition."

The second thumbnail sketch, *A Person I Know Well*, begins much the same as the first, but for this one I ask them to think of someone in their life they know so well they could probably predict what they would do in any circumstance. I instruct students to write four words just outside the second format shape that describes the person's personality. Then, I tell them to underline the word that best describes them in a general sense. "Now," I say, "you will draw what your person looks like from the inside, not the outside. It will be an abstract portrait of their personality. The underlined word is the focal point of your portrait composition, so consider how to express it. Will you use a shape or lines? Will they be large and dark to express a bold and aggressive personality or small and light to express a softer, more docile personality?" You get the picture. The remaining sketches unfold effortlessly into compositions as students consider the expressive value of the elements and principles of art (see Figure 4.3). Everyone is so engrossed in expressing their thoughts and feelings, drawing anxiety is forgotten. It is a lot like overcoming a fear of drowning by swimming in the beautiful Caribbean; the *pleasure* of the swirling surf dissuades the fear of *drowning* in it.

Final Drawing of One Selected Sketch

The next step in this assignment is for students to select the most successful composition of the four and enlarge it for a final drawing. To this end, we follow through with a silent Post-It Note Valentine Peer Critique (as described in Chapter Two) to help each artist select one sketch. The Post-It Note Critique leaves visible peer appraisal behind to help the artist select one for the final drawing. I must tell you that those Post-Its, the ones I call love note Valentines, do more to bolster drawing confidence than anything else involved in this assignment. I have never seen a negative comment left by a student on a Post-It. Most are positive, confidence bolstering, "way to go" statements that overcome the inertia of not drawing for so long.

With the selected sketch as a starting point, I guide students to enlarge their sketch to a 9" x 12" or 12" x 18" sheet of drawing paper (Evans-Palmer,

2015). I do *not* say "blow up the sketch" because we don't want anything blown up in schools these days. We use the width of a ruler to lightly draw a format border on all sides, then students follow me to add a value scale with 6 graded values in the outside margin. Seeing the range of gray, a good 9B Ebony Design Sketch pencil can render is enlightening to many. I explain that artists use specific tools to do certain things and a yellow number two pencil is NOT a tool an artist uses!

Students proceed to lightly draw shapes and lines similar to the sketch on their final drawing. I ask them to flip their paper over to see where their eyes land first, ensuring a dominant focal point adds emphasis for the drawing. Flipping over the drawing three times drives the point home. We begin at the focal point to add value (shading) and work through the rest of the drawing from there. I visit each table to demonstrate drawing methods they could use to finish their drawing: *subtractive drawing* (drawing with an eraser in an area which graphite has been applied), *frottage* (laying the paper over textured surfaces, like the bottom of sneakers or the lined grid on a paper cutter then rubbing with a graphite stick or side of a 6B pencil), *blending values* (gradual shading from a lighter to darker value). I encourage them to add contrast by using "black to push back" space and white to bring space forward (see Figure 4.4).

Class Critique of Final Drawings

The class gathers around the mounted final drawings and each student tells: (1) the most challenging part of the drawing process for them, (2) an aspect of the drawing of which they are the proudest, and (3) anything else they want to share. Seeing their drawings as acceptable, even successful perhaps for the first time as an adult, seals the proverbial deal on their drawing efficacy and they are more than willing to keep drawing.

The elevated efficacy students experience with the first drawing motivates them to attempt subsequent challenges. Toward this goal, I follow a simple set of criteria: (1) postpone observational drawing exercises until after simple mark-making, (2) present simple mark-making challenges that progress to more difficult, (3) introduce drawing as a record of expression, emotion, thoughts, and fears, (4) allow for freedom to choose drawing content, and (5) offer authentic, well-timed verbal encouragement during the drawing process.

When given options to choose what they draw, what scale and with what medium, students enjoy drawing more, gain more confidence in drawing and derive more personal meaning from their drawings than those with less choices (Ellenbecker, 2003). It is unfortunate that students are given fewer and fewer

HUMOR INVITES PLAY, DIVERGENT THINKING AND CREATIVITY | 123

A Problem in My Life	*A Person I Know Well*
An Emotion I Feel Now	*A Place I Like to Go*

Figure 4.3. Preliminary Thumbnail Sketches for the Analog Abstract Drawing

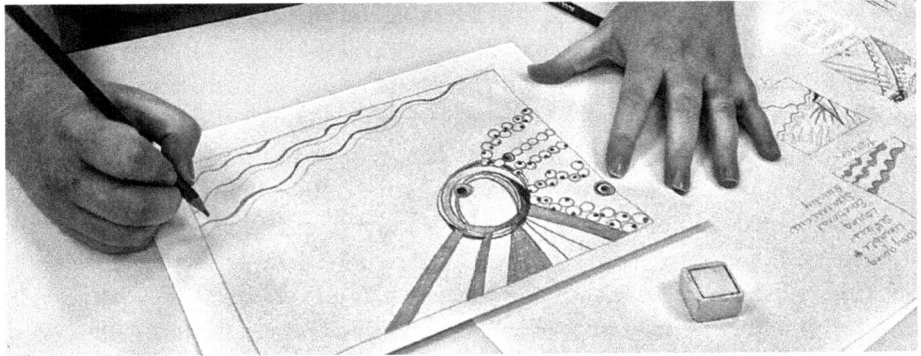

Figure 4.4. The Final Analog Abstract Drawing
Photos from p. 48 in Evans-Palmer, T. (2015) "I can't draw things that look real!" A 21st century non-traditional approach to raising learners' drawing efficacy. *Trends in Art Education*, 44–50.

opportunities to choose the content and style of their drawings as they advance through school (Anning, 2002). Middle and high school kids will tell you outright that their drawings would be more meaningful, more complex and of higher quality, if they were only allowed to choose what they drew (Rosenstiel & Gardner, 1977).

Teacher Feedback

I always approach a child's drawing with "Tell me about your drawing" rather than offer comments that my incriminate me for lack of knowledge. I remember saying that the dog in a child's drawing looked friendly only to be corrected by the child artist's admonishment, "That's not a dog, that's my father!" Our feedback can support or dismantle creativity. One day while supervising a student teacher, I sat in the back of a 4th grade art class watching a drawing lesson come to an end. A child sitting near me who had finished his artwork looked over and gleefully announced, "I am going to draw Sponge Bob Square Pants!" I whispered glumly, "Oh please don't! Someone has already created him. How about something new like the Grouchy Pickle Family?" I have nothing against the genius of Sponge Bob but replicating another artists' work is not original thinking to me. Some minutes later he came to show me a pickle family line-up stretching across the paper: Grandpa Pickle, Grandma Pickle, aunts, cousins and more, all cleverly detailed and not all grouchy. Rethinking the situation, I wish I leveraged the pickle situation with a challenge instead of a directive. One like, "I imagine there is a whole world of characters made from things around just waiting to be born. Why not design something new that no one has seen?"

Within a certain age in adolescence, the words children share with their peers does more to shape their behavior than anything the big people in their lives might say. It is no different with drawing. However, positive feedback from a teacher whom a middle or secondary student enjoys and reveres can also raise their belief in their creativity, so be mindful that what you say may tip the scale either way (Sternberg & Kaufman, 2010). Your best bet for their benefit is genuine interest in their work, not a grocery list of options that help them draw more realistically. Empathy joined with good natured humor can develop a relationship with a student that can transform them into a passionate learner committed to and skillfully engaged in life and the world around them. Just as powerful are the astute, scholarly insights other students offer to encourage their classmate. I often invite a team of three students to weigh in on a work of art a student is showing me. (After all, who made me the judge?) They seem to "get" the intentions of their peers much easier than I do and are able to candidly extrapolate the artist's execution of media.

Surprisingly, middle and high school student artists are open to peer review if a teacher is present to referee. Interactions with kids remind me that "common sense is the enemy of creativity and innovation. As soon as something seems the most obvious thing in the world, it means that we have abandoned all attempts at understanding it" (Azzam, 2009).

What Humor, Play, Inventiveness, and Divergent Thinking Means for Teachers

When we play, our behavior may look the same as when we are laughing with others (Martin, 2007), but both play and humor are emotional opposites of serious work. A teacher's perception of play in a place with students directly relates to creativity of those students in the space. In spaces where powerful, constraining authoritative leaders manage the environment, subordinates are expected to follow conventional rules. Spaces where flexible inspiring leaders manage, subordinates are expected to find unconventional, unique solutions to problems.

Tale of Two Teachers

For the sake of clarity, let's look at the spaces and dispositions of two very different leaders. In one room, there is a teacher we will call Mr. Rigid, a soberly serious soul who operates like a drill sergeant to keep unruly students in line. Mr. Rigid sees to it that his classroom is very clean, well-organized with everything in its place. Tables are grouped, but students work independently of others. There are set rules students must follow to ensure orderly behavior at all times. Mr. Rigid expects convergent thinking from his students and instructs them to search for one solution to achieve project assignment goals. To help them do this, he presents "model" samples of work to show his students so everyone understands what to do. One rule is "no talking while working" and another is "to work diligently during class to complete artwork assignments." Mr. Rigid considers laughter an indication of student play that is counterproductive to work. When student's walk into Mr. Rigid's static classroom and encounter his seriously restrained personality, they do not feel relaxed enough to generate innovative ideas nor do they feel they can safely take risks. Although the quality of artwork products generated in Mr. Rigid's classroom are technically excellent, products look the same year after year. Students remember technical processes they learned while making artwork but do not feel their artwork allowed their unique ideas or individual voices to be shown. In other words, their artwork and their learning experiences with Mr. Rigid were lifelessly detached from their real selves.

In another room is Mr. Supple, a cheerful teacher who enjoys teaching his students. Mr. Supple's classroom is set up like an art studio with grouped tables where students work together. His classroom is also clean and well-organized because his students initiate and follow their own procedures for material management. Mr. Supple sees each of his students as uniquely individual, nonconforming artists encouraged to take risks. Mr. Supple expects his students to question processes and to search out many original approaches to accomplish the artwork challenges he poses. He also expects them to fail every now and then, and, when they do fail, he asks them what they learned in the failing because Mr. Supple sees failing as a brief side trip of discovery, not a dead end. Mr. Supple has one rule: to be respectful of yourself, of others and your unique artistic gift.

He laughs a lot during classes and considers laughter an indication of joy, inventive play, positive feelings and students working together, which productively generate novel ideas. When student's walk into Mr. Supple's vibrant classroom and encounter his open, flexible and relaxed personality, they respond with ease and are willing to take risks. Consequently, the quality of artwork products generated in Mr. Supple's classroom is above average and student's artwork always represents investigative media application and authentically unique concepts year after year. Students remember how enjoyable learning was with Mr. Supple and they feel their artwork allowed them to find their style to express their thoughts, emotions, and concepts uniquely relevant to them. In other words, their artwork and their learning experiences with Mr. Supple were memorably happy times when they were joined to the subject of art and the ingenuity of others in a very real way.

Teachers, like organizational leaders possess capacities for humor and emotional intelligence that help them to be effective with their subordinates [students]. A national study conducted with personnel directors representing 100 of the largest corporations found 84% of the respondents believed leaders with a sense of humor were more creative, more flexible, and more willing to try new ideas (Scriven & Hefferin, 1998).

Artists Play to Create

When we are caught up in playful fun, we are given a free pass to step away from work and worry. Enjoying the act of art making is much like enjoying something funny, for no other reason than being away from reality allows us to be creative. Artists possess a childlike capacity to respond to the world seriously and playfully with materials they transform into products of art. They do not fret over skill and execution but jump into the middle of time while "in the zone" and

Table 4.1. Operational Definitions of Creativity-Related Terms

Term	Definition	Activities
Play	Intrinsically motivated, positive mood state which includes flexible, spontaneous behavior	Deeply engaging activities driven by children's own interests that invite interaction with didactic manipulatives and peers and is not extrinsically rewarded
Playful play	Play that generates new solutions to challenges set by the environment[1]	
Creativity	Coming up with a new idea	Spirited activities allowing for many novel ideas, unique iterations, flexible interpretations; not rewarded, noncompetitive,
Innovation	changing the way things are done	
Divergent thinking	generating many ideas from different directions to find a solution to a problem; spontaneous, playful, non-linear thinking	Playful learning activities with few restraints: open-ended games, challenges; problem-solving challenges that allow for play, humor, multiple answers, lists, brainstorming
Convergent thinking	bringing together concrete information to find the best solution to a problem; fast, logical, accurate thinking	Supervised and guided activities with restraints: multiple choice tests, one right answer or best solution challenges

[1] Definition attributed to Bateson (2014); Other definitions are derivatives of Merriam Webster (2020).

move organically with the making process. They operate with fluency, flexibility and originality. The creativity and humor that fortifies every human achievement begins with childlike imagination, imagination that illuminates the past, clarifies the present and foresees the future. But you can't see creativity unless an artist imagines, makes something new, or solves a problem. Creativity is imagination and play at work (Robinson, 2009).

The imagination of artists employs provocative incongruities to surprise us, much like comedians. The sudden visual—tactual shift in what we expect to see as we approach the work of art stimulates interest, fascination, amusement, confusion, indignation and even irritation (Ludden, Schifferstein, & Hekkert, 2012).

Artists not only sport a sense of humor but humor plays a major role in each stage of the creative process as they make the same kind of connections with arbitrary visual elements as comedians do with words and meanings (Blatner, 1988; Cousins, 1979; Koestler, 1964; Murdock & Ganim, 1992; Torrance, 1979). Where the artwork is the result of an artist's endeavor, a joke in itself is a kind of aesthetic experience, equal in value to any other aesthetic experience (Morreall, 1981).

Artists create, synthesize and empathize by thinking divergently, visually searching for relationships between small parts in order to form something new. These aptitudes rely on the symphonic ability to see relationships and join small pieces together, or "the aptitude to see the big picture—to sort out what really matters" detecting broad patterns as well as synthesizing pieces together (2007, p. 130).

Artists make creative connections with the help of the whole brain, interweaving high concepts and high-touch aptitudes to produce something externally new from within themselves. Creation calls for a full-fledged pronouncement of something not yet real, not quite born yet, existing only in the artist's mind. "The creative brain is not just right-brain: it involves the whole-brain, left-right-top-bottom, as the creative brain state accesses a large web of connections" (Goleman, 2011, p. 217). The structural difference between the right hemisphere and the left hemisphere of the brain is that the right has more neural connections to the rest of the brain than the left. The right is also directly connected to emotional centers. Conversely, the left hemisphere has fewer connections and is made of tidy, stacked columns that separate mental functions. Rational thinking springs from the left hemisphere where schematic images are stored by classification. By comparison, the right hemisphere is more of a structural mix. Humor involves the perception of cognitive synergy that includes current but contradictory interpretations of the same object.

The Call for Creativity from the Future

Artists who teach art are exceptional people. We teach the square kids in our schools who are frustrated by round holes. We know their plight because it was ours. We may be the only teacher in the school who truly understands the otherworldliness of square kids and surmise they may be among the few who will be ready for the future. We do not teach young artists discrete knowledge and mastered skills so they can reproduce them, we teach them how materials and skills can lead to deeper understanding of our human experiences. We help our students cross boundaries (operating well in several realms), invent (generating ideas beyond convention), and make metaphors (creating something that represents something else) to be competent agents in a future society we know little about (Pink, 2007).

We help them imagine with play and humor so they can climb to places they could not reach through logical, scientific processes.

Kids whose squareness does not prepare them for the round-shaped holes of mainstream society should take heart. There is a louder call for squareness in the next century than roundness. In his pioneering book, *Whole New Mind*, Daniel Pink claims the keys to the kingdom in the future "will belong to artists, inventors, and designers" (2007, p. 1). Pink projected 21st century workers who were innovative, empathetic and big picture visionaries would succeed in professional arenas of the next age. This is good news for art education. Our studio art making visual art programs indisputably develop these aptitudes because artists inherently combine incongruent concepts into something new and interact with joy and empathy. "Play, often regarded as a Cinderella subject, has come at last to the ball." (Bateson, 2013, p. 110). Hallelujah! (See Table 4.1 Operational Definitions of Creativity-Related Terms).

Just one more thing. I beg you to abandon the practice of giving your students "projects." Try calling them "challenges" or "problems" or "investigations," or even "research assignments." A project brings to mind a student following a described plan of action to assemble parts within a limited period of time to achieve a desirable end. Sounds like conventional work done with convergent thinking, right? Whereas, a challenge is more like a playful game, an enticement to investigate multiple solutions that solve a problem, meet a need or determine what a material will do. It sounds like unconventional play, invention, the creation of novelty with divergent thinking.

Bibliography

Azzam, A. M. (2009). Why creativity now? A conversation with Sir Ken Robinson. *Educational Leadership, 67*(1), 22–26.

Anning, A. (2002). Conversations around young children's drawing: The impact of the beliefs of significant others at home and school. *International Journal of Art & Design Education, 21*(3), 197–208.

Bateson, P., Bateson, P. P. G., & Martin, P. (2013). *Play, playfulness, creativity and innovation*. Cambridge University Press. 1-153.

Blatner. A. (1988). *The art of play*. New York, NY: Human Sciences Press.

Brophy, D. (2001). Comparing the attributes, activities, and performance of divergent, convergent, and combination thinkers. *Creativity Research Journal, 13*(3–4), 439–455.

Brown, S. (1998). Play as an organizing principle: Clinical evidence and personal observations. In M. Bekoff and J. A. Byers (Eds.), *Animal play: Evolutionary, comparative, and ecological perspectives* (pp. 243–259). Cambridge, UK: Cambridge University Press.

Cousins, N. (1979). *Anatomy of an illness as perceived by the patient: Reflections on healing and regeneration*. New York, NY: WW Norton & Company.

Edwards, B. (2013). *Drawing on the right side of the brain: A course in enhancing creativity and artistic confidence: Definitive 4th edition*. London, UK: Souvenir Press.

Ellenbecker, T. (2003). Effect of content choice freedom on drawer's creative engagement. *Art Therapy, 20*(1), 22–27.

Evans-Palmer, T. (2015). "I can't draw things that look real!" A 21st century non-traditional approach to raising learners' drawing efficacy. *Trends in Art Education*, 44–50.

Garrels, G. (2005). *Drawing from the Modern 1945–1975*. New York, NY: The Museum of Modern Art.

Goleman, D. (2011). *The brain and emotional intelligence: New insights*. More Than Sound.

Held, S. D., & Špinka, M. (2011). Animal play and animal welfare. *Animal Behaviour, 81*(5), 891–899.

Koestler, A. (1964). *The act of creation*. New York, NY: Macmillan.

Ludden, G., Schifferstein, H., & Hekkert, P. (2012). Beyond surprise: A longitudinal study on the experience of visual-tactual incongruities in products. *International Journal of Design, 6*(1).

Martin, R. (2007). *The psychology of humor; An integrative approach*. Burlington, MA: Elsevier Academic Press.

Martin, R., & Kuiper, N. (1999). Daily occurrence of laughter: Relationships with age, gender, and Type A personality. *Humor: International Journal of Humor Research, 12* (4), 355–384.

Morreall, J. (1981). Humor and aesthetic education. *Journal of Aesthetic Education*, 15(1), 55–70.

Murdock, M., & Ganim, R. (1992). Creativity and humor: Integration and incongruity. *Journal of Creative Behavior, 27*, 57–70.

Patton, A., & Bannerot, R. (2002). Chindogu: A problem solving strategy for transforming uselessness into fearlessness. *Paper IA, 2*, 20-22.

Pink, D. (2007). *A whole new mind*. New York, NY: Penguin Group.

Ramirez, A. (2015). *Encouraging the Einstein and Edison in everyone*. Blog. https://www.edutopia.org/blog/encouraging-einstein-edison-in-everyone-ainissa-ramirez

Robinson, K. (2009). *The element: How finding your passion changes everything*. New York, NY: Penguin.

Robinson, K. (2011). *Out of our minds*. Old Saybrook, CT: Tantor Media, Incorporated.

Rosenstiel, A., & Gardner, H. (1977). The effect of critical comparisons upon children's drawings. *Studies in Art Education, 19*(1), 36–44.

Scriven, J., & Hefferin, L. (1998). Humor: The "witting" edge in business. *Business Education Forum, 52*(3), 13.

Seelig, T. (2012). *inGenius: A crash course on creativity*. Carlsbad, CA: Hay House, Inc.

Shlesinger, B, Jr. (1982). An untapped resource of inventors: Gifted and talented children. *The Elementary School Journal, 82*(3), 215–220.

Skilbeck, A. (2017). Dewey on seriousness, playfulness and the role of the teacher. *Education Sciences, 7*(16).

Smith-Shank, D. (2014). Beyond this point there be dragons: pre-service elementary teachers' stories of art and education. *Art Education*, 46(5), 45–51.

Sternberg, R. J., & Kaufman, J. C. (Eds.). (2010). *The Cambridge handbook of creativity* (p. 132). Cambridge, UK: Cambridge University Press.

Torrance, E. (1972). Predictive validity of the Torrance tests of creative thinking. *The Journal of Creative Behavior*, 6(4), 236–262.

Torrance, E. (1979). *The search for Satori and creativity*. Buffalo, NY.

Conclusion: Our Best Bet for Teaching Tomorrow

Encouragement and Empathy for Educators

I am not convinced we are doing everything we can to support the emotional well-being of teachers in this era. Good teaching unfolds in an environment where learners want to learn and teachers want to teach. But teaching has become a delicate dance through an educational mine field that is planted with frustration, rejection, and assault. Every day, art teachers join self with students, and students with art, and we do it because we know art holds potential to change. Teaching is not easy. We have learned to mask our feelings to function, but what we really need is internal strength and the emotional agility to dance better. We need the power of joy to guard our full, well-meaning hearts because our hearts are what called us to teach in the first place (Palmer, 2007).

To Art Teachers

This book places the subject of humor as a priority for all educators whose job is to inspire innovation in learners. I pray that you will soon see teaching as the source of joy that it is and can be. Whether for a single minute or a string of moments, joy will change your perception of trials to opportunities for triumphs. Humor helps you do this. A sense of humor places us squarely in the present as those who are wholly alive and filled with joy. Giving away joy to others is key: "Our hearts ache, but we always have joy. We are poor, but we give spiritual riches to others. We own nothing, and yet we have everything" (2 Corinthians 6:10, New Living Translation).

The preceding chapters offer serious advice to art teachers for crafting laughter that releases us to be more flexible, more effective and more engaging. Specifically, I talk about humor's effect on resiliency, social connectedness, emotional intelligence, self-monitoring and divergent thinking. The interconnection of these teacher behaviors help us to use humor socially in our art classrooms to connect with students, connect students with art, to pick up emotional cues, monitor our teaching and leap over adversity. All of these raises what we believe about our teaching competency.

Truly, the payoff is big for you and your students if you are willing to bring humor into your classroom instruction and organization. Even if you are only able to turn your point of view toward playfulness, you will gain a most reliable instructional resource, an emotional lifesaver and a soft shroud to wear when the hard places in your teaching day leave you sore and tired. The learning that happens in your playful art studio classroom will be what John Dewey calls learning "permeated with the play attitude" (1916, p. 114). Art teaching is an art and teaching without play, according to Dewey, is not art.

You ask, "Ok, I get it, but where do I start?" Begin with play in your day, everyday. Get a magic wand, start lessons with impromptu stories about your students, introduce yourself as the reigning "Queen or King of Color" in your art studio/classroom realm. Make a paradigm detour off the scientific discovery trail where the hypothesis thing takes a systematic journey to a predetermined end. Instead, head toward the place where play helps your students move beyond disovering ideas that *are*, to inventing ideas that *are not yet*. You will be encouraging your students to think like artists and inventors, not navigators and discoverers.

A word of advice while you are contemplating embellishing your instruction with humor: take care that you do not overexert yourself with the emotional labor that comes with the job. Lighten your teaching load by looking for things in your job you enjoy, adore, relish, revel in, delight in, treasure and savor. Objectivity is crucial to your emotional health. Take care not to replay in your head today the angry student situation from the day before. Please do not go there. Compassion can be new every morning if you choose it to be. You might want to replace boiling emotions with full composure at the end of an emotionally taxing day. A few tips to help:

- Sit in your favorite place and breathe deeply. Distance yourself from angry thoughts by focusing on the wonderful blessings in your life that are so much more important to you than your teaching job (your family, the change of seasons and the fact that Christmas break is just a few weeks away).
- Consider that the students in your classes are in the process of finding their way through life. Being a kid is not for sissies these days. They have issues you may not know about causing them to act horrific in your class—issues that might have nothing to do with you.
- Seek out sources of laughter—standup comedian monologues, funny movies, videos or time with spirited friends. The miraculous effect of laughing releases enzymes that unravel the physiological, stress-induced knots in your body. Giggling is far better than gorging, chugging or drugging. Besides, laughter is free.
- Allow your now healthy sense of humor to wash over prickly situations with a student, a colleague, administrator or parent. Humor gives us strength.

A big shout out to those of you who are already exploiting humor as a social lubricant to ease into powerful interpersonal relationships with your students. You are the ones I herald as exemplars for healthy teaching! You have chosen to use appropriate, positive humor to illustrate and enhance content, to make lessons more dynamic and memorable, and to make your art classroom enjoyable and emancipating for everyone. Truly, successful teaching with humor "depends on employing the right type of humor, under the proper conditions, at the right time" (Bryant & Zillmann, 1989, p. 74). Optimistic educators have plenty of reasons to be optimistic, too. They have learned to let humor flip panic into pleasure and detachment into presence. Optimistic teachers become so supercharged by humor that they want their teaching friends to join them on their playful path to improved well-being and optimized teaching. It is rather like joining a high energy exercise class or a happy hour with friends who *stay* when happy hour is over.

To Teacher Educators

Heartfelt emotions, the most uniquely vibrant part of teachers, help us to interact with others more than any other human capacity. When humor is the epicenter of the emotional interaction, engagement is dynamically bonding. Why then are the emotions of preservice teachers dismissed as superfluous by teacher educators and professional development staff? I wholeheartedly contend that good teachers excel at their jobs because they do not suppress their feelings, but finely tune them to help them teach. Good teaching guided by the emotional capacity to work through problems is complicated by the emotions of other people. Therefore, teacher educators are charged to help candidates develop the emotional capacities and dispositions that guide them to mine the behaviors of learners for essential truth. We may even look at inculcating testing and training for emotional intelligence testing in our programs as an effort to cultivate teachers' emotional competence and longevity in the profession (Chechi, 2012; Edannur, 2010; Hen & Sharabi-Nov, 2014). And we must do it together.

Raising up teachers who will (re)shape the profession calls for our willingness to explain how emotional intelligence, self-appraisal and high self-efficacy beliefs have developed our own teaching practice:

> The new professional needs to know how to name and claim their feelings, neither denying or being dominated by them; discern whether and how they reflect in reality; ask if they have consequences for action; and, if so, explore them for clues to strategies for social change. (Palmer, 2007, p. 210)

We should seriously teach new teachers how to minimize their perceptions of "serious issues," given the expense of recruiting, training and retaining teachers. Some things are just not as serious as they seem. My experiences with young teachers tell me they are inclined to big drama over small problems. I hold myself back from responding with, "So you are saying your life is really hard?" to long-winded stressful complaints about stacked up life tasks demanding too much of their attention. (Perhaps we should include measures of resilience in our admission procedure to the profession?) At any rate, affective dispositions ushered in with humor certify an enduring state of emotional and physiological balance for new teachers if they choose. As educators ourselves, we know how shared laughter and an unexpected shift of perspective activates social, emotional, cognitive processes. I am quite sure that modeling personal skills that help us manage stress would not only equip candidates with similar coping behaviors to support their well-being, but also inform their instruction (Klusmann, Kunter, Trautwein, Lüdtke, & Baumert, 2008).

Not surprising for art education students becoming art teachers are dispositions they develop as exploring, imagining, playful artists; dispositions that accentuate teaching as an art (Gradle, 2007). We can help our candidates understand that their positive self-efficacy comes from the interplay of emotions with their unique teaching identity. Toward this goal, I use an egg metaphor to explain the "teacher self" identity to preservice teachers. The central yoke is the core of their identity, their beliefs, convictions, and personal attributes. The egg white surrounding the yolk comprises the uncooked, teacher self that is becoming. I tell them that I may "scramble their whites" on a burner of dedicated feedback to help them congeal into the teacher they will be, but I will never "mess" with their yokes. Then, we engage in resilience-building activities that call for intuition and emotionally guided perceptions of their "teacher selves." These include important role-playing scenarios directing their social skills, assertiveness, self-regulation, and empathy. They also interact with K-12 learners and art teachers in situated field engagements within the context of coursework several years before student teaching. Often, humor is a major player in these engagements, as it helps candidates detect and monitor their emotional behavior with learners. Exiting the program are young art teachers, well acquainted with their teacher selves, confident because they have had positive feedback about their knowledge, skills. intuition, emotional capacities and sense of humor to the extent that they believe they will teach well.

To Educational Policy Makers

Education as we know it doesn't need reforming—it needs transforming (Robinson, 2009). If we continue to devalue, demean and dishearten the hearts of teachers—our greatest resource in education—we will never reach transformation. We must do something—and something is where we must begin. I challenge those with the power to alter education's trajectory, to make the changes we need to see in the teaching profession and in the schools where teachers work. We must rebrand teaching as an esteemed and venerable position in society, one that is admired, valued and respected, and yes, even enjoyed. Initiate congruent school communities where the emotional skills of teachers, our greatest agents of change, are nurtured and supported. We know keeping teachers in teaching is challenged by many factors urging them to leave, but factors holding teachers steadfast to their calling, factors sustaining motivation, commitment, satisfaction and contentment can be instituted in educational policy. At the pinnacle of teaching enjoyment is the freedom that humor makes possible.

    Second, reframe education in schools as places of open-ended wonder, investigation and innovation by removing the oppressive practice of testing that brands schools as entities beholden to government accountability. Let's replace rigid, right-answer, conventional thinking with flexible, open-ended, divergent thinking. If teachers are to accomplish social reform in schools, we must replace accountability tests of group performance with celebrated individual innovation. Students are under pressure to memorize and recall right answers and teachers are under pressure to deliver them. The deleterious practice of promoting rigid thinking does not help our economy. Those in first-place position for the best jobs of the future will be artists, inventors, designers and big picture thinkers (Pink, 2007, p. 1), yet educational policy is directed to reward the virtue of knowledge keeping (linear, logical, accurate thinking). Third, we need teacher education with a focus on identifying creativity, play and humor behaviors unique to each teacher. Novice and experienced teachers would benefit from training of high-touch capacities that maximize student-teacher rapport (immediacy), from pedagogical humor instruction to enable them to "empathize and elicit joy in oneself and others and appreciate the subtleties of human interaction" (p. 52). "The tools are everywhere—humor and art, games and stories, protest and spectacle, the quiet, patient intervention and the angry and urgent thrust" (Ayers & Ayers, 2018, p. 68).

Bibliography

Ayers, W., & Ayers, R. (2018). Singing in dark times. Taboo: *The Journal of Culture and Education*, *17*(1). https://digitalcommons.lsu.edu/taboo/vol17/iss1/7

Bryant, J., & Zillmann, D. (1989). Using humor to promote learning in the classroom. In J. H. McGhee (Ed.), *Humor and children's development: A guide to practical applications* (pp. 49–78). Philadelphia, PA: Haworth Press.

Chechi, K. V. (2012). Emotional intelligence and teaching. *International Journal of Research in Economics & Social Sciences*, *2*(2), 297–304.

Dewey, J. (1916). Democracy and education. Hollywood, FL: Simon and Brown.

Edannur, S. (2010). Emotional intelligence of teacher educators. *International Journal of Educational Sciences*, *2*(2), 115–121.

Gradle, S. (2007). Random weave: Developing dispositions to teach art. *Art Education, 60*(4), 6–11, DOI: 10.1080/00043125.2007.11651646

Hen, M., & Sharabi-Nov, A. (2014) Teaching the teachers: emotional intelligence training for teachers, *Teaching Education*, *25*(4), 375–390.

Klusmann, U., Kunter, M., Trautwein, U., Lüdtke, O., & Baumert, J. (2008). Teachers' occupational well-being and quality of instruction: The important role of self-regulatory patterns. *Journal of Educational Psychology*, *100*(3), 702–715.

Palmer, P. (2007). *The courage to teach: Exploring the inner landscape of a teacher's life*. San Francisco, CA: Jossey-Bass.

Pink, D. (2005). *A whole new mind: Why right-brainers will rule the future*. New York, NY: Riverhead Books.

Robinson, K. (2009). *The element: How finding your passion changes everything*. New York, NY: Penguin.

Bibliography

Abel, M. (1998). Interaction of humor and gender in moderating relationships between stress and outcomes. *The Journal of Psychology, 132,* 267–276.
Abel, M. (2002). Humor, stress, and coping strategies. *Humor, 15*(4), 365–381.
Abel, M., & Sewell, J. (1999). Stress and burnout in rural and urban secondary school teachers. *The Journal of Educational Research, 92*(5), 287–293.
Allinder, R. (1994). The relationship between efficacy and the instructional practices of special education teachers and consultants. *Teacher Education and Special Education, 17,* 86–95.
Alwin, D., & Krosnick, J. (1991). The reliability of survey attitude measurement: The influence of question and respondent attributes. *Sociological Methods Research, 20,* 139–181.
Andrei, S. (2012). Psychologists at the gate: A Review of Daniel Kahneman's "Thinking, Fast and Slow," *Journal of Economic Literature, 4,* 1080.
Anderson, T., & Milbrandt, M. (2005). *Art for life: Authentic instruction in art.* New York, NY: McGraw-Hill.
Anning, A. (2002). Conversations around young children's drawing: The impact of the beliefs of significant others at home and school. *International Journal of Art & Design Education, 21*(3), 197–208.
Ansaldo, J., & Kopf, R. (2016). Camp yes and: An improv camp for teens and teachers. *The Reporter, 21*(6). Retrieved from https://www.iidc.indiana.edu/pages/camp-yes-and-animprov-camp-for-teens-with-asd-and-teachers

Apter, M. (1991). A structural-phenomenology of play. In J. H. Kerr & M. J. Apter (Eds.), *Adult play: A reversal theory approach* (pp. 13–29). Amsterdam, the Netherlands: Swets & Zeitlinger.

Apter, M. (Ed.). (2001). *Motivational styles in everyday life: A guide to reversal theory.* Washington, DC: American Psychological Association.

Apter, M., & Smith, K. (1977). Humour and the theory of psychological reversals. In A. Chapman & H. Foote (Eds.), *It's a funny thing, humour* (pp. 95–100). Oxford, UK: Pergamon Press.

Arendt, L. (2006). *Leaders' use of positive humor: Effects on followers' self-efficacy and creative performance* (Unpublished doctoral dissertation). The University of Wisconsin-Milwaukee, Milwaukee, WI.

Armor, D., Conroy-Oseguera, P., Cox, M., King, N., McDonnell, L., & Pascal, A. (1976). *Analysis of the school preferred reading programs in selected Los Angeles minority schools* (Report No. R-2007-LAUSD). Rand Corporation. (ERIC Document Reproduction Service No. 130–243).

Ashley, Sheila S., (2009). *Self-efficacy beliefs of elementary general education teachers in inclusive classrooms and the role of professional development* (Dissertations, Theses, and Masters Projects). Paper 1539618704. https://dx.doi.org/doi:10.25774/w4-a2mg-gh30

Ashton, P., Buhr, D., & Crocker, L. (1984). Teachers' sense of efficacy: A self- or norm-influenced construct? *Florida Journal of Educational Research, 26*(1), 29–41.

Ashton, P., Olejnik, S., Crocker, L., & McAuliffe, M. (1982). *Measurement problems in the study of teachers' sense of efficacy.* Paper presented at the Annual Meeting of the American Educational Research Association, New York.

Axelson, R., & Flick, A. (2011). Defining student engagement. *Change, 43,* 38–43. https://dx.doi.org/doi:10.1080/00091383.2011.533096

Ayers, W., & Ayers, R. (2018). Singing in dark times. Taboo: *The Journal of Culture and Education, 17*(1). https://digitalcommons.lsu.edu/taboo/vol17/iss1/7

Azzam, A. M. (2009). Why creativity now? A conversation with Sir Ken Robinson. *Educational Leadership, 67*(1), 22–26.

Bagakas, J., & Scott, C. (2006). Teacher efficacy, school reform, and state tests. *Academic Exchange Quarterly, 22*(1).

Bains, G., Berk, L., Lohman, E., Daher, N., Petrofsky, J., Schwab, E., & Deshpande, P. (2015). Humor's effect on short-term memory in healthy and diabetic older adults. *Alternative Therapy Health Medicine, 21*(3), 16–25.

Balonon-Rosen, P. (2017, February 13). Using improv to help kids with Autism show and read emotion. Retrieved from https://www.npr.org/sections/ed/2017/02/13/508978540/using-improv-to-helpkids-with-autism-show-and-read-emotion

Banas, J., Dunbar, N., Rodgriquez, D., & Liu, S. (2011). A review of humor in educational settings. *Communication Education, 60,* 115–144.

Bandura, A. (Ed.). (1976). *Modeling theory.* Chicago, IL: Rand McNally.

Bandura, A. (1977). Self-efficacy: Toward a unifying theory of behavioral change. *Psychological Review, 84,* 191–215.

Bandura, A. (1986). *Social foundations of thought and action: A social cognitive theory.* Hoboken, NJ: Prentice-Hall.

Bandura, A. (1993). Perceived self-efficacy in cognitive development and functioning. *Educational Psychologist, 28*(2), 117–148.

Bandura, A. (1997). *Self-efficacy: The exercise of control.* New York, NY: W. H. Freeman.

Bandura, A. (1998). Self-efficacy. In V. Ramachaudran (Ed.), *Encyclopedia of human behavior* (pp.71–81), Vol. 4. New York, NY: Academic Press.

Bandura, A. (2006). *Self-efficacy beliefs of adolescents.* Charlotte, NC: Information Age Publishing.

Bargh, J., Chaiken, S., Raymond, P., & Hymes, C. (1996). The automatic activation effect: Unconditional automatic attitude activation with a pronunciation task. *Journal of Experimental Social Psychology, 32*, 104–128.

Bateson, P., Bateson, P.P.G., & Martin, P. (2013). *Play, playfulness, creativity and innovation.* Cambridge University Press. 1–153.

Bell, N., McGhee, P., & Duffey, N. (1986). Interpersonal competence, social assertiveness and the development of humour. *British Journal of Developmental Psychology, 4*(1), 51–55.

Beltman, S., Mansfield, C., & Price, A. (2011). Thriving not just surviving: A review of research on teacher resilience. *Educational Research Review, 6*(3), 185–207.

Berk, R. (2002). *Humor as an instructional defibrillator.* Sterling, VA: Stylus Publishing.

Berk, R. (2003). *Professors are from Mars, students are from Snickers.* Sterling, VA: Stylus Publishing.

Berk, R., Tan, S., Fry, W., Napier, B., Lee, J., Hubbard, R., et al. (1989). Neuroendocrine and stress hormone changes during mirthful laughter. *American Journal of the Medical Sciences, 298*, 390–396.

Berlyne, D. (Ed.). (1969). *Laughter, humor, and play.* Reading, MA: Addison-Wesley.

Berlyne, D. (Ed.). (1971). *Humor and its kin.* New York, NY: Academic Press.

Bertoch, M., Nielsen, E., Curley, J., & Borg, A. (1988). Reducing teacher stress. *Journal of Experimental Education, 57*(1), 117–128.

Biderman, A., & Cantor, D. (1984*). A longitudinal analysis of bounding, respondent conditioning and mobility as sources of panel bias in the national crime survey.* Proceedings of the Section on Survey Research Methods, Bureau of Social Science Research, Inc., Washington, DC.

Bieg, S., & Dresel, M. (2018). Relevance of perceived teacher humor types for instruction and student learning. *Social Psychology of Education, 21*(4), 805–825. https://doi-org.libproxy.txstate.edu/10.1007/s11218-018-9428-z

Bieg, S., Grassinger, R., & Dresel, M. (2017). Humor as a magic bullet? Associations of different teacher humor types with student emotions. *Learning and Individual Differences, 56*(2107). 24–33.

Blatner. A. (1988). *The art of play.* New York, NY: Human Sciences Press.

Bobek, B. (2002). Teachers' resiliency: A key to career longevity. *Clearing House, 70*(4), 176–178.

Bolkan, S., & Goodboy, A. K. (2010). Transformational leadership in the classroom: The development and validation of the student intellectual stimulation scale. *Communication Reports, 23*(2), 91–105.

Booth-Butterfield, M., & Booth-Butterfield, S. (1991). Individual differences in communication of humorous messages. *Southern Communication Journal, 56*, 43–50.

Boyle, G., & Joss-Reid, J. (2004). Relationship of humour to health: A psychometric investigation. *British Journal of Health Psychology, 9*(1), 51–66.

Brackett, M., Reyes, M., Rivers, S., Elbertson, N., & Salovey, P. (2011). Classroom emotional climate, teacher affiliation, and student conduct. *The Journal of Classroom Interaction*, (1), 27–36.

Brauer, K., Pryor, R., & Ruch, W. (2019). Extending the study of gelotophobia, gelotophilia, and katagelasticism in romantic life towards romantic attachment. *Journal of Individual Differences.* https://www.researchgate.net/publication/334084815_Extending_the_Study_of_Gelotophobia_Gelotophilia_and_Katagelasticism_in_Romantic_Life_Towards_Romantic_Attachment

Brophy, D. (2001). Comparing the attributes, activities, and performance of divergent, convergent, and combination thinkers. *Creativity Research Journal, 13*(3–4), 439–455.

Brophy, J. (1996). *Teaching problem students.* New York, NY: Guilford.

Brotheridge, C. (2006). A review of emotional labour and its nomological network: Practical and research implications. *Ergonomia, 28*(4), 295–309.

Brotheridge, C., & Grandey, A. (2002). Emotional labor and burnout: Comparing two perspectives of people work. *Journal of Vocational Behavior, 60*, 17–39. https://doi.org/10.1006/jvbe.2001.1815.

Brotheridge, C., & Lee, R. (2003). Development and validation of the Emotional Labour Scale. *Journal of Occupational and Organizational Psychology, 76*(3), 365–379.

Brouwers, A., & Tomic, W. (2000). A longitudinal study of teacher burn-out and perceived self-efficacy in classroom management. *Teaching and Teacher Education, 16*, 239–253.

Brown, S. (1998). Play as an organizing principle: Clinical evidence and personal observations. In M. Bekoff and J. A. Byers (Eds.), *Animal play: Evolutionary, comparative, and ecological perspectives* (pp. 243–259). Cambridge, UK: Cambridge University Press.

Brown, N., & Thomas, K. (1999, September). *Creativity as collective misrecognition in the relationships between art students and their teachers.* Paper presented at the Annual World Congress of the International Society for Education through Art (InSEA), Brisbane, Australia.

Brunsting, N., Sreckovic, M., & Lane, K. (2014). Special education teacher burnout: A synthesis of research from 1979 to 2013. *Education and Treatment of Children, 37*(4), 681–711.

Bryant, J., Brown, D., Parks, S., & Zillmann, D. (1983). Children's imitation of a ridiculed model. *Human Communication Research 10*(2), 243–255.

Bryant, J., Comisky, P., Crane, J., & Zillmann, D. (1980). Relationship between college teachers' use of humor in the classroom and students' evaluations of their teachers. *Journal of Educational Psychology, 72*(4), 511–519.

Bryant, J., Comisky, P., & Zillmann, D. (1979). Teachers' humor in the college classroom. *Communication Education, 28*, 110–118.Bryant, J., & Zillmann, D. (1989). Using humor to promote learning in the classroom. In J. H. McGhee (Ed.), *Humor and children's development: A guide to practical applications* (pp. 49–78). Philadelphia, PA: Haworth Press.

Byrne, B. (1992, April). *Investigating causal links to burnout for elementary, intermediate, and secondary teachers.* Paper presented at the Annual Meeting of the American Educational Research Association, San Francisco, CA.

Byrne, B. (1993). The Maslach Burnout Inventory: Testing for factorial validity and invariance across elementary, intermediate, and secondary teachers. *Journal of Occupational Psychology, 66*(3), 197–212.

Burkman, A. (2012). Preparing novice teachers for success in elementary classrooms through professional development. *Delta Kappa Gamma Bulletin, 78*(3), 23–33.

Burić, I. (2019). The role of emotional labor in explaining teachers' enthusiasm and students' outcomes: A multilevel mediational analysis. *Learning and Individual Differences, 70,* 12–20.

Cann, A., Cann, A., & Jordan, J. (2016). Understanding the effects of exposure to humor expressing affiliative and aggressive motivations. *Motivation & Emotion, 40*(2), 258–267. https://doi-org.libproxy.txstate.edu/10.1007/s11031-015-9524-8

Castro, A. J., Kelly, J., & Shih, M. (2010). Resilience strategies for new teachers in high-needs areas. *Teaching and Teacher Education, 26*(3), 622–629.

Cayirdat, N., & Acar, S. (2010). Relationship between styles of humor and divergent thinking. *Procedia-Social and Behavioral Science, 2*(2), 3236–3240.

Chacon, C. (2005). Teachers' perceived efficacy among English as a foreign language teacher in middle schools in Venezuela. *Teaching and Teacher Education, 21,* 257–272.

Chang, J. H., Chen, H. C., Hsu, C. C., Chan, Y. C., & Chang, Y. L. (2015). Flexible humor styles and the creative mind: Using a typological approach to investigate the relationship between humor styles and creativity. *Psychology of Aesthetics, Creativity, and the Arts, 9*(3), 306.

Chapman, A., & Foot, H. (Eds.) (1996). *Humor and laughter: Theory, research, and applications.* Piscataway, NJ: Transaction Publishers.

Chapman, L., (2005). No child left behind in art? *Art Education, 58*(1), 6–15.

Chechi, K. (2012). Emotional intelligence and teaching. *International Journal of Research in Economics & Social Sciences, 2*(2), 297–304.

Chen, H. C., Su, C.-L., & Ye, J.-R. (2011). A study on the types of humor appreciation, humor styles, creative ability, and creative tendency [in Chinese]. *Journal of Chinese Creativity, 2,* 53–78.

Cherniss, C. (Ed.) (1993). *Role of professional self-efficacy in the etiology and amelioration of burnout.* Boca Raton, FL: Taylor & Francis.

Chesnut, S., & Cullen, T. (2014) Effects of self-efficacy, emotional intelligence, and perceptions of future work environment on preservice teacher commitment. *The Teacher Educator, 49*(2), 116–132. http://dx.doi.org/10.1080/08878730.2014.887168

Civikly, J. (1986). Humor and the enjoyment of college teaching. In J. Civikly (Ed.) *Communicating in college classrooms: New directions for teaching and learning,* (pp. 61–70). San Francisco, CA: Jossey-Bass.

Cohen, J. (1988). *Statistical power analysis for the behavioral sciences* (2nd ed.). Mahwah, NJ: Lawrence Erlbaum Associates.Coladarci, T. (1992). Teachers' sense of efficacy and commitment to teaching. *Journal of Experimental Education, 60*(4), 323–337.

Coladarci, T., & Bretton, W. (1997). Teacher efficacy, supervision, and the special education resource room teacher. *The Journal of Educational Research, 90*(4), 230–239.

Coleman, J. (1992). All seriousness aside: The laughing-learning connection. The International *Journal of Instructional Media, 19*(3), 269–276.

Converse, P. (1964). The nature of belief systems in mass publics. In D. Apter (Ed.), *Ideology and discontent* (pp. 206–261). New York, NY: Free Press.

Converse, P. (1970). Attitudes and non-attitudes: Continuation of a dialogue. In E. Tufte (Ed.), *The quantitative analysis of social problems* (pp. 168–189). Reading, MA: Addison-Wesley.

Cooper, C. (2008). Elucidating the bonds of workplace humor: a relational process model, *Human Relations,* 61(8), 1087–1115.

Coser, R. (1960). Laughter among colleagues. *Psychiatry, 2,* 81–95.

Cousins, N. (1991). *Anatomy of an illness as perceived by the patient.* New York, NY: Norton.

Crocco, S., & Costigan, A. (2007). The narrowing of curriculum and pedagogy in the age of accountability: Urban educators speak out. *Urban Education 42*(6), 512–535.

Crowe, J. (2002). *A conversation about choice-based art education: Whit is it so effective? Knowledgeloom.* Available at https://www.brown.edu/academics/education-alliance/sites/brown.edu.academics.education-alliance/files/uploads/KLOOM_tab_entire.pdf

Csikszentmihalyi, M., & McCormack, J. (1995). The influence of teachers. In K. Ryan and J. Cooper (Eds.), *Kaleidoscope: Readings in education* (pp. 2–8). Boston, MA: Houghton Mifflin.

Cundy, D. (1979). Affect, cue-giving and political attitude formation: Survey evidence in support of a social conditioning interpretation. *The Journal of Politics, 41*(1), 75–105.

Curwin, R., & Mendler, A. (1988). *Discipline with dignity.* Alexandria, VA: Association for Supervision and Curriculum Development.

Darling, A., & Civikly, J. (1987). The effect of teacher humor on students' perceptions of classroom communicative climate. *Journal of Classroom Interaction, 22,* 24–30.

Darwich, L. (2018). New academic year, new beginning: What a teacher does for renewal. *Northwest Journal of Teacher Education, 13*(1), 1–22.

Davies, A., & Apter, M. (1980). Humour and its effect on learning in children. In P. McGhee & A. Chapman (Eds.), *Children's humour* (pp. 237–253). Hoboken, NJ: John Wiley & Sons.

Davis, G. A. (1999). Barriers to creativity and creative attitudes. In M. A. Runco, & S. R. Pritzker (Eds.), *Encyclopedia of creativity* (pp. 165–174). Burlington, MA: Elsevier Academic Press.

Day, C. (2008). Committed for life? Variations in teachers' work, lives and effectiveness. *Journal of Educational Change, 9*(3), 243–260.

Deci, E., Koestner, R., & Ryan, R. (1999). A meta-analytic review of experiments examining the effects of extrinsic rewards on intrinsic motivation. *Psychological bulletin, 125*(6), 627.

Dellinger, A., Bobbett, J., Olivier, D., & Ellett, C. (2008). Measuring teachers' self-efficacy beliefs: Development and use of the TEBS-Self. *Teaching and Teacher Education, 24,* 751–766.

Derks, P. (1996). Twenty years of research on humor: A view from the edge. In A. Chapman & H. Foot (Eds.), *Humor and laughter: Theory, research, and applications*. Piscataway, NJ: Transaction Publishers.

DeVon, H., Block, M., Moyle-Wright, P., Ernst, D., Hayden, S., & Lazzara, D. (2007). A psychometric toolbox for testing validity and reliability. *Journal of Nursing Scholarship. 39*(2), 155–164.

Dewey, J. (1894). The theory of emotion. *Psychological Review, 1*, 553–569.

Dewey, J. (1910). *How we think*. Lexington, MA: D.C. Heath & Co.

Dewey, J. (1916). Democracy and education. Hollywood, FL: Simon and Brown

Dewitte, S., & Verguts, T. (2001). Being funny: A selectionist account of humor production. *Humor: International Journal of Humor Research*, 14(1), 37–53.

Dickmeyer, S. (1993, April). *Humor as an instructional practice: A longitudinal content analysis of humor use in the classroom*. Paper presented at the annual meeting of the Eastern Communication Association, New Haven, CT.

Doebler, L., Roberson, T., & Ponder, C. (1998). Pre-service teacher case study responses: A preliminary attempt to describe program impact. *Education, 119*(2), 349–358.

Donahue, R., Kher, N., & Molstad, S. (1999). Using humor in the college classroom to enhance teaching effectiveness in dread courses. *College Student Journal, 33*(3), 400–436.

Doskoch, P. (1996). New frontiers of happiness … Happily ever laughter. *Psychology Today, 29*(4), 32–35.

Douglas, K., Crowe, J., Jaquith, D., & Brannigan, R. (2002). Promising practices for a choice-based approach to art education. Knowledgeloom: http://knowledgeloom. org/tab/index.jsp.

Douglas, K., & Jaquith, D. (2018). *Engaging learners through artmaking: Choice-based art education in the classroom (TAB)*. New York, NY: Teachers College Press.

Downs, V., Javidi, M., & Nussbaum, J. (1988). An analysis of teachers' verbal communication within the college classroom: Use of humor, self-disclosure, and narratives. *Communication Education, 37*, 127–141.

Duffy, M., & Sperry, L. (2012). *Mobbing: Causes, consequences, and solutions*. New York, NY: University Oxford Press.

Edannur, S. (2010). Emotional intelligence of teacher educators. *International Journal of Educational Sciences, 2*(2), 115–121.

Edwards, B. (2013). *Drawing on the right side of the brain: A course in enhancing creativity and artistic confidence: Definitive 4th edition*. London, UK: Souvenir Press.

Egan, K. (2005). *An imaginative approach to teaching*. San Francisco, CA: Jossey-Bass.

Ellenbecker, T. K. (2003). Effect of content choice freedom on Drawer's creative engagement. *Art Therapy, 20*(1), 22–27.

Ennis, C. (2003). "Can you hear me now?" Expert teachers' use of humor to enhance student learning. *Research Quarterly for Exercise and Sport*, 3. http://www.highbeam.com

Epstein, B. (1998, November 1). *Humor in behavioral and cognitive therapies*. Paper presented at the annual meeting of the Association for the Advancement of Behavior Therapy, Washington, DC.

Ersfjord, E. (2018). Taking children's humor seriously: A study of humor in children diagnosed with obesity and the medicalization of body weight. *Childhood*, 25(2), 189–202.

Eysenck, H. (1942). The appreciation of humour: An experimental and theoretical study. *The British Journal of Psychology, 32*, 295–309.

Eysenck, H. (1972). Foreword. In J. Goldstein & P. McGhee (Eds.), *The psychology of humor: Theoretical perspectives and empirical issues* (pp. xii–xvii). New York, NY: Academic Press.

Evans-Palmer, T. (2009). *The relationship between sense of humor and self-efficacy: An exploration of the beliefs of art teachers* (Doctoral dissertation). University of the Incarnate Word, San Antonio, TX. Available from ProQuest Digital Dissertation. (TX 6-697-683).

Evans-Palmer, T. (2010). The potency of humor and instructional self-efficacy on art teacher stress. *Studies in Art Education, 52*(1), 69–83.

Evans-Palmer, T. (2013). Raising docent confidence in engaging students on school tours. *Journal of Museum Education, 38*(3) October 2013, 364–378.

Evans-Palmer, T. (2015a). Humor and self-efficacy traits that support the emotional well-being of educators. *Journal of Research in Innovative Teaching, 8(1)*, 21–36.

Evans-Palmer, T. (2015b). "I can't draw things that look real!" A 21st century non-traditional approach to raising learners' drawing efficacy. *Trends in Art Education*, 44–50.

Evans-Palmer, T. (2016). Building dispositions and self-efficacy in pre-service art teachers. *Studies in Art Education, 57*(3), 265–278.

Evans-Palmer, T. (2017). *The significance of teacher humor and self-efficacy beliefs to enhance instruction*. Paper presented at Annual International Conference of Education, Research and Innovation (ICERI2017), Seville, Spain.

Fazio, R. (1989). On the power and functionality of attitudes: The role of attitude accessibility. In S. Pratkanis & A. Greenwalds (Eds.), *Attitude structure and function* (pp. 153–179). Mahwah, NJ: Erlbaum.

Fazio, R., Sanbonmatsu, D., Powell, M., & Kardes, F. (1986). On the automatic activation of attitudes. *Journal of Personality and Social Psychology, 37*, 229–238.

Feingold, A., & Mazzella, R. (1993). Primary validation of a multidimensional model of witness. *Journal of Personality, 61*(3), 439–456.

Field, A. (2009). *Discovering statistics using SPSS* (3rd ed.). Thousand Oaks, CA: Sage.

Fluegge, E. (2008). *Who put the fun in functional? Fun at work and its effects on job performance* (PhD thesis), ProQuest UMI, Ann Arbor, MI, Vol. 3322919.

Foley, C. (2014). Why creativity? Articulating and championing a museum's social mission. *Journal of Museum Education, 39*(2), 139–151.

Ford, R., McLaughlin, F., & Newstrom, J. (2003). Questions and answers about fun at work. *Human Resource Planning, 26*(4), 18–33.

Ford, T., Ford, B., Boxer, C., & Armstrong, J. (2012). Effect of humor on state anxiety and math performance. *Humor, 25*, 59–74.

Fortson, S., & Brown, W. (1998). Best and worst university instructors: The opinions of graduate students. *College Student Journal, 32*(4), 572–576.

Freda, P., & Csikszentmihalyi, M. (1995). *The influence of teachers.* Boston, MA: Houghton-Mifflin.

Freda, P., Fry, W., Jr., & Allen, M. (1996). Humor as a creative experience: The development of a Hollywood humorist. In R. Chapman & H. Foot (Eds.), *Humor and laughter: Theory, research, and applications* (pp. 245–258). New Brunswick, NJ: Transaction.

Freedman, K. (2007). Art making/troublemaking: Creativity, policy, and leadership in art education. *Studies in Art Education, 48*(2), 204–217.

Freitas, T. (2018). *Student perceptions of instructor humor as a predictor of student intellectual stimulation, academic interest and engagement* (Thesis). University of the Pacific, Stockton, CA. https://scholarlycommons.pacific.edu/uop_etds/3117

Freud, S. (1928). Humour. *International Journal of Psychoanalysis, 9*, 1–6.

Freud, S. (1960). *Jokes and their relation to the unconscious.* New York, NY: Norton.

Friere, P. (1970). *Pedagogy of the oppressed* (M.B. Ramos, Trans.). New York, NY: Continuum, 2007.

Fry, W. (1994). The biology of humor. *Humor: International Journal of Humor Research, 7*(2), 111–126.

Frymier, A., & Houser, M. (2000). The teacher-student relationship as an interpersonal relationship. *Communication Education, 49*, 207–219.

Frymier, A., Wanzer, M., & Wojtaszczyk, A. (2008). Assessing students' perceptions of inappropriate and appropriate teacher humor. *Communication Education, 57*, 266–288.

Garner, R. (2006). Humor in pedagogy: How ha-ha can lead to aha! *College Teaching, 51*(1), 177–180.

Garrels, G. (2005). *Drawing from the Modern 1945–1975.* New York, NY: The Museum of Modern Art.

Gerberich, S., Nachreiner, N., Ryan, A., Church, T., McGovern, P., Geisser, M., & Pinder, E. (2014). Case-control study of student-perpetrated physical violence against educators. *Annals of Epidemiology, 24*(5), 325–332. http://doi.org/10.1016/j.annepidem.2014.02.006

Gibson, S., & Dembo, M. (1984). Teacher efficacy: A construct validation. *Journal of Educational Psychology, 76*(4), 569–582.

Gignac, G., Karatamoglou, A., Wee, S., & Palacios, G. (2014). Emotional intelligence as a unique predictor of individual differences in humour styles and humour appreciation. *Personality and Individual Differences, 56*, 34–39.

Glasser, W. (1986). *Control theory in the classroom.* New York, NY: Harper and Row.

Glasser, W. (1997). Choice theory and student success. *The Education Digest, 63*, 16–21.

Godkewitsch, M. (1974). Correlates of humor: Verbal and nonverbal aesthetic reactions as functions of semantic distance within adjective-noun pairs. In D. Berlyne (Ed.), *Studies in the new experimental aesthetics: Steps toward an objective psychology of aesthetic appreciation* (pp. 279–304). London: Hemisphere.

Goleman, D. (1995). *Emotional intelligence.* New York, NY: Bantam Books.

Goleman, D. (2011). *The Brain and Emotional Intelligence: New Insights.* More Than Sound Publishing. http://www.morethansound.net

Goodreads (2019). Emotion quotes. Retrieved from https://www.goodreads.com/quotes/tag/emotions

Gordon, D. (2017). Understanding the constant dialogue that goes on between our gut and our brain. *UCLA Newsroom.* Retrieved from http://newsroom.ucla.edu/stories/understanding-the-constant-dialogue-that-goes-on-between-our-gut-and-our-brain

Gordon, K., & Coscarelli, W. (1996). Recognizing and fostering resilience. *Performance Improvement, 35*(9), 14–17.

Gordon, M. (2012). Exploring the relationship between humor and aesthetic experience. *The Journal of Aesthetic Education, 46*(1), 110–121. https://dx.doi.org/doi:10.5406/jaesteduc.46.1.0110

Gordon, M. (2014). Friendship, intimacy and humor. *Educational Philosophy and Theory, 46*(2), 162–174.

Greenberg, J., Putman, H., & Walsh, K. (2013). Training our future teachers: Classroom management. *National Council on Teacher Quality.* Retrieved from http://www.nctq.org/dmsStage/Future_Teachers_Classroom_Management_NCTQReport

Greengross, G., Martin, R., & Miller, G. (2012). Personality traits, intelligence, humor styles, and humor production ability of professional stand-up comedians compared to college students. *Psychology of Aesthetics, Creativity, and the Arts, 6*(1), 74.

Greenwood, G., Olejnik, S., & Parkay, F. (1990). Relationships between four teacher efficacy belief patterns and selected teacher characteristics. *Journal of Research and Development in Education, 23*(2), 102–106.

Griffith, A., & Burns, M. (2012) *Outstanding teaching: Engaging learners.* Carmarthen, UK: Crown House Publishing.Gross, J. (2002). Emotion regulation: Affective, cognitive, and social consequences. *Psychophysiology, 39,* 281–291. https://doi.org/10.1017//S0048577201393198.

Gruner, C. (1976). Humor and laughter: Theroy, research, and applications. In A. Chapman & H. Foot (Eds.), *Wit and humor in mass communication* (pp. 287–311). Hoboken, NJ: John Wiley & Sons.

Gruner, C. (1997). *The game of humor: A comprehensive theory of why we laugh.* Piscataway, NJ: Transaction Publishers.

Guilford, J. (1961). *Factorial angles to psychology. Psychological Review, 68*(1), 1–20. http://dx.doi.org/10.1037/h0045887

Guskey, T. (1981). Measurement of responsibility teachers assume for academic successes and failures in the classroom. *Journal of Teacher Education, 32,* 44–51.

Guskey, T., & Passaro, P. (1994). Teacher efficacy: A study of constructs. *American Educational Research Journal, 31*(3), 627–643.

Hadani, H., & Jaeger, G. J. (2015). *Inspiring a generation to create: Critical components of creativity in children* [White paper]. Sausalito, CA: Center for Childhood Creativity. http://www.csus.edu/coe/profiles/assets/jaeger-garret-j.pdf

Hafenstein, N., Haines, K., & Cramond, B. (2009). *Perspectives in gifted education: Creativity. Perspectives in Gifted Education, 5,* Institute for the Development of Gifted Education,

Ricks Center for Gifted Children, University of Denver. https://digitalcommons du.edu/perspectivesingifteded/5/

Hauck, W., & Thomas, J. (1972). The relationship of humor to intelligence, creativity, and incidental learning. *Journal of Experimental Education, 40*(4), 52–55.

Henman, L. (2001). Humor as a coping mechanism: Lessons from POWs. *Humor: International Journal of Humor Research, 14*(1), 83–94.

Henricks, T. (2015). *Play and the human condition.* Champaign, IL: University of Illinois Press.

Henson, R. (2001, January 26). *Teacher self-efficacy: Substantive implications and measurement dilemmas.* Paper presented at the meeting of the Educational Research Exchange, Texas A. & M. University, College Station, TX.

Ho, S. (2016). Relationships among humour, self-esteem, and social support to burnout in school teachers. *Social Psychology of Education, 19*, 41–59.

Hoenigman Meyer, E. (2018, May 7). The secret to likeability [*Career News*]. https://www.higheredjobs.com/Articles/articleDisplay.cfm?ID=1621&utm_source=05_16_2018&utm_medium=email&utm_campaign=InsiderUpdate

Holzer P. (2017) Interoception and gut feelings: Unconscious body signals' impact on brain function, behavior and belief processes. In H. F. Angel, L. Oviedo, R. Paloutzian, A. Runehov, & R. Seitz (Eds.), *Processes of believing: The acquisition, maintenance, and change in creditions. new approaches to the scientific study of religion, Vol 1.* Cham, Switzerland: Springer.

Houser, M. L., Cowan, R. L., & West, D. A. (2007). Investigating a new education frontier: Instructor communication behavior in CD-ROM Texts—Do traditionally positive behaviors translate into this new environment? *Communication Quarterly, 55*(1), 19–38.

Hoy, W., & Woolfolk Hoy, A. (1993). Teachers' sense of efficacy and the organizational health of schools. *The Elementary School Journal, 93*, 356–372.

Hudak, D., Dale, J., Hudak, M., & DeGood, D. (1991). Effects of humorous stimuli and sense of humor on discomfort. *Psychological Reports, 69*, 779–786.

Infante, D., Riddle, B., Horvath, C., & Tumlin, S. (1992). Verbal aggressiveness: Messages and reasons. *Communication Quarterly, 40*, 116–126.

Intrator, S. & Kunzman, R. (2007). The person in the profession: Renewing teacher vitality. *Educational Forum, 71*(1), 16–32.

James, T., Minor, L., Onwuegbuzie, A., & Witcher, A. (2002). Preservice teachers' educational beliefs and their perceptions of characteristics of effective teachers. *The Journal of Educational Research, 96*(2), 116–127.

Javidi, M., Downs, V., & Nussbaum, J. (1988). A comparative analysis of teachers' use of dramatic style behaviors at higher and secondary educational levels. *Communication Education, 37*, 278–288.

Javidi, M., & Long, L. (1988). Teachers use of self-disclosure and narrative activity as a function of experience. *Communication Research Reports, 6*, 46–52.

Jennings, P., & Greenberg, M. (2009). The prosocial classroom: Teacher social and emotional competence in relation to student and classroom outcomes. *Review of Educational Research, 79*(1), 491–525.

Johnson, P. (2007, July). *High stakes testing and no child left behind: Conceptual and empirical considerations.* Paper presented at the Long Island Economic & Social Policy Institute, Dowling College School of Education, Oakdale, NY.

Jonas, P. (2004). *Secrets of connecting leadership and learning with humor.* Lanham, MD: Scarecrow Education.

Kane, T., Suls, J., & Tedeschi, J. (1977). Humor as a tool of social interaction. In A. Chapman & H. Foot (Eds.), *It's a funny thing, humor* (pp. 13–16). Oxford, UK: Pergamon Press.

Kahneman, D. (2011). *Thinking, fast and slow.* New York, NY: Macmillan.

Kang, S., & Neitzel, C. (2005). Teacher efficacy research from an agentic view. *Academic Exchange Quarterly, 22*(12), 219–223.

Kaplan, R., & Pascoe, G. (1977). Humorous lectures and humorous examples: Some effects upon comprehension and retention. *Journal of Educational Psychology, 69*, 61–15.

Kaufeldt, M. (2009). *Begin with the brain: Orchestrating the learner-centered classroom.* Thousand Oaks, CA: Sage.

Kaufman, J., & Baer, J. (2012). Beyond new and appropriate: Who decides what is creative? *Creativity Research Journal, 24*(1), 83–91. https://doi.org/10.1080/10400419.2012.649237

Keith-Spiegel, P. (1972). Early conceptions of humor: Varieties and issues. In J. H. Goldstein & P. E. McGhee (Eds.), *The psychology of humor: Theoretical perspectives and empirical issues* (pp. 3–39). New York, NY: Academic Press.

Kennedy, M., Ahn, S., & Choi, J. (2008). The value added by teacher education. In M. Cochran-Smith, S. Feiman-Nemser, & J. McIntyre (Eds.), *Handbook of research on teacher education* (pp. 1249–1273). New York, NY: Macmillan.

Kerr, J., & Apter, M. (Eds.). (1991). *A structural phenomenology of play.* Amsterdam, the Netherlands: Swets & Zeitlinger.

Kher, N., Molstad, S., & Donahue, R. (1999). Using humor in the college classroom to enhance teaching effectiveness in "dread courses." *College Student Journal 33*(3), 400–406.

Kipper, S., & Todt, D. (2001). Variation of sound parameters affects the evaluation of human laughter. *Behaviour, 138*(9), 116. http://search.ebscohost.com.libproxy.txstate.edu/login.aspx?direct=true&db=edsjsr&AN=edsjsr.4535881&site=eds-live&scope=site

Klauer, K. (1985). Framework for a theory of teaching. *Teaching and Teacher Education, 1*, 5–17.

Klusmann, U., Kunter, M., Trautwein, U., Lüdtke, O., & Baumert, J. (2008a). Engagement and emotional exhaustion in teachers: Does the school context make a difference? *Applied Psychology, 57*, 127–151.

Klusmann, U., Kunter, M., Trautwein, U., Lüdtke, O., & Baumert, J. (2008b). Teachers' occupational well-being and quality of instruction: The important role of self-regulatory patterns. *Journal of Educational Psychology, 100*(3), 702–715.

Koestler, A. (1964). *The act of creation.* New York, NY: Macmillan.

Köhler, G., & Ruch, W. (1996). Sources of variance in current sense of humor inventories: How much substance, how much method variance? *Humor: International Journal of Humor Research 9*(3/4), 363–397.

Kohn, A. (1996). The trouble with character education. *Yearbook-National Society for The Study of Education, 96*, 154–162.

Korobkin, D. (1988). Humor in the classroom: Considerations and strategies. *College Teaching, 36*, 154–158.

Kuan-Chen, T. (2018). An empirical examination of the relationships among creativity, the evaluation of creative products, and cognitive style among Chinese undergraduates. *International Journal of Cognitive Research in Science, Engineering and Education, 6*(1), 53.

Kuiper, N., McKenzie, S., & Belanger K. (1995). Cognitive appraisals and individual differences in sense of humor: Motivational and affective implications. *Personality and Individual Differences, 19*, 359–372.

Kunter, M., Klusmann, U., Baumert, J., Richter, D., Voss, T., & Hachfeld, A. (2013). Professional competence of teachers: Effects on instructional quality and student development. *Journal of Educational Psychology, 105*, 805–820.

Kyriacou, C. (1987). Teacher stress and burnout: An international review. *Educational Research, 29*, 146–152.

La Favre, L., Haddad, J., & Maesen, W. (1996). Superiority, enhanced self-esteem, and perceived incongruity humour theory. In A. Chapman & H. Foot (Eds.), *Humor and laughter: Theory, research, and applications* (pp. 63–93). Piscataway, NJ: Transaction Publishers.

Labatt, S. (1990). The physiological and psychological effects of the expression and inhibition of emotion. *Behavioral Medicine, 16*(4), 182–189.

Lamm, E., & Meeks, M. (2009). Workplace fun: the moderating effects of generational differences. *Employee Relations*, 31(6), 613–631.

Latta, R. (1999). *The basic humor process: A cognitive-shift theory and the case against incongruity.* Berlin, Germany: Mouton de Gruyter.

Lefcourt, H. (2001). *Humor: The psychology of living buoyantly.* Hingham, MA: Kluwer Academic.

Lefcourt, H., Davidson, K., Shepherd, R., Phillips, M., Prkachin, K., & Mills, D. (1995). Perspective-taking humor: Accounting for stress moderation. *Journal of Social & Clinical Psychology, 14*(4), 373–391.

Leist, A. K., & Müller, D. (2013). Humor types show different patterns of self-regulation, self- esteem, and well-being. *Journal of Happiness Studies, 14*, 551–569. http://dx.doi.org/10.1007/s10902-012-9342-6

Leithwood, K., & McAdie, P. (2007). Teacher working conditions that matter. *Education Canada, 47*(2), 42–45.

Lippitt, G. (1982). Humor: a laugh a day keeps the incongruities at bay. *Training and Development Journal, 36*(11), 98–100.

Lloyd, G., Wilson, M., Wilkins, J., & Behm, S. (Eds.). (2005). *Teachers' beliefs in their instructional capacity: The effects of in-service.* Paper presented at the 27th Annual meeting of the North American Chapter of the International Group for Psychology of Mathematics Education.

Long, P. (1987). Minding your health: Laugh and be well? *Psychology Today, 21*(10), 28–29.

Loosveldt, G., Carton, A., & Billiet, J. (2004). Assessment of survey data quality: A pragmatic approach focused on interviewer tasks. *International Journal of Market Research, 46*(1), 65–82.

Ludden, G., Schifferstein, H., & Hekkert, P. (2012). Beyond surprise: A longitudinal study on the experience of visual-tactual incongruities in products. *International Journal of Design*, *6*(1), 1–10.

Magnuson, C., & Barnett, L. (2013). The playful advantage: How playfulness enhances coping with stress. *Leisure Sciences*, *35*(2), 129–144.

Mahony, D., Burroughs, W., & Hieatt, A. (2001). The effects of laughter on discomfort thresholds: Does expectation become reality? *Journal of General Psychology*, *128*(2), 217–226.

Mahony, D., Burroughs, W., & Lippman, L. (2002). Perceived attributes of health-promoting laughter: a cross-generational comparison, *The Journal of Psychology*, *136*(2), 171–181.

Manning, K. (1982). *Lighten up! An analysis of the role of humor as an instructional practice in the urban and/or culturally diverse middle school* (Unpublished doctoral dissertation). Cleveland State University, Cleveland, OH.

Martin, M. (1987). Humor and aesthetic enjoyment of incongruities. In J. Morreall (Ed.), *The philosophy of humor and laughter* (pp. 172–186), Albany, NY: SUNY Press.

Martin, R. (1988). Sense of humor, hassles, and immunoglobulin: Evidence for a stress-moderating effect on humor. *International Journal of Psychiatry in Medicine*, *18*, 93–105.

Martin, R. (1996). The Situational Humor Response Questionnaire (SHRQ) and Coping Humor Scale (CHS): A decade of research findings. *Humor: International Journal of Humor Research*, *9*(3–4), 251–272.

Martin, R. (2001). Humor, laughter, and physical health: Methodological issues and research findings. *Psychological Bulletin*, *127*(4), 504–519.

Martin, R. (2002). Is laughter the best medicine? Humor, laughter, and physical health. *Current Directions in Psychological Science*, *11*(6), 216–220.

Martin, R. (2007). *The psychology of humor; An integrative approach*. Burlington, MA: Elsevier Academic Press.

Martin, R., & Kuiper, N. (1999). Daily occurrence of laughter: Relationships with age, gender, and Type A personality. *Humor: International Journal of Humor Research*, *12* (4), 355–384.

Martin, R., & Lefcourt, H. (1983). Sense of humor as a moderator of the relation between stressors and moods. *Journal of Personality and Social Psychology*, *45*, 1313–1324.

Martin, R., & Lefcourt, H. (1984). Sense of humor as a moderator of the relation between stressors and moods. *Journal of Personality and Social Psychology*, *47*, 145–155.

Marzano, R., Marzano, J. & Pickering, D. (2003). *Classroom management that works: Research-based strategies for every teacher*. Alexandria, VA: Association for Supervision and Curriculum Development.

Maslach, C. (2003). Job burnout: New directions in research and intervention. *Current Directions in Psychological Science*, *12*, 189–192.

Maslow, A. (1968). *Toward a psychology of being*. New York, NY: D. Van Nostrand Company.

Mayer, J., & Salovey, P. (1993). The intelligence of emotional intelligence. *Intelligence*, *17*, 433–442.

McCarron, K., & Savin-Baden, M. (2008). Compering and comparing: Stand-up comedy and pedagogy. *Innovations in Education and Teaching International*, *45*(4), 355–363.

McGhee, P. (1979). *Humor: Its origins and development.* New York, NY: W. H. Freeman.

McGhee, P. (1983). Humor development: Toward a life span approach. In P. E. McGhee & J. H. Goldstein (Eds.), *Handbook of humor research, Vol. 1, Basic issues* (pp. 109–134). Berlin, Germany: Springer-Verlag.

McGhee, P. (1986). Humor across the life span: Sources of developmental change and individual differences. In L. Nahemow, K. McCluskey-Fawcett, & P. E. McGhee (Eds.), *Humor and aging* (pp. 27–51). New York, NY: Academic Press.

McGhee, P., & Goldstein, J. (1983). *Handbook of humor research, applied studies (Vol. II).* Berlin, Germany: Springer-Verlag.

McKinney, S., Campbell-Whately, G., & Kea, C. (2005). Managing student behavior in urban classrooms: The role of teacher ABC assessments. *Clearing House 79*(1), 16–20. https://dx.doi.org/doi: 10.3200/TCHS.79.1.16-20

McLaughlin, M. (1990). The rand change agent study revisited: Macro perspectives and micro realities. *Educational Researcher, 19*(9), 11–16.

McLeod, S. A. (2007). *Maslow's hierarchy of needs.* http://www.simplypsychology.org/maslow.html

McNeill, P., & Chapman, S. (2005). *Research methods* (3rd ed.). London, UK: Routledge.Merolla, A. (2006). Decoding ability and humor production. *Communication Quarterly, 54*(2), 175–190.

Merriam, S., Caffarella, R., & Baumgartner, L. (2007). *Learning in adulthood.* San Francisco, CA: Jossey-Bass.

Mertler, C., & Vannatta, R. (2005). *Advanced and multivariate statistical methods* (3rd ed.). Los Angeles, CA: Pyrczak Publishing.

Mesmer-Magnus, J., & Glew, D. (2012). A meta-analysis of positive humor in the workplace. *Journal of Managerial Psychology, 27*(2), 155–190.

Meyer, J. (1990). Ronald Reagan and humor: A politician's velvet weapon. *Communication Studies, 41*(1), 76–88.

Microsoft Corporation (2007). *Encarta Dictionary* (North America).

Miller, D. (1991). *Handbook of research design and social measurement.* Thousand Oaks, CA: Sage.

Milner, H., & Hoy, A. (2003). A case study of an African American teacher's self-efficacy, stereotype threat, and persistence. *Teaching and Teacher Education, 19*(2), 263–276.

Minor, D. (2014). The captain of the ship: Classroom management. In N. López-Burton & D. Minor (Eds.), *On being a language teacher: A personal and practical guide to success* (pp. 178–201). New Haven, CT: Yale University Press. http://www.jstor.org.libproxy.txstate.edu/stable/j.ctt13x1swk.14

Moore, R. (2013). *Pedagogical stressors and coping strategies for bolstering teacher resilience* (Doctoral dissertation) Walden University, Minneapolis, MN. Available from ProQuest Dissertations & Theses Global. (1428739220).

Moore, T., Wehby, J., Oliver, R., Chow, J., Gordon, J., & Mahany, L. (2017). Teachers' reported knowledge and implementation of research-based classroom and behavior management strategies. *Remedial and Special Education, 38*(4), 222–232.

Morreall, J. (1981). Humor and aesthetic education. *Journal of Aesthetic Education, 15*(1), 55–70.
Morreall, J. (1983). *Taking laughter seriously.* Albany, NY: State University of New York.
Morreall, J. (1997). *Humor works.* Amherst, MA: HRD Press.
Morreall, J. (2009). *Comic relief: A comprehensive philosophy of humor.* Hoboken, NJ: Wiley-Blackwell.
Morton, M. (2005) Practicing praxis: mentoring teachers in a low-income school through collaborative action research and transformative pedagogy, *Mentoring & Tutoring: Partnership in Learning, 13*(1), 53–72, DOI: 10.1080/13611260500040278
Mottet, T. P., McCroskey, J. C., & Richmond, V. P. (2016). *Handbook of instructional communication: Rhetorical and relational perspectives.* Abingdon, England: Routledge.
Mulkay, M. J. (1988). *On humor: Its nature and its place in modern society.* Cambridge, UK: Polity Press.
Murdock, M., & Ganim, R. (1992). Creativity and humor: Integration and incongruity. *Journal of Creative Behavior, 27*, 57–70.
Murphy, K., & Myors, B. (1998). *Statistical power analysis: A simple and general model for traditional and modern hypothesis tests.* Mahwah, NJ: Erlbaum.
Nagel, S., & Brown, S. (2003). The ABC's of managing teacher stress. *Clearing House, 5*(1), 255–258.
Nasiri, F., & Mafakheri, F. (2015). Higher education lecturing and humor: From perspectives to strategies. *Higher Education Studies, 5*(5), 26–31.
National Commission on Excellence in Education (1983). A nation at risk: The imperative for educational reform [Electronic version]. A Report to the Nation and the Secretary of Education, United States Department of Education, Washington, DC.
Nesi, H. (2015). Laughter in university lectures. *Journal of English for Academic Purposes, 11*, 79–89.
Neuliep, J. (1991). An examination of the content of high school teachers' humor in the classroom and the development of an inductively derived taxonomy of classroom humor. *Communication Education, 40*(4), 343–355.
No Child Left Behind Act of 2001, Pub. L. No. 107–110, 115 Stat. 1425 (2002).
Nouri, A., & Sajjadi, S. M. (2014). Emancipatory pedagogy in practice: Aims, principles and curriculum orientation. *The International Journal of Critical Pedagogy, 5*(2), 76-87.
Nutt, L., & Hardman, L. (2019). *Complete the agenda in higher education: Challenge beliefs about student success.* Lanham, MD: Rowman & Littlefield.
Opplinger, P., & Zillman, D. (1997). Humor and learning. *International Journal of Humor Research, 10*(4), 421–437.
Opplinger, P., & Zillman, D. (2003). Humor and learning. In J. Bryant, D. Roskos-Ewoldsen & J. Cantor (Eds.), *Communication and emotion: Essays in honor of Dolf Zillman* (pp. 255–273). NYC, New York: Routledge.
O'Quin, K., & Derks, P. (2017). Humor and creativity. Reference module in neuroscience and biobehavioral psychology science direct, EBSCOhost (accessed June 29, 2018).

Oshima K. (2018). Functions of humor in intercultural communication and educational environments. In A. Curtis & Sussex R. (Eds.), *Intercultural communication in asia: education, language and values* (*Multilingual education*, 24). Cham, Switzerland: Springer.

Pajares, F. (1996). Self-efficacy beliefs in academic settings. *Review of Educational Research, 66*, 543–578.

Pajares, F. (2002). Overview of social cognitive theory and self-efficacy. http://www.emory.edu/EDUCATION/mfp/eff.html

Palmer, P. (2007). *The courage to teach: Exploring the inner landscape of a teacher's life.* San Francisco, CA: Jossey-Bass.

Pannell, E. (2009, July 30). Bryant teacher of the year uses humor in classes. Arkansas Democrat-Gazette [Electronic version]. http://www2.arkansasonline.com

Patrick, C. (2014, January 13). 11 Ways to handle a heckler. http://mentalfloss.com/article/54496/11-ways-handle-heckler

Patton, A., & Bannerot, R. (2002). Chindogu: a problem solving strategy for transforming uselessness into fearlessness. *Paper IA, 2*, 20-22.

Penrose, A., Perry, C., & Ball, I. (2007). Emotional intelligence and teacher self-efficacy: The contribution of teacher status and length of experience. *Issues in Educational Research, 17.*

Perrez, M., Huber G., & Geissler, K. (2001). Psychologie der pädagogischen interaktion. [Psychology of pedagogical interaction]. In A. Krapp & B. Weidenmann (Eds.), *Educational Psychology* (pp. 357–413). Weinheim, Germany: Beltz.

Petty, R., & Cacioppo, J. (1981). *Attitudes and persuasion: Classical and contemporary approaches.* Dubuque, IA: Brown.

Phillips, K., Johnson, F., & Maddala, T. (2002). Measuring what people value: A comparison of "attitude" and "preference" surveys. *Health Services Research, 37*(6), 1659–1679.

Pigford, T. (2001). Improving teacher-student relationships: What's up with that? *Clearing House, 74*(6), 337–339.

Pink, D. (2005). *A whole new mind: Why right-brainers will rule the future.* New York, NY: Riverhead Books.

Pollack, J., & Freda, P. (1997). Humor, learning, and socialization in middle level classrooms. *Clearing House, 70*(4), 176–178.

Pollio, H., & Edgerly, J. (1996). Comedians and comic style. In A. Chapman & H. Foot (Eds.). *Humor and laughter: Theory, research, and applications* (pp. 215–241). Piscataway, NJ: Transaction Publishers.

Pollio, H., & Humphreys, W. (1996). What award-winning lecturers say about their teaching: It's all about connection. *College Teaching 44*(3), 101–106.

Powell, J., & Andresen, L. (1985). Humor and teaching in higher education. *Studies in Higher Education, 10*(1), 79–90. http://dx.doi.org/10.1080/03075078512331378726

Prosser, B. (2008). The role of the personal domain in middle years teachers' work. *Australian Journal of Middle Schooling, 8*(2), 11–16.

Provine, R. (1992). Contagious laughter: Laughter is a sufficient stimulus for laughs and smiles. *Bulletin of the Psychonomic Society, 30*(1), 1–4.

Provine, R. (2000). *Laughter: A scientific investigation*. New York, NY: Penguin.

Pryor, M., Singleton, L., Taneja, S., & Humphreys, J. (2010). Workplace fun and its correlates: a conceptual inquiry. *International Journal of Management*, 27(2), 294–302.

Pugliese, C. (2013). *Creative teaching. Being Creative-The Challenge of Change in the Classroom.* Surrey, UK: Delta Publishing.

Pullin, D. (2004). Accountability, autonomy, and academic freedom in education preparation programs. *Journal of Teacher Education*, 55(4), 300–312.

Ramirez, A. (2015). *Encouraging the Einstein and Edison in everyone.* Blog. https://www.edutopia.org/blog/encouraging-einstein-edison-in-everyone-ainissa-ramirez

Rao, P., Beidel, D., & Murray, M. (2008). Social skills interventions for children with Asperger's Syndrome or High-Functioning Autism: A review and recommendations. *Journal of Autism and Developmental Disorders*, 38, 353–361. http://dx.doi.org/10.1007/s10803-007-0402-4

Rea, L., & Parker, R. (1992). *Designing and conducting survey research: A comprehensive guide.* San Francisco, CA: Jossey-Bass.

Reglin, G., & Reitzammer, A. (1998). Dealing with the stress of teachers. *Education*, 118(4), 590–596.

Rimm-Kaufman, S., & Sawyer, B. (2004). Primary-grade teachers' self-efficacy beliefs, attitudes toward teaching, and discipline and teaching practice priorities in relation to the Responsive Classroom approach. *The Elementary School Journal*, 104(4), 321–341.

Robinson, K. (2006). *Do schools kill creativity?* https://www.ted.com/talks/ken_robinson_says_schools_kill_creativity?utm_campaign=tedspread&utm_medium=referral&utm_source=tedcomshare

Robinson, K. (2009). *The element: How finding your passion changes everything*. New York, NY: Penguin.

Robinson, S. (2017). *Consciousness in clay* (Bachelor's thesis). Stephen F. Austin University, Nacogdoches, TX. Electronic theses and dissertations, SFA Scholar Works. https://scholarworks.sfasu.edu/etds

Romero, E., & Pescosolido, A. (2008). Humor and group effectiveness, *Human Relations*, 61(3), 395–418.

Rose, J., & Medway, F. (1981). Measurement of teachers' beliefs in their control over student outcome. *Journal of Educational Research*, 74, 185–190.

Ross, J., & Bruce, C. (2007). Professional development effects on teachers' efficacy: Results of randomized field trial. *Journal of Educational Research*, 101(1), 50–60.

Rotter, J. (1966). Generalized expectancies for internal versus external control of reinforcement. *Psychological Monographs*, 80, 1–28.

Rowe, A., & Regehr, C. (2010) Whatever gets you through today: An examination of cynical humor among emergency service professionals, *Journal of Loss and Trauma*, 15(5), 448–464, https://dx.doi.org/doi:10.1080/15325024.2010.507661

Ruch, W. (1998). *Humor research 3: The sense of humor—Explorations of a personality characteristic.* Berlin, Germany: Mouton de Gruyter.

Ruch, W., Attardo, S., & Raskin, V. (1993). Toward an empirical verification of the General Theory of Verbal Humor. *International Journal of Humor Research, 6*(2), 123–136.

Ruch, W., & Köhler, G. (1999). The measurement of state and trait cheerfulness. In I. Marvielde, I. Deary, F. De Fruyt & F. Ostendorf (Eds.). *Personality, psychology in Europe* (pp. 67–83). Tilburg, the Netherlands: Tilburg University.

Runco, M. A. (2014). *Creativity: Theories and themes: Research, development, and practice.* NYC, New York: Elsevier.

Sala, F. (2003). Laughing all the way to the bank. *Harvard Business Review, 81,* 16–17.

Salkind, N. (2000). *Statistics for people who think they hate statistics.* Thousand Oaks, CA: Sage.

Salovey, P., Bedell, B., Detweiler, J., & Mayer, J. (2000). Current directions in emotional intelligence research. In M. Lewis & J. M. Haviland-Jones (Eds.), *Handbook of emotions* (2nd ed., pp. 504–520). New York, NY: Guilford.

Sapsford, R. (1999). *Survey research.* Thousand Oaks, CA: Sage.

Schmidt, S. R. (2002). The humor effect: Differential processing and privileged retrieval. *Memory, 10,* 127–138. https://dx.doi.org/doi:10.1080/09658210143000263

Schonfeld, I. (2001). Stress in first-year women teachers: The context of social support and coping. *Genetic, Social, and General Psychology Monographs, 127,* 133–168.

Schrecengost, A. (2001). Does humorous preoperative teaching work? D. *AORN Journal, 74*(5), 683–689.

Scot, T., Callahan, C., & Urquhart, J. (2009). Paint-by-number teachers and cookie-cutter students: the unintended effects of high-stakes testing on the education of gifted students. *Roeper Review, 31,* 40–52.

Scriven, J., & Hefferin, L. (1998). Humor: The "witting" edge in business. *Business Education Forum, 52*(3), 13.

Seelig, T. (2012). *inGenius: A crash course on creativity.* Carlsbad, CA: Hay House, Inc.

Seidman, A. (2005). The learning killer: Disruptive student behavior in the classroom. *Reading Improvement, 42*(1), 40+.

Senge, P., (2004). *Presence: Exploring profound change in people, organizations, and society.* New York, NY: Random House.

Shade, R. (1996). *License to laugh.* Englewood, CO: Teacher Ideas Press.

Sheldon, K., & Biddle, B. (1998). Standards, accountability, and school reform: Perils and pitfalls. *Teachers College Record, 100*(1), 164–180.

Shibinski, K., & Martin, M. (2010). The role of humour in enhancing the classroom climate *Human Kinetics, 15*(5), 27–29.

Shih, Y. (2018). Rethinking Paulo Freire's dialogic pedagogy and its implications for teachers' teaching. *Journal of Education and Learning, 7*(4), 230–235.

Shlesinger, B., Jr. (1982). An untapped resource of inventors: Gifted and talented children. *The Elementary School Journal, 82*(3), 215–220.

Shor, I., & Freire, P. (1987). What is the "dialogical method" of teaching? *Journal of Education, 169*(3), 11–31.

Sim, I. (2015). Humor intervention program for children with chronic diseases. *Applied Nursing Research, 28*(4), 404–412.

Skilbeck, A. (2017). Dewey on seriousness, playfulness and the role of the teacher. *Education Sciences, 7*(1), 16.

Smith, M. (2016). Playful invention, inventive play. *International Journal of Play, 5*(3), 244–261. https://doi-org.libproxy.txstate.edu/10.1080/21594937.2016.1203549

Smith-Shank, D. (2014). Beyond this point there be dragons: pre-service elementary teachers' stories of art and education, *Art Education, 46*(5), 45–51.

Smylie, M. (1990). *Teacher efficacy at work in teachers and their workplace.* Thousand Oaks, CA: Sage.

SPSS. (2004). Sample power: Get the right sample size the first time. Retrieved June 9, 2009, from http://www.spss.com/PDFs/SP2SPC-0704hr.pdf

Stajkovic, A., & Luthaus, F. (1998). *Self-efficacy and work-related performance: A meta-analysis. Psychological Bulletin, 124*(2), 240–261.

Steele, K. (1998). *The positive and negative effects of the use of humor in the classroom setting* (Unpublished doctoral dissertation). Salem-Teikyo University, Salem, WV.

Steffens, P. (1990). *Characteristics of teacher efficacy as perceived by teachers of the year* (Unpublished doctoral dissertation). Northern Arizona University, Flagstaff, AZ.

Sternberg, R. J., & Kaufman, J. C. (Eds.). (2010). *The Cambridge handbook of creativity* (p. 132). Cambridge, UK: Cambridge University Press.

Stoycheva, K. (1996, October 19). *The school: A place for children's creativity?* Paper presented at the European Council for High Ability Conference, Vienna, Austria.

Strean, W. (2008). Evolving toward laughter in learning. *Collected Essays on Learning and Teaching, 1*, 165–171.

Strean, W. (2011). Creating student engagement? HMM: Teaching and learning with humor, music and movement. *Creative Education, 2*(3), 189–192.

Sultanoff, S. (1995). Humor: An antidote to stress. *Therapeutic Humor, Publication of the American Association for Therapeutic Humor, 9*(3), 1–2.

Sveback, S. (1974). A theory of sense of humor. *Scandinavian Journal of Psychology, 15*, 99–107.

Sveback, S. (1975). Styles in humor and social self-images. *Scandinavian Journal of Psychology, 16*, 79–84.

Sveback, S. (1977). Some characteristics of resting respiration as predictors of laughter. In A. Chapman & H. Foot (Eds.), *It's a funny thing, humour* (pp. 101–104). Oxford, UK: Pergamon Press.

Sveback, S. (1996). The development of the sense of humor questionnaire: From SHQ to SHQ-6. *Humor: International Journal of Humor Research, 9*(3–4), 341–361.

Szekely, G. (1988). *Encouraging creativity in art lessons.* New York, NY: Teachers College Press.

Tabachnick, B., & Fidell, L. (1996). *Using multivariate statistics* (3rd ed.). New York, NY: Harper Collins.

TAEA. (2009). Texas Art Education Association. http://www.taea.org/taea/default.asp

Tait, G., Lampert, J., Bahr, N., & Bennett, P. (2015). Laughing with the lecturer: the use of humour in shaping university teaching. *Journal of University Teaching & Learning Practice*, *12*(3), 7.

Taupin, A. (2018). *Humor: A bridge to social skills for individuals with high-functioning autism.* Chester, PA: Widener University.

Teslow, J. (1995). Humor me: A call for research. *Educational Technology Research and Development*, *43*(3), 6–28.

Thibodeaux, J. (2014). Three versions of constructionism and their reliance on social conditions in social problems research. *Sociology*, *48*(4), 829–837.

Thorson, J., & Powell, F. (1993a). Development and validation of a multidimensional sense of humor scale. *Journal of Clinical Psychology*, *49*(1), 13–23.

Thorson, J., & Powell, F. (1993b). Sense of humor and dimensions of personality. *Journal of Clinical Psychology*, *49*(6), 799–809.

Thorson, J., Powell, F., Sarmany-Schuller, I., & Hampes, W. (1997). Psychological health and sense of humor. *Journal of Clinical Psychology*, *53*(6), 605–619.

Tickle-Degnon, L., & Rosenthal, R. (1990). The nature of rapport and its nonverbal correlates. *Psychological Inquiry*, *1*(4), pp. 285–293

Todt, D., & Kipper, S. (2001). Variation of sound parameters affects the evaluation of human laughter. *Behaviour*, *138*(9), 1161–1178.

Torok, S., McMorris, R., & Lin, W. (2004). Is humor an appreciated teacher tool? Perceptions of professors' teaching styles and use of humor. *College Teaching*, *52*(1), 14–20.

Torrance, E. (1966). *The Torrance tests of creative thinking: Norms—Technical manual* (Research edition). Lexington, MA: Personnel Press. https://books.google.com.tw/books/about/Torrance_Tests_of_Creative_Thinking.html?id=_4dUYAAACAAJ&redir_esc=y

Torrance, E. (1972). Predictive validity of the Torrance tests of creative thinking. *The Journal of creative behavior*, *6*(4), 236–262.

Torrance, E. (1979). The search for satori and creativity. Buffalo. NY: Creative Education Foundation.

Torrance, E., & Ball, O. (1978). Streamlined scoring guide and norms manual for figural form B. 7TCT. Athens, GA: University of Georgia.

Torrance, E., & Myers, R. E. (1970). *Creative learning and teaching.* New York, NY: Dodd, Mead.

Tourganeau, R., Rips, L., & Rasinki, K. (2000). *The psychology of survey response.* Cambridge, UK: Cambridge University Press.

Tournaki, N., & Podell, D. M. (2005). The impact of student characteristics and teacher efficacy on teachers' predictions of student success. *Teaching and Teacher Education*, *21*, 299–314.

Tsai, K. (2018). Evaluation of creative products, and cognitive style among Chinese undergraduates, *International Journal of Cognitive Research in Science, Engineering and Education*, *6*(1), 2018

Tschannen-Moran, M., & Woolfolk Hoy, A. (1998). Teacher efficacy: Its meaning and measure. *Review of Educational Research*, *68*, 202–248.

Tschannen-Moran, M., & Woolfolk Hoy, A. (2001). Teacher efficacy: Capturing an elusive construct. *Teacher and Teacher Education, 17,* 783–805.

Tschannen-Moran, M., & Woolfolk Hoy, A. (2002). The influence of resources and support on teachers' efficacy beliefs. *Review of Educational Research, 68,* 202–248.

Tschannen-Moran, M., & Woolfolk Hoy, A. (2007). The differential antecedents of the self-efficacy beliefs of novice and experienced teachers. *Teaching and Teacher Education, 23*(6), 944–956.

Tsigilis, N., Grammatikopoulos. J., & Koustelios, A. (2007). Applicability of the teachers' sense of efficacy scale to educators teaching innovative programs. *International Journal of Educational Management, 21*(7), 634–642.

VanBeselaere, C. (2004, May). Survey response behavior. Paper presented at the meeting of the American Association for Public Opinion Research, Phoenix, AZ.

Wakshlag, J., Day, K., & Zillmann, D. (1981). Selective exposure to educational television programs as a function of differently paced humorous inserts. *Journal of Educational Psychology, 73*(1), 27.

Walker, B. E. (2006). Using humor in library instruction. *Reference Services Review,* 34(1), 117–128. http://libproxy.txstate.edu/login?url=https://search-proquest-com.libproxy.txstate.edu/docview/200504821?accountid=5683

Walonik, D. (2004). *Survival statistics.* Lauder Cowansville, Canada: Stat Pac.

Wambach, C., & Brothen, T. (1997). Teacher self-disclosure and student classroom participation revisited. *Teaching of Psychology, 24,* 263–265.

Wanzer, M., & Frymier, A. (1999). The relationship between students' perceptions of instructor humor and students' reports of learning. *Communication Education, 48,* 48–62.

Wanzer, M., Frymier, A., & Irwin, J. (2010). An explanation of the relationship between instruction humor and student learning: Instructional humor processing theory. *Communication Education, 59,* 1–18.

Watts, R. (2005). Making art in primary school. *International Journal of Art & Design Education, 24*(3), 243–53.

Watzke, J. (2003). Longitudinal study of stages of beginning teacher development in a field-based teacher education program. *The Teacher Educator, 38*(3), 209–229.

Weasmer, J., & Woods, A. (1998). I think I can: The role of personal teaching efficacy in bringing about change. *Clearing House, 71*(4), 245–247.

Webb, G. (2001). Teachers' report of how they used humor with students perceived use of such humor. *Education, 122*(2), 337–347.

Welch, A. (1995). The self-efficacy of primary teachers in art education. *Issues in Educational Research, 5*(1), 71–84.

Wentland, E., & Smith, K. (1993). *Survey responses: An evaluation of their validity.* New York, NY: Academic Press.

Wiley, C. (2000). A synthesis of research on the causes, effects, and reduction of strategies of teacher stress. *Journal of Instructional Psychology, 27*(2), 80–87.

Williams, T., Billingsley, B., & Banks, A. (2018). Incidences of student-on-teacher threats and attacks: a comparison of special and general education teachers. *Journal of Special Education Leadership, 31*(1), 39-49.

Wilson, T., & Hodges, S. (1992). Attitudes as temporary constructions. In L. Martin & A. Tesser (Eds.), The construction of social judgments. (pp. 37–66). Berlin, Germany: Springer-Verlag.

Wong, H., Wong, R., Rogers, K., & Brooks, A. (2012). Managing your classroom for success. *Science and Children, 49*(10), 60–64.

Woolfolk, A., & Hoy, W. (1990). Prospective teachers' sense of efficacy and beliefs about control. *Journal of Educational Psychology, 52*, 81–91.

Wrench, J., & McCroskey, J. (2001). A temperamental understanding of humor communication and exhilaratability. *Communication Quarterly, 49*(2), 142–159.

Wright, W. (2002). The effects of high stakes test in an inner-city elementary school: The curriculum, the teachers, and the English language learners. *Current Issues in Education*. http://cie.ed.asu.edu/volume5/number5/.html

Yatvin, J. (2008). 2007 NCTE presidential address: Where ignorant armies clash by night. *Research in Teaching of English, 42*(3), 363–372.

Yoo, J., & Carter, D. (2017). Teacher emotion and learning as praxis: Professional development that matters. *Australian Journal of Teacher Education, 42*, 38–52.

Yost, D. (2006). Reflection and self-efficacy: Enhancing the retention of qualified teachers from a teacher education perspective. *Teacher Education Quarterly, 33*(4), 59–72.

Zillmann, D. (1977). Humor and communication. In A. J. Chapman & H. Foot (Eds.), *It's a funny thing, humor.* Oxford, UK: Pergamon Press.

Zillmann, D., & Bryant, J. (Eds.). (1983). *Uses and effects of humor in educational venues.* Berlin, Germany: Springer-Verlag.

Ziv, A. (1976). Facilitating effects of humor on creativity. *Journal of Educational Psychology, 68*(3), 318–322.

Ziv, A. (1981). The self-concept of adolescent humorists. *Journal of Adolescence, 4*, 187–197.

Ziv, A. (1984). *Personality and sense of humor.* Berlin, Germany: Springer.

Ziv, A. (1989). Using humor to develop creative thinking. In P. E. McGhee (Ed.), *Humor and children's development: a guide to practical applications* (pp. 99–116). Philadelphia, PA: Haworth Press Inc.

Relevant Websites

http://www.psychologie.uzh.ch/perspsy/gelotophobia/—Gelotophobia (fear of being laughed at) research page.

http://www.degruyter.com/journals/humor/detailEn.cfm—*Humor: International Journal of Humor Research.*

http://www.humorresearch.org/—Humor research site.

http://www.hnu.edu/ishs/index.htm—International Society for Humor Studies.

http://www.unc.edu/peplab/home.html—Positive Emotions and Psychophysiology Lab (Barbara Frederickson).

www.ingramcontent.com/pod-product-compliance
Ingram Content Group UK Ltd.
Pitfield, Milton Keynes, MK11 3LW, UK
UKHW022122230426
12048UKWH00011BA/660